The pattern here and throughout the book is inspired by piña cloth, which is made from the thorny leaves left over from harvested pineapples, whose innermost fibers are woven into a delicate material, light and cool against the skin in a hot climate. It's a testament to frugality and the insistence on wasting nothing, and a marker, too, of the colonial history of the Philippines: From the sixteenth through the nineteenth centuries, the Spanish mandated that native Filipino men wear a shirt of piña cloth, the barong tagalog, untucked—a humble and humbling uniform, whose translucency ensured that they could not carry concealed weapons and rise against their foreign rulers. For the Filipinos, embroidery became a way to take ownership of what they wore, to express their character as individuals, and to make themselves seen and known.

Filipinx

fi • luh • pee • NEKS

A gender-inclusive term for people of Philippine origin or descent. From Filipino/Filipina, words first used to describe natives of the Philippines in the late nineteenth century.

Filipinx

HERITAGE RECIPES
FROM THE DIASPORA

BY ANGELA DIMAYUGA AND LIGAYA MISHAN

PHOTOGRAPHS BY ALEX LAU

ABRAMS, NEW YORK

For my mom and dad,
who always trusted me to know myself.

Angela

For my mom, who waited so patiently
for me to find my way home.

Ligaya

"We are made of blood, earth, and stardust. The ancient sources of life that built our bones and pulse through our veins proclaim that we are because someone, many ones, gave us life. We do not get here on our own."

Chani Nicholas

CONTENTS

COME INSIDE AND *Eat*

Our annual ritual: Mom and I make time to bake ensaymadas every year.

"We tried to teach you Tagalog, remember," my mom says with a laugh. I do: The babysitter was deputized to teach all six of us kids—I'm the second youngest—and it was chaos. That was life in the diaspora in northern California. Even today, I'm humbled in the presence of native speakers; I can't keep up with an entire conversation in Tagalog, let alone any of the Philippines' other indigenous languages (there are close to two hundred of them). What I know are the phrases and words that my parents and their friends slip so effortlessly and instinctively into English, taken from Tagalog, Kapampangan, Ilocano, and Pangasinan, each language getting its shot, sometimes three at once in a single sentence, without a hitch, as if it were all one clamorous tongue.

I am a Filipino, a Filipina, and a Filipinx—I'm comfortable being identified by any of those terms, from the traditional to the more inclusive (see "Siya: Decolonizing the Language," page 208)—but I am also a Filipino American, one of more than four million. My parents are Americans, too: They emigrated from the Philippines in 1976 and have lived in the U.S. for most of their lives. But I was born here and have never known another home.

In second grade, a boy asked me, "Are you white?" I thought the right answer was yes. Still, I knew I was different, if not exactly how. Growing up in San Jose, California, where the population is a third Asian and a third Hispanic, I eventually found a sense of belonging in a brown culture that brought together kids of Filipino and Mexican heritage. As teens in the nineties, my older sisters and I wore black eyeliner and brown lipstick (I still do), and our regalia was cut-off Dickies, Nike Cortezes, and Adidas Sambas.

Cooking was the shining thread. Whenever I went to a Filipino home, even just to drop off something for a friend, I was told: "Come inside and eat." No matter how my parents struggled, scrimping and making do with squashed Wonder Bread from the discount store, there was always food in our house, and always more than enough. Love was expressed not in words but abundance. I happily ate everything: sinigang, PBJs, Taco Bell, instant ramen. Every Saturday morning, when my brothers and sisters wanted to watch cartoons, I commandeered the TV and set it to Julia Child and Jacques Pépin. I stood vigil in the kitchen while my mom and my titas prepared feasts so gigantic, they set an impossibly high standard for every party I've attended since. Above all I kept my eyes on the tiny, nimble, shamanistic hands of my lola Josefina, whose recipes were our family's wealth and deepest secrets.

At the same time I was impatient for another life, and for the person I might discover myself to be out on my own. After college, I headed to New York and landed a job as a line cook at a rustic-elegant restaurant whose dishes traced an arc from Europe to the American South. For three years I deveined lobes of foie gras and banged out terrines like my life depended on it, each one a little better than the one before, until I was the only one trusted to make them. I was supposed to do this, I thought. This was sophistication: not just cooking, but *cuisine*.

Then I was recruited to open and run an outpost of the San Francisco–based Mission Chinese Food in New York. Suddenly I was deploying Sichuan peppercorns and Chinkiang vinegar in dishes that were irreverently inauthentic but true to a distinctly Asian American experience, one that celebrated Asian ingredients not as "exotics" but bedrock.

I hadn't forgotten the food of my childhood—I made it for myself and friends at home, when we were all broke and needed to eke out big meals from cheap groceries—but I realized that I'd never given it proper respect. I could cook it from memory, but did I really know it? Somewhat abashed, I turned to my lola Josefina. She took me into her kitchen and gently, firmly, with her hair pinned under a black shower cap like a revolutionary's beret, she walked me through one of the trickiest dishes in her repertoire: a whole chicken, divested of its rib cage and thigh bones, filled with a pork and sausage stuffing, then sewed up with twine and roasted until it dripped gold. It was as meticulously engineered as a French galantine. (You can learn more about Lola on page 42; to try this dish for yourself, see page 147.)

This was my initiation, with all the weight of a religious rite. Once I'd been a cook; now I was a chef.

The next generation.

I started sneaking Filipino flavors into dishes at Mission, wondering if anyone would notice, and was thrilled when they did. I wanted to learn more, and so the work of this book began. And as I researched the Philippines' ancient, precolonial history, trying to understand my ancestry, I thought about my living, breathing relatives and all they might have to teach me. I'd put myself at a bit of a distance, not just by crossing the country but in the life I chose to lead; when I began to identify as queer, I had no reference points at home for what that meant. For my own survival, I had to go out in the world and find my people.

Writing this book has been a form of coming home—a way to try to get to know my family better, and to have them get to know me, as a complete person, beyond the daughter and sister whom I know they're proud of.

This is a personal cookbook. I don't claim to speak for Filipinos or Filipino Americans; I can only offer my story. Sometimes I use the Tagalog names of dishes, sometimes English, because the distinction between those languages wasn't always clear in our house. Purists may decry departures from tradition, but I don't believe in treating recipes like relics, preserved in amber. Part of the joy of cooking is that we each bring to the kitchen our own imagination and sense of play. If these flavors are familiar, I hope you'll enjoy where I take them; and if they're new to you, welcome—come inside and eat.

Me, age 6.

My kitchen in Brooklyn.

Sharing THE TABLE

With six kids in the family, we almost never used the dining table for a formal meal. Instead, we helped ourselves directly from giant pots on the stove, then jostled for places around the kitchen counter or sat cross-legged at the coffee table to eat. My mom tried to cook a week's worth of dinners at a time, so they'd be ready to go when she got home from work and my dad had to head to his night shift at McDonald's.

Filipino food is built for a crowd. My mom was one of nine kids; my lola Josefina, the eldest of eleven. Our definition of immediate family includes second and third cousins and people we've called tito and tita for so long, we forget we're not actually related. Everyone brings food—potluck is our way of life—and this is when the dining table finally gets its due, as the stage for a great patchwork of baking dishes and foil bins, packed edge to edge, more than we could ever eat. All day we graze, pausing between plates until hungry again, lunch blurring into dinner. The food holds up, somehow as good six hours in as it was at the start. No one is allowed to go home without leftovers.

When I first started testing recipes for this cookbook, I realized that many of my measurements were calibrated to feed a dozen people. I scaled most of them down, except for the biggest celebration dishes, because if you're going to take the time to debone and stuff a whole chicken, you want an audience to gasp in awe. There will be leftovers—it's a feature, not a bug—since almost everything keeps well: This is a cuisine developed to withstand a hot climate.

And the spirit of inclusion goes beyond abundance. The chef is not an autocrat. Every Filipino meal is a collaboration between cook and diner. Dishes are finished not in the kitchen but at the table, where the sawsawan (dipping sauce) and condiments await— what the cultural historian Doreen Gamboa Fernandez called a "galaxy of flavor-adjusters," and evidence, she wrote, of "the sense of community of the Filipino, the bond between all cooks and their clients, all the backstage crew and the guys onstage, the farmer and the neighbors and relatives who form his support network."

In keeping with that sense of community, it was important for me to put this book together with a Filipino team: Ligaya Mishan, my co-writer, and Jenn de la Vega, a fellow chef who meticulously tested the recipes. It was a privilege to take this journey together, all three of us children of the diaspora (and, by coincidence or fate, all born in California).

I hope that you too will collaborate with me. People outside the Filipino community often first encounter our food not at a restaurant but through a friend, who shows up at a party with what turns out to be the best dish you've ever had. That's what I'd like this book to be: the friend in the kitchen ready to offer suggestions for alternate ingredients and techniques, draw connections with dishes in other cultures, and talk you through flavors and textures you might not be familiar with—and (if I do my job right!) make them your new favorites.

My family at my childhood home in northern California, 2017.

SEASONING MATRIX

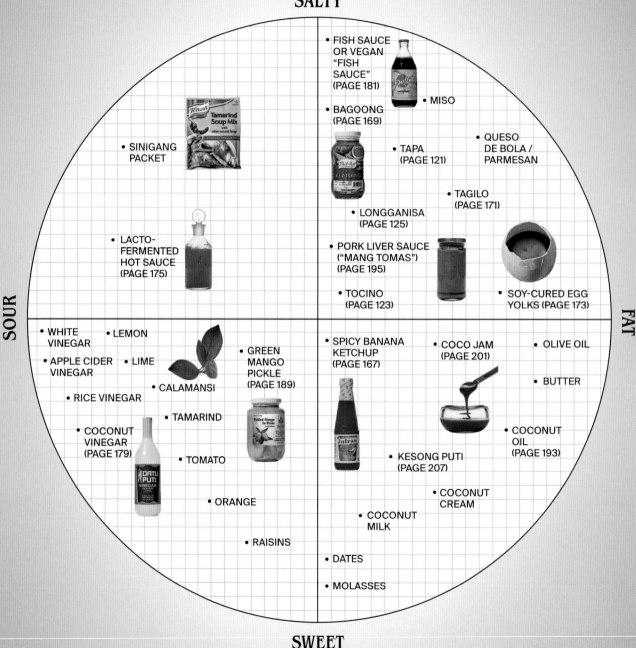

SALTY

SOUR

FAT

SWEET

- FISH SAUCE OR VEGAN "FISH SAUCE" (PAGE 181)
- MISO
- BAGOONG (PAGE 169)
- SINIGANG PACKET
- TAPA (PAGE 121)
- QUESO DE BOLA / PARMESAN
- TAGILO (PAGE 171)
- LONGGANISA (PAGE 125)
- LACTO-FERMENTED HOT SAUCE (PAGE 175)
- PORK LIVER SAUCE ("MANG TOMAS") (PAGE 195)
- TOCINO (PAGE 123)
- SOY-CURED EGG YOLKS (PAGE 173)
- WHITE VINEGAR
- LEMON
- APPLE CIDER VINEGAR
- LIME
- GREEN MANGO PICKLE (PAGE 189)
- SPICY BANANA KETCHUP (PAGE 167)
- COCO JAM (PAGE 201)
- OLIVE OIL
- CALAMANSI
- RICE VINEGAR
- BUTTER
- TAMARIND
- COCONUT VINEGAR (PAGE 179)
- COCONUT OIL (PAGE 193)
- TOMATO
- KESONG PUTI (PAGE 207)
- ORANGE
- COCONUT CREAM
- COCONUT MILK
- RAISINS
- DATES
- MOLASSES

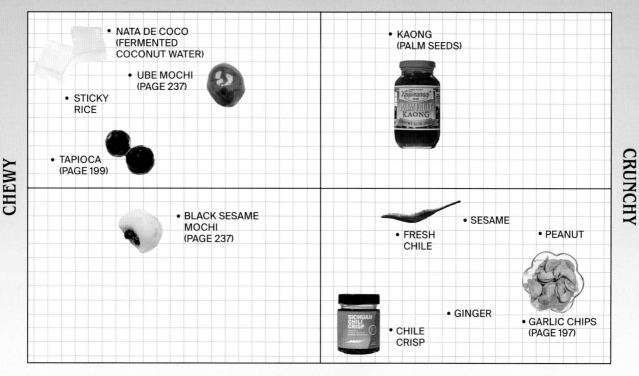

SWEET

CHEWY

- NATA DE COCO (FERMENTED COCONUT WATER)
- UBE MOCHI (PAGE 237)
- STICKY RICE
- TAPIOCA (PAGE 199)
- KAONG (PALM SEEDS)

- BLACK SESAME MOCHI (PAGE 237)
- FRESH CHILE
- SESAME
- PEANUT
- CHILE CRISP
- GINGER
- GARLIC CHIPS (PAGE 197)

CRUNCHY

SALT/SPICE

Immigrant cooking is an art of making do. When my parents and grandparents came to the United States, they had to adapt to the ingredients they found; so too have the estimated ten to twelve million Filipino overseas workers around the world, who leave their families behind to seek jobs abroad—as nannies and nurses, construction workers and engineers, at hotels and in oil fields and on ships—and send billions of dollars home each year, making up about ten percent of the country's gross domestic product.

It turns out that our cuisine is pretty resilient: You can capture that distinctly Filipino flavor mostly using goods already in your larder or available at the local supermarket. Throughout this book I've included substitutions for the more difficult-to-find ingredients, or suggestions on how you can make your own staples, like Latik and coconut oil (page 193), Homemade Coconut Vinegar (page 179), and Bagoong (page 169). But these days many cities and towns are home to at least one well-stocked Filipino or more general Asian grocery, from mega-chains like H Mart and 99 Ranch to family-owned businesses from Boise, Idaho; to Mobile, Alabama—and almost everything can be purchased online.

In making substitutions, it's helpful to know what an ingredient brings to a recipe. So I've arranged a number of the most important ones here in a seasoning matrix, along axes of salty and sweet, sour and fat, chewy and crunchy. Don't worry if you don't recognize some of them now—you'll encounter them again in the recipes that follow, with specific notes on how to use them, and you can always flip back to this page to check the chart and come up with your own sweet-sour-salty-fat-chewy-crunchy adaptations.

It's there if you know where to look—in a strip mall, behind a car wash, at the back of a grocery store, in the Philippines or northern California, or anyplace Filipinos call home—this bare-bones canteen where, if you listen close, you can hear the low, steady hiss of steam. Food awaits in steel bins, warm and replenished as needed. Turo-turo means "point-point," and that's how you order. Prices are kept reasonable by low overhead: There might be just one or two people on staff at any time, moving between stove and cash register. You clear your own plate; you do your part. In return, you get abundance. Almost everything in this cookbook could fit in this chapter. What I've included here are the recipes that in my experience hold up the best over time, so you can linger and forget that you have anything to do but eat.

TURO-TURO

TOO•roh TOO•roh

The buffet at Rene Rose Island Cuisine,
a beloved turo-turo in Sunnyvale, Northern California.

In the 1970s, the chef Nora Daza opened the restaurant Aux Îles Philippines in Paris, in the Latin Quarter on the Left Bank, and the luminaries descended. Brigitte Bardot came for the lumpia (page 107); Simone de Beauvoir put in an appearance, and reportedly so did a Bourbon prince. Among the specialties was tenderloin anointed with soy sauce and calamansi (an indigenous citrus with a bit of the sweetness of an orange but tart as a lime), touted on the menu as Steak Philippin.

This was bistek, and it was one of my lola's signature dishes, too (see "Listening to Lola," page 42). She'd take London broil, a cheaper cut of meat, and pound it into tenderness with a mallet. Then she'd cut onions into rounds ½-inch (12 mm) thick and give them a quick sear before tossing a little water in the pan so it flared up and the onions got extra crisp. I like to use rib eye, which is a splurge but worth it, with the pillowy fat cap and lush marbling of the meat–enough fat to coat your lips–and the bright sting of citrus cutting through it. The dish has only a few ingredients, so each one matters, especially good olive oil. (And use calamansi instead of lemon, if you can find it.)

When the pan is hot, be ready to move quickly–the mini-steaks should barely kiss the skillet, just enough that the meat keeps its blush at the center.

BISTEK *bee • STEHK*
SEARED RIB EYE WITH LEMON AND ONIONS SERVES 4 TO 6

2 rib eye steaks, 1-inch (2.5 cm) thick (about 1½ pounds/680 g)

4 tablespoons (60 ml) olive oil

10 bay leaves, fresh or dried

8 cloves garlic, smashed and peeled

1 large white onion, peeled and sliced crosswise into ¾-inch-thick (2 cm) disks

Kosher salt and coarsely cracked black pepper

2 tablespoons unsalted butter

½ cup (120 ml) calamansi juice, frozen or squeezed fresh (from around 12 calamansi), or ½ cup (120 ml) lemon juice (from 2 to 3 lemons)

3 tablespoons (45 ml) fresh orange juice (from ½ orange)

¼ cup (60 ml) soy sauce

Steamed rice, for serving

Trim and discard any excess fat from the steaks if you wish. (I like a lot of fat, especially on a rib eye.) Cut each steak horizontally into 2 thinner steaks, ½-inch (12 mm) thick, then cut each of those into 5 or 6 pieces. No need for the pieces to be the same size–they can be roughly chopped rectangles and triangles. What matters is that they're all even in thickness. Set aside in the refrigerator to keep the meat cold; this will keep it from overcooking.

•

Pour 2 tablespoons of the olive oil into a large skillet over medium heat. Add the bay leaves, pressing to flatten them, and fry for 30 seconds to 1 minute–flipping them halfway through–until they're toasted at the edges and fragrant. Transfer the bay leaves to a plate.

•

Raise the heat to medium high, add the garlic cloves to the skillet, and sear for 1 to 2 minutes, flipping frequently, until gilded on both sides. Transfer to the plate with the bay leaves.

•

Add the onion to the skillet, keeping the rounds intact so the rings don't separate. Season with salt and let cook undisturbed for about 2 minutes, until the undersides of the onions begin to steam and bronze. Flip the onion rounds, add 2 tablespoons water, cover the skillet with a lid, and continue to steam for 2 minutes. Remove the lid and continue cooking for about 2 minutes, until the onions are tender but still have a bit of crunch and the liquid has almost evaporated. Transfer the onions to a plate.

•

Add the remaining 2 tablespoons olive oil to the skillet and heat over medium high until ripping hot. Take the beef out of the refrigerator and season all over with salt and pepper. Working quickly with kitchen tweezers or tongs, sear the beef–in 2 to 3 batches to avoid crowding–until caramelized and golden brown but not fully cooked through, 1 to 2 minutes per side for medium or medium-rare. When done, each piece should look like a mini-steak. Transfer to a platter and repeat with the remaining pieces. Arrange the steaks on the platter so that no pieces overlap.

→

Add the butter to the skillet and cook over medium high for 1 to 2 minutes, swirling the pan, until browned. Add the calamansi or lemon juice, orange juice, and soy sauce and cook for another 2 to 3 minutes, stirring frequently with a small rubber spatula, scraping up what French chefs call fond—the brown seared bits stuck to the pan—until the sauce is glossy and slightly looser than maple syrup.

•

Drizzle and drape the pan sauce over the steaks. Top with the onions and garlic and tuck the bay leaves around and under the steaks as decoration (not to be eaten). Serve immediately with rice.

COCONUT MILK CHICKEN ADOBO
ah • DOH • boh SERVES 6 TO 8

Adobo is probably the Filipino dish best known and least understood by Westerners. Like the name of the Philippines itself—imposed by Spanish colonialists in the sixteenth century in honor of their king, Philip II—it bears the lexical imprint of a foreign empire. In 1613, a Franciscan friar, attempting to compile a Tagalog dictionary, reached for the Spanish verb adobar to describe the dousing of ingredients with vinegar, to season and pickle. But that technique of preservation, essential in a tropical climate, long predated his arrival. Adobo is an indigenous dish, and one that contains multitudes, with no two recipes alike.

Vinegar is the constant. Here I use coconut vinegar (see page 179 if you're feeling ambitious and want to make your own!), along with coconut milk and coconut oil—three forms of coconut, to bring silkiness without heaviness. (Coconut milk adobo, or adobo sa gata, is a tried and true variation in the Philippines but a little less common in the U.S.) It's just as good if you substitute rice vinegar or diluted white or apple cider vinegar.

And the chicken is just a suggestion: You could roast or steam a whole fish and pour the adobo over it, or sear mushrooms, fresh langka (jackfruit), or big meaty chunks of cauliflower and throw them in as the stew simmers down and turns thick.

2 tablespoons coconut oil, store-bought or homemade (page 193)

2 teaspoons whole black peppercorns

1 teaspoon coarsely cracked black pepper

½ teaspoon red pepper flakes

4 pounds (1.8 kg) chicken drumsticks and thighs, bone in and skin on

15 garlic cloves, smashed and peeled

1 cup (240 ml) unsweetened, full-fat coconut milk

½ cup (120 ml) coconut vinegar (store-bought or homemade, page 179) or rice vinegar

½ cup (120 ml) soy sauce

8 bay leaves, fresh or dried

1 whole fresh serrano chile

Steamed rice, for serving

In a large pot, heat the coconut oil on medium until shimmering. Add the whole peppercorns, coarsely cracked black pepper, and red pepper flakes. Lay the drumsticks and thighs in the pan, skin side down, and raise the heat to medium high. Cook for about 5 minutes, resisting the urge to poke and prod; just let the chicken cook undisturbed, until the fat starts to render, melting into the pan, and the skin turns slightly brown. Using kitchen tweezers or tongs, flip over the chicken.

•

Add the garlic, coconut milk, vinegar, soy sauce, bay leaves, serrano chile, and 1 cup (240 ml) water. Let the mixture come to a boil. Put a lid on the pot, reduce the heat to medium low, and simmer for 1 to 1½ hours, stirring occasionally. The chicken should feel loose, almost—but not yet—ready to slip off the bone.

•

Remove the lid, raise the temperature to medium high, and reduce the sauce by cooking uncovered for another 15 minutes, stirring occasionally, until the sauce is thick as velvet.

•

Serve over rice, to soak up the sauce.

Some might consider this the OG adobo, a duel between vinegar and soy sauce, sour and salt, with whole black peppercorns that soften as they braise and pop in the mouth. Then again, purists would reject the addition of soy sauce as an outside influence, since it was introduced to the Philippines by Chinese traders—although this took place possibly as far back as the second century A.D., so it's been around a long time.

Keep in mind that the recipe is really just a starting point. For the meat, you might go for all pork belly, with its stripes of fat, or mix shoulder, ribs, and belly, or pair pork with chicken (remembering that they have different cooking times). I call for apple cider or white vinegar, but you can use more delicate rice vinegar or the traditional coconut vinegar (page 179); just be sure to add a bit more, to balance out the salt and cut through the richness of the fat. And try tossing in hunks of potato or whole hard-boiled eggs toward the end. As the novelist Gina Apostol says, adobo "has the most leeway for a cook's imagination, hubris, art, or bigoted sense of one's own mother's love-and-greatness."

I like to double the numbers because leftovers keep a long time; after all, vinegar and salt were a means of preserving meat in the time before refrigeration. If you reduce the sauce to a more syrupy consistency and shred the pork, it makes a great filling for Siopao (steamed buns, page 113) or a base for fried rice.

PORK ADOBO *ah • D O H • boh*

SERVES 4

1 pound (455 g) pork shoulder, boneless pork ribs, or pork belly, cut into 1½ inch (4 cm) dice
Kosher salt and coarsely cracked black pepper
2 tablespoons olive oil
½ teaspoon whole black peppercorns
4 cloves garlic, smashed and peeled
4 bay leaves, fresh or dried
⅓ cup (75 ml) apple cider or white vinegar
⅓ cup (75 ml) soy sauce
Steamed rice, for serving

Season the diced pork on both sides with salt and pepper.

•

Heat the olive oil in a 3-quart (2.8 L) saucepan over medium high. Add the pork chunks and sear for 2 minutes, then flip them over and sear the other side for 2 minutes. While the pork is cooking, season it in the pan with more pepper. After searing both sides, add the whole black peppercorns and garlic and let them toast until fragrant, another minute or two.

•

Add the bay leaves, apple cider vinegar, soy sauce, and 2 cups (480 ml) water. Stir and bring to a boil. Cover and braise by simmering on low heat for 1½ to 1¾ hours, lifting the lid to stir occasionally.

•

When the pork chunks are fork-tender and the fat is soft and jiggly, remove the lid, raise the heat to medium high, and continue to cook until the sauce is reduced to a light syrupy consistency, coating and clinging to the pork. (Although the sauce consistency is really a matter of taste—some like it loose, others very syrupy; my preference is right in the middle.)

•

And always: Serve over rice.

I loved squid when I was a kid, especially in adobo, with its briny ink staining the sauce black. The ink is full of glutamate, the source of that elusive fifth flavor, umami. Later in life, I fell for shiokara, a small, rich Japanese dish of fermented squid guts studded with nubs of raw squid, the perfect slippery, salty counterpoint to beer or sake. It inspired me to add squid guts here, alongside the rings, tentacles, and ink, all quickly poached at the very end, no more than a minute. The guts melt beautifully into the sauce—but if that's not to your taste, there's no shame in skipping that step!

ADOBONG PUSIT
ah • D O H • bohng poo • S E E T
SQUID INK ADOBO

SERVES 2

8 ounces (225 g) cleaned squid or baby squid,
    beak and cuttlebone discarded (see note),
    ink and half the guts reserved (optional)
2 tablespoons olive oil
¼ teaspoon coarsely cracked black pepper
4 cloves garlic, smashed and peeled
1 whole fresh serrano chile
2 bay leaves, fresh or dried
1 tablespoon soy sauce
1 tablespoon Suka at Bawang (page 177) or apple
    cider vinegar
Steamed rice, for serving

Note: If cleaning your own squid, start by pulling the head off the body. Reserve the ink sac and guts, if using. With kitchen shears, cut the head below the eyes and separate the arms and tentacles. Squeeze the center of the tentacles to remove the bony nub of beak. Pluck the thin, glass-like sliver of cuttlebone from the tube. Discard the eyes, beak, and cuttlebone, and rinse and dry the remaining parts.

Cut the squid into rings, arms, and tentacles—unless using baby squid, which may be tossed in whole.

•

Heat a 2-quart (2 L) saucepan over medium high. Add the olive oil, black pepper, and garlic and cook for about 2 minutes, until softened. Add the serrano chile, bay leaves, soy sauce, and vinegar, then simmer for another minute.

•

Finally, add the squid, then the ink, squeezed from the sac, and half the reserved guts, if using (discard the rest). Cook in the liquid for just 1 minute; the sauce should thicken instantaneously. Turn off the heat and transfer to a serving bowl.

•

Serve over hot rice and present the serrano chile to someone who will appreciate the extra heat.

ilipinos are fond of repeating syllables to make new words, like Halo-Halo (page 263), a dessert named for its mix-mix of ingredients, and Turo-Turo (page 16), steam-table joints where you point-point at the dishes you want. (Linguists call this reduplication, and it's characteristic of Austronesian languages like Tagalog, although English speakers do it too: no-no, hush-hush, boo-boo.) So bola-bola, little deep-fried garlicky meatballs, get their name from the word for ball, said twice—fitting, because you never eat just one.

As in Mexican albóndigas, these meatballs have a high ratio of starch to meat, which means they're both nourishing and inexpensive to make. When I was starting out as a line cook, I used to feed them to my roommate straight out of the fryer. For the ground beef mixture, I prefer russet potatoes—the potato of choice for French fries—because they crisp up the best. If you double the recipe, you can save the leftovers for up to two days, to add to chicken broth for Bola-Bola Soup (page 54) or eat straight from the refrigerator as a snack: When cold, they're just as delicious.

BOLA-BOLA
BOH•lah BOH•lah
BEEF MEATBALLS

MAKES 20 MEATBALLS (1½ INCHES/4 CM IN DIAMETER)

8 ounces (225 g) russet potatoes, unpeeled

2½ teaspoons kosher salt

1 pound (455 g) ground beef

4 cloves garlic (about ½ ounce/12 g), peeled and minced

1 tablespoon soy sauce

1½ teaspoons fish sauce

1 large egg, beaten

1½ teaspoons coarsely cracked black pepper

1 tablespoon all-purpose flour

½ cup (120 ml) canola or other neutral oil

Steamed rice, for serving

Banana ketchup, store-bought or homemade (page 167), or tomato ketchup, for serving

Put the potatoes in a small saucepan, cover with water, and add 1½ teaspoons of the salt. Bring to a boil, then simmer over medium low for about 20 minutes, until the potatoes are tender enough that a knife can slip in without resistance. Drain the potatoes and rest on a plate in the freezer for about 5 minutes (or 10 minutes in the refrigerator), until cool enough to handle.

•

Slide the skins off with your fingers and discard. In a large mixing bowl, break the potatoes one by one into small pieces, again just using your fingers. Look over the broken potato bits and crush the largest ones until they are no more than ½ inch (12 mm).

•

Add the ground beef, garlic, soy sauce, fish sauce, egg, pepper, and remaining 1 teaspoon salt. Sprinkle the flour over the beef mixture and combine gently with your fingers, being careful not to overwork the beef. Shape into 20 meatballs, each about the size of a Ping-Pong ball, and set on a sheet tray or plate.

•

In a large saucepan, heat the oil on medium high until it shimmers. Add 10 meatballs to the pan, allowing for about ½ inch (12 mm) of breathing space between meatballs, so they can sear evenly. Shallow-fry on each side for 4 to 5 minutes, until the meatballs turn dark brown, a few shades past caramel. They should be crispy on the outside while still juicy within. Transfer to a plate lined with a paper towel. Repeat with a second batch of 10 meatballs.

•

Serve immediately with rice and banana ketchup. Or store the meatballs raw or cooked, up to 2 days in the refrigerator, to make Bola-Bola Soup (page 54).

In Tagalog, the name of this dish tells you how it's made: Giniling comes from the verb meaning "to grind." A Cuban friend of mine calls it picadillo, from the Spanish picar, to chop; for both of us, the recipe is a legacy of foreign occupation that we made our own.

I remember it as an after-school meal, a simple hash of ground beef, onions, and garlic, with raisins for little pops of sweetness, all bound together by ketchup—not unlike the American sloppy joe. Sometimes we'd toss in a hot dog or Vienna sausage, minced into a salty rubble. (Try it!)

My dad liked to add, on the side, a plank of fried banana, ripe enough that the sugars ran in the pan. A saba banana from the Philippines is best, stout with squarish edges, small and sweet, but a more readily available Cavendish banana or an extra-ripe plantain would be fine.

BEEF GINILING
ghee • NEE • leeng
SPICED TOMATO-STEWED GROUND BEEF, POTATO, AND RAISINS SERVES 4

4 tablespoons (60 ml) olive oil

1 clove garlic, coarsely chopped

½ small yellow onion, cut into ½ inch (12 mm) dice

½ red bell pepper, cut into ¼ inch (6 mm) dice

½ teaspoon sweet paprika

1 pound (455 g) ground beef

⅓ cup (75 ml) tomato ketchup or banana ketchup, store-bought or homemade (page 167)

2 teaspoons tomato paste

¼ cup (35 g) black raisins

Kosher salt

½ teaspoon coarsely cracked black pepper

2 ripe saba bananas or Cavendish bananas or very ripe plantains, sliced in half lengthwise

Steamed rice, for serving

4 large eggs, fried sunny-side-up (optional)

Heat a large sauté pan over medium high. Add 2 tablespoons of the olive oil, and when the oil shimmers, add the garlic, onion, bell pepper, and paprika. Cook, stirring occasionally, for about 4 minutes, until the onion turns translucent and sweet.

•

Add the ground beef, ketchup, tomato paste, raisins, salt, and pepper. Continue to cook, stirring occasionally, for 6 to 7 minutes, until the ground beef has browned, the sauce has slightly thickened, and the raisins have plumped with the cooking juices. Turn the heat off and leave the sautéed beef in the pan to keep warm.

•

Heat another sauté pan over medium high and add the remaining 2 tablespoons olive oil. When the oil shimmers, add 2 halves of the bananas in an even layer, starting with the cut side down. Sear the banana halves to a deep golden brown, 2 to 3 minutes on each side. Transfer to a plate lined with paper towels and repeat with the remaining banana halves.

•

Serve the sautéed beef with warm rice, the fried banana halves, and, if you like, an egg fried sunny-side-up on every plate.

When I was coming up through Brooklyn kitchens, everyone was reading *The Whole Beast* by the English chef Fergus Henderson and getting excited about nose-to-tail cooking—which to many in the Philippines is just a way of life: If you don't have much, you use everything you have.

I was already comfortable with offal, because I grew up eating dinuguan, pork blood stew, which my and pretty much every Fil-Am kid's parents tried to pass off as "chocolate meat," thinking that the presence of blood would make us squeamish. Not me. I always loved the richness of dinuguan, just as I now love French boudin noir, British black pudding with its whiff of warming spices, and the iron tang of Korean soondae, a purple-black sausage that has an almost even ratio of rice and noodles to blood.

You can ask your butcher for pork blood or look out for it in the frozen section at an Asian grocery. The braise works beautifully with fatty cuts of pork, and I like to add the skin for texture and extra thickening from the collagen. If you have leftovers, try wrapping a spoonful or two in rice and nori as a sushi roll. You could even tuck in bonus offal, braised until tender: tripe, tendon, liver, heart, kidneys—the "nasty" but oh so lovely bits.

DINUGUAN
dee•noo•goo•AHN
PORK BLOOD STEW SERVES 5

1½ teaspoons kosher salt

1 whole star anise

3 whole cloves

1 teaspoon coarsely cracked black pepper

1½ pounds (680 g) skin-on pork shoulder or pork belly, cut into 1-inch (2.5 cm) dice

1 tablespoon olive oil

2 cloves garlic, peeled and coarsely chopped

1 (1-inch/2.5 cm) piece fresh ginger, peeled and coarsely chopped

1 medium yellow onion, finely minced

2 bay leaves, fresh or dried

½ cup (120 ml) apple cider vinegar

1½ teaspoons fish sauce

1 whole fresh long green chile or jalapeño

5 ounces (150 ml) frozen pork blood, thawed

In a spice grinder or mortar and pestle, combine the salt, anise, and cloves and grind to a powder. Season the pork with the black pepper and ground spices and mix to distribute.

•

Heat a large saucepan over high. Add the olive oil, then the pork. Brown for about 15 minutes, stirring occasionally but resting in between to develop a nice fond—the dark caramelized bits that bring depth of flavor to the dish—and to help render the pork fat for a richer, more velvety sauce.

•

Add the garlic, ginger, onion, and bay leaves and sauté while stirring for about 5 minutes. Add the vinegar, ½ cup (120 ml) water, the fish sauce, and the chile. Bring to a boil, then lower the heat to medium low and cover with a lid.

•

Simmer for 1½ to 2 hours, until the pork is tender. The fat should be wobbly and break easily with a spoon. Drop the heat to low and slowly drizzle the pork blood into the pot and stir. The sauce should thicken within 2 to 3 minutes and coat your spoon. Add a couple tablespoons water to loosen if necessary.

•

Serve immediately. This also makes great reheated leftovers—like most Filipino dishes!—and keeps in the refrigerator for up to 1 week.

For a brief twenty months in the middle of the eighteenth century, Manila was part of the British empire, a pawn between England and Spain. As the cultural historian Felice Prudente Sta. Maria has written, the kare in kare-kare and karinderia (small restaurant) is believed to derive from the Tamil kari or curry, brought to the Philippines by the Indian cooks who served with the Royal Navy. But the kare-kare of today shares little with its South Asian namesake beyond a golden hue, achieved with annatto (known in the Philippines as achuete).

Working on this recipe, I realized it had more in common with mafe, a peanut stew from West Africa. As I've learned from the chefs Precious Okoyomon and Yewande Komolafe, there are many resonances between our cuisines, from the long braising of meats to the frequent use of brine for umami and depth: stockfish and ground crayfish in West Africa, bagoong and patis (fish sauce) in the Philippines.

In homage to mafe, I use palm oil here, which lends a smoky and almost carrot-like flavor; you can substitute coconut oil (see page 193), or canola or other neutral oil, if you prefer. Toasted chiles yield more smoke, making it practically an ingredient in itself, evoking for me the thrilling smokiness of Nigerian party jollof rice, cooked over fire in giant half-burnt pots.

The oxtail needs 3 hours on the stove to fully unknit—or just 40 minutes in a pressure cooker: a worthy investment.

KARE-KARE
kah • REH kah • REH
OXTAIL PEANUT STEW SERVES 6

2 large onions, one whole and unpeeled, the other cut into a large dice

2½ pounds (1.2 kg) oxtail, cut into 1-inch (2.5 cm) medallions

2 bay leaves, fresh or dried

2 teaspoons kosher salt

5 dried Thai chiles

1 cup (170 to 200 g) toasted rice from Rice Coffee (page 275), ground into a fine powder

4 teaspoons finely ground annatto seed

2 teaspoons coarsely cracked black pepper

3 tablespoons (45 ml) palm oil

1 cup (128 g) coarsely ground peanuts

1 (2-inch/5 cm) piece fresh ginger, peeled and finely minced

6 cloves garlic, smashed and peeled

2 large carrots, cut into large dice

2 whole fresh Fresno or serrano chiles

⅓ cup (75 ml) fish sauce

½ cup (120 ml) peanut butter

1 medium Japanese eggplant, cut into 1½-inch (4 cm) pieces

½ bunch long beans, cut into 3-inch (7.5 cm) pieces (about 1½ cups/165 g)

12 pods okra

1 large red bell pepper, cut into 1-inch (2.5 mm) dice

½ head small green cabbage, chopped into 1½-inch (4 cm) pieces

1 bunch kangkong (water spinach) or spinach

Bagoong, store-bought or homemade (page 169)

Steamed rice, for serving

Turn a stovetop gas burner to medium high. Cut the whole onion in half and, keeping the skin on, char each half directly on the burner, rotating every 2 minutes, until the exterior of the onion has blackened.

•

Fill a stockpot with 3 quarts (2.8 L) water. Add the charred onion halves, oxtail, bay leaves, and salt. Bring to a boil over high heat, then reduce to medium low and simmer with the lid on—occasionally skimming off the foam—for about 3 hours, or until the meat is tender, just shy of falling off the bone.

•

Turn off the heat and set the pot aside. Put a strainer over a bowl or a large heat-safe glass measuring cup and pour the cooking liquid through the strainer until you have about 4 cups (960 ml).

•

Heat another large pot over medium high. Once hot, add the dried chiles, toasted rice powder, annatto seed, and black pepper. Stir for about 5 minutes, until light brown and fragrant. Add the palm oil and ground peanuts, and toast for another 3 minutes, or until deeply browned. Add the ginger, garlic, carrots, diced onion, fresh chiles, fish sauce, and peanut butter, and cook for about 8 minutes, stirring occasionally.

•

Add the oxtail from the stockpot and the strained cooking liquid. Then add the eggplant, long beans, okra, bell pepper, and cabbage, and simmer covered for about 25 minutes, until the sauce has thickened into a gravy that clings to the oxtail and vegetables. Five minutes before serving, stir in the kangkong and bagoong, to taste.

•

Ladle over warm rice with some of each of the vegetables.

The only fried chicken I knew as a kid came from KFC and Banquet frozen family packs. So it was a revelation when one day my dad made dry fried chicken à la Max's, a Philippine chain founded in the wake of World War II, which today has outposts from Milpitas and Waipahu to Las Vegas and Dubai. The chicken was steamed whole before it got dunked in the deep fryer, making it extra juicy and miraculously crispy without a batter.

This recipe draws from both Max's and my time at Mission Chinese Food in New York, where I experimented with rice koji—an essential ingredient in the making of soy sauce, sake, and miso: steamed rice inoculated with spores of *Aspergillus oryzae* (kin to the mold that gives blue cheese its veins and funk)—to tenderize the chicken, before dusting it with rice flour for a subtle crust. Here I prime the chicken with a marinade of raw rice pulverized into a sort of coarse rice flour, then air-dry it in the refrigerator overnight, for maximal crisp.

Although I suggest a whole chicken (in the true Max's style), feel free to split it in two or use your favorite cut pieces. Just be sure to follow the same air-drying process: The extra step makes all the difference.

MAX'S STYLE FRIED CHICKEN

SERVES 3 OR 4

2 scallions, trimmed and chopped

1 (2-inch/5 cm) piece fresh ginger, peeled and chopped

2 bay leaves, fresh or dried

3 cloves garlic, smashed and peeled

1 tablespoon fish sauce

1 teaspoon soy sauce

1 teaspoon kosher salt

2 teaspoons whole black peppercorns

¼ cup (40 g) uncooked white rice

1 chicken (3 pounds/1.4 kg), giblets removed, rinsed, and patted dry with paper towels

4 cups (960 ml) canola or other neutral oil, for frying

Steamed rice, for serving

Banana ketchup, store-bought or homemade (page 167), or Suka at Bawang (page 177), for serving

In a blender, combine ¼ cup water with the scallions, ginger, bay leaves, garlic, fish sauce, soy sauce, salt, peppercorns, and uncooked rice. Blend for about 2 minutes, until the mixture is smooth.
•

Rub the marinade all over the chicken, including inside the cavity.
•

Lay a folded paper towel on a plate large enough to hold the chicken. Cover a beer or soda can or can of beans with plastic wrap and set it on the plate on top of the paper towel. Hold the chicken upright and lower the cavity over the can, so that the chicken appears to be standing. (The paper towel underneath will keep the can from slipping and collect any juices.) Let the chicken marinate in this standing position in the refrigerator overnight or up to 24 hours, until the marinade is dry to the touch. (Propping up the chicken helps the skin to air-dry, but it's okay to lay the chicken on a baking tray with a rack, if that's easier.)
•

In a large pot, set up a steaming basket over 1 inch (2.5 cm) of water. Put the chicken in the steamer and cook over medium high heat for 20 to 25 minutes. Remove the chicken and let it rest and cool on a plate for about 15 minutes.
•

In a pot large enough to accommodate the chicken, heat the oil over medium high, until it reaches 375°F (190°C). Carefully lower the whole chicken into the hot oil and fry for 8 to 10 minutes, until the skin is crisp. (If the chicken is not entirely submerged in the oil, very carefully turn it over with tongs after 8 to 10 minutes—you might want to use two sets of tongs for a more secure grip, so the chicken won't slip and splash the hot oil—then fry the other side for 8 to 10 minutes.) Remove from the oil and let drain on paper towels for about 10 minutes.
•

Carve the chicken into 10 parts: 2 drumsticks, 2 thighs, 2 wings, and the 2 breasts, each cut in half.
•

Serve with steamed rice and your choice of banana ketchup or a sawsawan (dipping sauce) like suka at bawang.

I was a child when I last ate my mom's croquettes, but when it came time to set down the recipe, I could cook them from memory. Mashed potatoes—fortified with just enough milk to lend creaminess without heft—make a cozy little pocket for a simple filling of ground beef with a flourish of garlic and onion, brought to seething in the pan, and bright pops of green peas. (I add Parmesan for more depth of flavor, and panko to give the crust some crackle.) I remember helping my mom shape the balls, studiously palming each one until it was as round as a planet, having honed my skills with Play-Doh. This is a food born of frugality, a means of repurposing leftovers; it can be just a snack, but with rice, it's a meal.

CROQUETTES

MAKES 5 CROQUETTES, ABOUT 2 INCHES (5 CM) IN DIAMETER

1 pound (455 g) russet potatoes, not peeled

1½ teaspoons kosher salt, plus more for finishing

⅓ cup (75 ml) milk

¼ cup (25 g) freshly grated Parmesan

2 tablespoons olive oil

4 cloves garlic, peeled and coarsely chopped

½ white onion, finely minced

12 ounces (340 g) ground beef

½ cup (65 g) frozen green peas

½ teaspoon coarsely cracked black pepper

1 cup (125 g) all-purpose flour

2 large eggs, beaten

1 cup (70 g) panko breadcrumbs

3 cups (720 ml) canola or other neutral oil, for frying

Banana ketchup, store-bought or homemade (page 167), or tomato ketchup, for serving

In a 2-quart (2 L) saucepan, combine the potatoes, 1 teaspoon of the salt, and water to cover. Bring to a boil, then drop the heat to medium and cook for 40 minutes, or until the potatoes have softened and offer little resistance when you poke them with a paring knife.

•

Drain the water from the pan and let the potatoes rest for about 5 minutes, or until cool enough to peel with your fingertips. Mash the potatoes in a mixing bowl using a whisk or potato masher, and mix in the milk and Parmesan until combined. (Leaving a few chunks of the potatoes is fine.) Chill in the refrigerator.

•

Heat a medium sauté pan over medium high. Add the olive oil, swirl the pan, then add the garlic and onion. Cook and stir until softened, about 3 minutes. Add the ground beef, frozen peas, remaining ½ teaspoon salt, and the pepper and cook for another 3 minutes, or until the beef has browned. Transfer to a plate and let cool.

•

Scoop about ½ cup (120 g) of the mashed potatoes and, using clean hands, make an indent in the center of the potatoes and fill it with about 1½ tablespoons of the meat filling. Enclose the meat completely with mashed potatoes, then roll into a neat ball and set aside. Repeat until you have 5 pieces.

•

Set up three bowls and fill them with the flour, beaten egg, and panko, respectively. This is your breading station. Roll each potato ball in flour, followed by egg wash, then panko. Repeat with all the potato balls and set aside.

•

Line a plate with paper towels. Fill a 2-quart (2 L) saucepan with the neutral oil and heat over medium high. Fry the croquettes two at a time—making sure there's enough space between croquettes to fry evenly—90 seconds on each side, for a total of 3 minutes.

•

Transfer the fried croquettes to the paper towel–lined plate and sprinkle a little salt on each. Cool for a few minutes before serving with banana ketchup.

*I*n high-end professional kitchens, a pork chop is almost always double-cut, as thick as a dictionary, and seared just enough to get a crust on the outside, with the juices still surging within. But my mom liked her chops thin and fried hard; she served them in stacks, with nothing but rice, and I could easily eat two at a pop. My version is somewhere in the middle: crispy and juicy, dressed in bronzed garlic and a shower of hot butter. You can serve the chops with the sides of your choice, but I like pairing them with Laing (taro leaves stewed in coconut milk, page 67).

FRIED PORK CHOP STACK

SERVES 4

4 bone-in pork chops, ½-inch (12 mm) thick
Kosher salt and coarsely cracked black pepper
8 cloves garlic, smashed and peeled
1 cup (240 ml) apple cider vinegar
4 tablespoons (60 ml) olive oil
4 tablespoons (½ stick/55 g) cold unsalted butter,
      cut into 1-tablespoon pats
Steamed rice, for serving

On a cutting board, season each pork chop generously with the salt and pepper. Layer the pork chops in a large sealable plastic bag, alternating with a couple cloves of the smashed garlic between each pork chop. Pour in the vinegar. Press each corner of the bag to squeeze out any air, then seal. Set the bag of pork chops on a large plate and let marinate in the refrigerator for 2 to 3 hours or overnight.

Scoop the garlic cloves and pork chops out of the marinade and transfer to paper towels. (Discard the vinegar.) Pat down each chop with additional paper towels; the drier the chops are, the quicker they'll brown in the pan. If preparing the chops in the morning for dinner that night or the following day, let them rest in the refrigerator on paper towels to keep them dry. Reserve the marinated garlic cloves for frying.

Right before serving, heat a large skillet over medium high and add 1 tablespoon of the oil. Wait to remove the pork chops from the refrigerator until you're ready to cook. (The chill will help keep the meat tender and juicy.) Quickly transfer one marinated chop to the pan and lower the heat to medium.

Using a fish spatula, gently press down the pork chop as it browns, about 2 minutes. (Because the fish spatula has a larger surface area than a spoon, it can press down the meat all at once, which helps to get a better crust.)

Switching to a metal tablespoon, flip the pork chop over. Add 1 tablespoon of the cold butter to the pan, followed by 2 of the smashed and marinated garlic cloves. Swirl the pan slightly to help melt the butter, then immediately start basting the pork chop with the butter, tilting the pan so the butter pools and flicking the spoon quickly so it doesn't burn. There's no need to flip the pork chop again; as you baste, some of the butter will sizzle across the top while the rest glides underneath, so you're browning both sides at once. Flip the garlic until softened and lightly browned all around, then lay it on top of the pork chop to season it.

After another 1½ minutes of cooking, transfer the pork chop and smashed garlic cloves to a plate and pour the garlic-butter sauce from the hot pan over the top. The garlic should look burnished and the pork chop should be medium well, juicy and golden on the outside, with the fat partially melted and crispy at the edges.

Clean out the pan with a paper towel and scrape off any charred bits with the fish spatula.

Repeat the process with each pork chop and the remaining garlic cloves. When you finish each chop, add it to the stack on the plate, along with the garlic, and let rest for 10 minutes. This is a crucial step: If you cut into the chops too soon, their juices, still hot and seething from the pan, will spill out; the fibers in the meat need time to relax and allow the juices to soak back in.

Serve immediately with warm rice.

When I was little, my brothers and sisters and I went to a small Catholic school, and at the start of summer, we'd have a carnival—we called it a fiesta—and everyone would line up at the Filipino BBQ stall and then wander around tearing meat off the skewers with their teeth. My parents volunteered at the Italian sausage booth, and because we were friends with the people cooking the BBQ, we got to bypass the line by surreptitiously trading sausages for skewers: the magic of the Filipino discount (see page 278).

Here pork belly is cut thin and left overnight in a sticky-sweet marinade with just enough vinegar to stand up to the sugar. I douse the charred skewers with extra suka at bawang afterwards, and eat them with rice and Atsara (green papaya pickle, page 183), Smoky Charred Eggplant (page 187), or Lacto-Fermented Green Mango (page 189). Two skewers make a meal, although it's hard not to go for three.

A note on grilling: When I was in the Philippines, I loved watching cooks get a fire really hot by waving at the coals with a bamboo fan. These days I always keep one in my grill kit. You can also make a little square with your index finger and thumb and blow through the square to direct air toward coals that need extra attention.

FILIPINO PORK BBQ

MAKES 10 TO 14 SKEWERS

1 onion, diced

12 cloves garlic, peeled

Juice of 1 lemon

2 tablespoons Suka at Bawang (page 177) or apple cider vinegar

1 whole fresh chile (jalapeño, serrano, Thai), or to taste

¼ cup (56 g) tomato paste

½ cup (110 g) packed brown sugar

2 teaspoons coarsely cracked black pepper

Kosher salt

2 pounds (910 g) boneless pork belly, skin removed, cut into rough 1-inch (2.5 cm) squares, ½-inch (12 mm) thick

In a blender, puree the onion, garlic cloves, lemon juice, suka at bawang, chile, tomato paste, brown sugar, and black pepper for about 3 minutes, until very smooth.

•

Salt the pork belly pieces generously, making sure to season all sides, then transfer the meat to a large airtight container. Pour the marinade from the blender over the pork belly and stir to combine. Cover and refrigerate overnight.

•

The next day, prepare a charcoal grill. While the grill is heating, soak 10 wooden skewers in water. (This will keep them from catching fire.) Take the marinated pork belly from the refrigerator and spear 4 to 5 pieces on each skewer, aligning them in a neat stack with spaces in between. You should have 10 to 14 skewers in all. Set aside on a plate.

•

Pour the remaining marinade, about 1 cup (240 ml), into a small saucepan. Bring the liquid up to a boil, then drop the heat to medium low and let the marinade simmer until it thickens into a loose syrup. (Add water to dilute if necessary.) Transfer to a bowl and set near the grill, along with a heatproof pastry brush.

•

When the fire is evenly hot, arrange the skewers on the grill so they don't touch each other; grill in batches if necessary. Watch to make sure the pork belly doesn't char too quickly; fan the coals to keep them hot. (You can use a simple bamboo fan or just a piece of cardboard.) Grill the skewers for about 2 minutes, until the meat starts to brown, then flip. While the other side browns (again, about 2 minutes), baste the just grilled sides with the marinade-turned-syrup, using the pastry brush. Then flip and baste the other sides, letting the just basted sides caramelize and char for 30 seconds to 1 minute. (It's quicker when the coals are fresh.) Flip one last time and let the just basted sides caramelize and char (again, 30 seconds to 1 minute). Repeat with any remaining skewers.

•

Serve immediately or leave out at room temperature for a BBQ buffet.

Listening TO LOLA

his cookbook—and my true life as a chef—began when my lola Josefina decided to entrust me with her recipe for Chicken Relleno (page 147).

It was a recipe she'd shared with no one. Friends who asked were rebuffed and sent off sulking. Even within the family, she kept it a closely guarded secret. But I had just been tapped to open the New York outpost of San Francisco's Mission Chinese Food, and she thought I was ready. "You're an executive chef now," she said—and so the real cooking lesson could begin.

First she pulled a shower cap over her hair, tucking in any stray strands. Then she laid out two cutting boards and a set of knives. From a professional cook's perspective, they were terrible knives, stubby-handled, unwieldy, and battered from years of use, but somehow she made them glide. With her tiny hands, she liberated the chicken from its bones so fast, for a moment I didn't know what parts were left. When she made the embutido (pork and sausage stuffing), I could've been watching Jacques Pépin: It required the precision of a French farce (finely puréed meat). Then she nested hard-boiled eggs in the stuffing and sewed the bird shut, as calm and steady as a surgeon.

For three years I'd trained in a restaurant kitchen, trying to master high-end French techniques, when Lola had been doing it all along, breezily turning out three stuffed chickens at a time for a party. I'd bought

Lola at age 94, teaching me how to make chicken relleno, 2012.

Lola resting post-tutorial in a sillon, or "lazy chair," with arms long enough that you can lean back and put your feet on them.

Me taking a break from making terrines in Brooklyn to say hello to my visiting sister Mimi, 2010.

Top left: Stuffing the chicken. Top middle: A portrait of Lola from the 1940s, with Lolo's handwriting. Bottom left: Lolo and Lola outside their house in Quezon City, the Philippines. Middle right: the finished chicken relleno.

Deboning the chicken.

into the idea that Western cuisine was elegant while the food of my childhood was just that, food for comfort, simple and straightforward.

I wanted people to know how complex Filipino food could be. So I put Josefina's House Special Chicken on the menu at Mission. (This was a bit of bravado: The first time I cooked it at the restaurant was only the third time I'd ever made it, and my audience was René Redzepi, David Chang, and Wylie Dufresne, three of the most prominent chefs in the world.) We sold it for $75 a bird, and in 2015 it was voted best chicken in the city by *New York* magazine.

By then, Lola had started to suffer from dementia. She always asked me the same questions about her House Special, and I loved how astonished she was by the answers each time. "So expensive!" she'd say, and then she'd scold me if I wasn't using the right chorizo.

Born in Manila in 1918, Lola worked for years as a pharmacist, mixing medicines and piping them into little bottles. To make ends meet, she sometimes set up long tables in the house and cooked big batches of adobo and sinigang for students from the nearby university. In her retirement in California, she tended African violets, canaries, and us. I'm just one of her forty-seven descendants—children, grandchildren, great-grandchildren. Every year, at the family Christmas party, I'd feel awe looking at her and my lolo, knowing that these two small people were responsible for all the life and energy in that room.

She died in 2018, a few days after her hundredth birthday. At her funeral, every eulogy ended in an ode to her cooking and the bounty she'd fed us. When I cook, I like to think that she's still with me, and that these flavors will last me all my life.

I learned to love vegetables from eating Sinigang (page 47), a soup potent enough to be a meal. So much attention is paid to meat in our cooking because it's a luxury, a sign that your host really splashed out. Vegetables are stealthier, unnoticed but everywhere, the humble ingredients that keep us going. They bring heartiness to soups and stews that are essentially folk medicine, and take the lead in two of my favorite dishes, Laing (page 67) and Tortang Talong (page 63). People sometimes joke that it's impossible to be Filipino and vegetarian, but I was able to come up with a vegan Sinigang sa Kamatis (page 49) using English breakfast tea, miso, and a Vegan "Fish Sauce" (page 181) that you can use throughout this book whenever fish sauce, or Bagoong (page 169), is called for, or just as an umami boost.

SOUP AND

VEGETABLES

To the cultural historian Doreen Gamboa Fernandez, sinigang was our archetypal dish, found everywhere from the humblest dulang (low hardwood table) to the elaborate feasts of the ilustrados (the educated elite). Above all, it is sour, and by sourness it is judged and loved: Does it bring a pucker to your mouth, or do you all-out flinch? (The calibration is up to you.)

What *makes* it sour is where the artistry comes in. Fernandez wrote, "The cook who sours with kalamansi or vinegar suffers, in the folk view, from 'abysmal poverty of mind,' for these are to be used only in extreme necessity, being too obvious. Instead, one uses mashed sampalok or kamias; guavas or green pineapple; alibangbang leaves or the tenderly green sampaloc leaves and flowers. . . . This bounty becomes habit, then taste."

Without the bounty of all those fruits, leaves, and flowers at hand, this recipe relies on tamarind, but feel free to experiment. Instead of pork, add extra body to the soup by using water reserved from washing rice and then, with the last batch of vegetables, throw in a favorite fish, whole or fillets (I like fish head); or swap in Vegan "Fish Sauce" (page 181), miso, and some starchier, more substantial vegetables to make it a vegan centerpiece (see Sinigang sa Kamatis, page 49).

SINIGANG *sih•nee•*GAHNG
SOUR TAMARIND BROTH WITH PORK AND VEGETABLES

SERVES 6 TO 8

2 pounds (910 g) boneless pork shoulder

2 medium yellow onions

2 tablespoons canola or other neutral oil

12 cloves garlic, smashed and peeled

Kosher salt and coarsely cracked black pepper

2 cups (454 g) tamarind concentrate, like Vietnamese nước me chua, or one 14-ounce (400 g) block tamarind paste, liquefied (see note)

¼ cup (60 ml) fish sauce

2 whole fresh serrano chiles

1 daikon (about 1¾ pounds/800 g)

8 ounces (225 g) long beans

1 Japanese eggplant (about 5 ounces/140 g)

2 medium tomatoes

10 ounces (280 g) whole baby spinach leaves (about 8 packed cups)

½ cup (120 ml) lemon juice (from 2 to 3 lemons)

Steamed rice, for serving

Note: To liquefy a block of tamarind paste, first break up the block into 1-inch (2.5 cm) chunks, then put the chunks in a mixing bowl and add 2½ cups (600 ml) boiling water. After 5 minutes, break up the chunks further with a fork, and let soften for another 15 minutes. Mash up the tamarind again and pour everything through a fine-mesh strainer into another mixing bowl, pressing and mashing the solids in the strainer to extract as much jammy tamarind pulp as possible. (Be sure to scrape off the back of the strainer, where the pulp will collect.) Whisk together the resulting liquid, then transfer to a measuring cup. You should have about 2 cups (480 ml); if not, add water to top it off.

Cut the pork shoulder into 1½-inch (4 cm) pieces, trimming any excess fat as you wish. Slice the onions in half from tip to tip, then cut each half into 4 roughly equal-sized cubes.

●

In a large pot, heat the oil on medium high until shimmering. Add the garlic and cook for 1 minute, or until toasted. Add the pork, season with the salt and pepper, and cook for about 4 minutes, stirring occasionally, until the pork is lightly browned.

●

Add the tamarind, onion, fish sauce, chiles, and 10 cups (2.5 L) water, increase the heat to high, and bring to a boil. Drop the heat to medium, then cover and simmer for about 1½ hours, until the pork is softened but not fully tender.

●

While the soup is simmering, peel the daikon and slice it into 1½-inch (4 cm) pieces. Cut the beans into 2-inch (5 cm) lengths. Slice the eggplant into 1-inch (2.5 cm) disks. Take the tomatoes, cut them in half, then cut each half into 4 roughly equal-sized cubes.

●

Stir the daikon into the pork mixture, then replace the lid and continue to simmer for another 30 minutes, or until the daikon grows soft and the pork is yielding.

●

Remove the lid and scoop the chiles out of the soup. (These may be discarded.) Add the long beans, eggplant, tomatoes, and spinach and cook for about another 20 minutes, stirring occasionally, until the vegetables are tender.

●

Stir in the lemon juice. Serve by ladling a generous scoop over rice—just a small mound if the soup is one of several dishes on the table, or more if it's the main course. This is a great way to use leftover rice, since there's no need to warm it up beforehand: The hot sinigang will bring it back to life.

Sinigang is sinigang so long as the broth is sour; there are no rules about which ingredients are used to bring that telltale shudder to the lips. So when I was in the Cayman Islands during the COVID-19 pandemic—far from home and family, waiting for a seat to open up on an evacuation flight—and woke up one morning longing for that hot sour broth, I decided to improvise. I was holed up in a hotel room under renovation, with only a bare-bones kitchenette: bar sink, self-heating tea kettle, mini-fridge. But I had a packet of grocery store–brand instant red miso soup on hand, and inside it was a foil-wrapped mini-puck of desiccated miso, seaweed, and freeze-dried tofu, just enough for a

punch of brine and umami. I boiled water in the kettle, dropped the puck in a bowl, squished the pulp out of some cherry tomatoes, and squeezed a leftover half lemon into it. When I poured the hot water into the bowl, I could smell sinigang.

My friend and fellow chef Gerardo Gonzalez taught me a tip from his time cooking vegan food in San Francisco: Start a broth with tea, to give it some tannins. When I finally had access to a full kitchen again, I tried this and saw how the tannins helped elongate the flavor. On their own, the acid, salt, and umami strike like power chords, then fade away. But with the tannins, you get another hit of acid after the umami, and the sourness stays on your tongue longer.

SINIGANG SA KAMATIS
sih • nee • GAHNG sah kah • MAH • tees
VEGAN SOUR TOMATO BROTH with VEGETABLES SERVES 6

3 sachets English breakfast tea

5 tablespoons (90 g) miso paste, preferably red

6 tablespoons (90 g) Vegan "Fish Sauce" (page 181)

8 cloves garlic, smashed and peeled

3 bay leaves, fresh or dried

1 whole fresh green chile, such as jalapeño or serrano

1 large white onion, cut into 1-inch (2.5 mm) chunks

½ daikon (13 ounces/370 g), peeled and cut into 1-inch (2.5 cm) chunks

10 ounces (280 g) long beans, cut into 2-inch (5 mm) pieces

6 ounces (170 g) okra

6 ounces (170 g) eggplant, cut into 1-inch (2.5 mm) pieces

Juice of 2 lemons

2 large and very ripe tomatoes, grated on the large holes of a cheese grater

3 cups (60 g) loosely packed baby spinach

Steamed rice, for serving

In a 4-quart (3.8 L) stockpot, bring 2 quarts (2 L) water to a boil, then turn off the heat but keep the pot on the burner. Steep the tea bags in the hot water for about 3 minutes. Remove the tea bags, squeeze gently over the pot to get all the liquid out, then discard.

•

In a small bowl, combine the miso and a couple ladles of the tea water. Whisk to break up the miso clumps, until completely dissolved. Add the miso mixture to the stockpot, then add the vegan "fish sauce," garlic, bay leaves, chile, onion, and daikon. Turn on the heat and bring the broth back up to a boil.

Once boiling, reduce the heat to low and simmer for about 25 minutes, or until the daikon has softened.

•

Add the long beans and okra. After 5 minutes, add the eggplant, lemon juice, grated tomatoes, and baby spinach. Continue simmering for about 7 minutes, until the eggplant and okra have softened and the long beans have lost their "squeak" when you bite into them.

•

Serve in bowls, ladled over rice, as much or as little as you wish, with a bit of every vegetable and plenty of sabaw (the liquid of the soup).

The same dish in the Philippines may go under different names, depending on where it's eaten and the slightest changes in ingredients, which can be confusing to an outsider (and sometimes even to us!). So: The genre of rice porridge is called lugaw, which at its most basic is simply rice boiled down until the grains lose their individual contours and become one. A cousin to Chinese congee and Korean juk, lugaw might be seasoned with nothing more than patis (fish sauce) and still soothe the soul.

There are more sumptuous variations: pale honey-comb strips of tripe make it goto; with chicken and a gilding of saffron, it's arroz caldo. I add collard greens so it's a balanced meal, and toss in chicken wings whole, letting the bones and jiggly skin fatten the broth. Each bowl gets the luxurious touch of a Soy-Cured Egg Yolk (page 173), ready to spill its gold.

ARROZ CALDO
ahr • ROHZ KAL • doh
CHICKEN RICE PORRIDGE WITH SAFFRON, COLLARDS, AND SOY-CURED EGG YOLKS SERVES 6

2 tablespoons canola oil or other neutral oil

1 medium yellow onion, minced

8 cloves garlic, peeled and minced

2½ pounds (1.2 kg) bone-in, skin-on chicken wings

Kosher salt and coarsely cracked black pepper

1 cup (185 g) uncooked jasmine or other long-grain rice

10 cups (2.5 L) chicken stock, store-bought or homemade (see headnote, Sinigang Roast Chicken, page 141)

1 pound (455 g) collard greens, stems ripped off and discarded, leaves roughly chopped

2 (2-inch/5 cm) pieces fresh ginger, not peeled, each crushed into a few pieces

2 large pinches saffron

FOR SERVING:

2 tablespoons fish sauce

3 calamansi (see headnote for Pulpy Salty Citrus Soda, page 271), halved, or 6 lemon wedges (from 1 lemon), plus extra calamansi halves or lemon wedges for serving

6 Soy-Cured Egg Yolks (page 173)

Garlic Chips (page 197)

1 bunch scallions, trimmed and thinly sliced

1 (1-inch/2.5 cm) piece fresh ginger, peeled and julienned

Put a large pot over medium. Add the oil and let warm, then add the onion and garlic and cook, stirring occasionally, for about 7 minutes, until soft and translucent.

•

Add the chicken wings and season with the salt and pepper. Cook for about 5 minutes, rotating the wings a few times to brown and render the skin, so the fat starts to melt. Add the rice and stir to coat the grains with the rendered fat. Raise the heat to medium high and continue cooking, with the occasional stir, until the rice is glossy with chicken fat, about 2 minutes.

•

Add the chicken stock, collards, crushed ginger, and saffron. Bring to a boil on high, then reduce the heat to low and simmer for about 1½ hours. There's no need to stand vigil; the liquid just needs an occasional stir. When it's ready, the chicken will be tender and almost falling off the bone, and the rice will be obliterated to the point that individual grains are no longer distinguishable. The broth should be thinner than Chinese congee; if it seems too thick, add up to 1 cup (240 ml) water and stir. (If still too thick, repeat.) Now is the time to scoop out and discard the crushed ginger.

•

Season the broth with the fish sauce, then divide among bowls. Squeeze the citrus over each bowl—I like to serve extra on the side, in case diners want more acid—and then top with a soy-cured egg yolk and a scattering of garlic chips, scallions, and julienned ginger.

As a young chef, I was struck by how this comfort dish of my childhood—a lush, long-simmered broth of bone-in beef shank—kept turning up in other cultures in different forms, like Korean seolleongtang, milky from ox bones and leached marrow, and French pot-au-feu, crystalline and crowded with vegetables. What makes nilaga special is the touch of surf alongside the turf from the fish sauce, giving contour to the broth.

This recipe marries the nilaga of my memory and the pot-au-feu of brasseries in Paris, with each serving carefully constructed to showcase each ingredient, from the delicate cabbage and bright corn to the beautifully braised hunks of beef. It's simple yet sumptuous, and the great thing is that you don't have to be fussy about it. While a French cook would discard the first pot of boiled water and bring a second pot to boil, for a clearer broth,

I usually skip that step, because we all have busy lives. A little cloudiness is okay.

Beef shanks are readily available at most markets. My Tita Lulu taught me to choose the ones with the most marrow (her favorite part), to make the broth sweeter. For a special occasion, I suggest buying extra beef marrowbones, enough to allot one to each guest's bowl. Ask the butcher to cut the bones crosswise into medallions 1½ inches (4 cm) in length. It's important that the bones aren't split in half, otherwise the marrow will just fall out in the broth. Soak the medallions for 12 to 24 hours in heavily salted cold water. (It should taste like the ocean.) Change the water a few times as it turns pink; this will help remove any trace of blood and yield a clean marrow.

Nilaga can be made ahead and reheated. If leftovers are saved for another day, add fresh leek, corn, and cabbage and let simmer 15 minutes before serving, just enough to cook the vegetables without their losing shape.

NILAGA *nee•LAH•gah*
TENDER OSSO BUCO, BONE MARROW, AND VEGETABLES IN BEEF BROTH SERVES 6

Kosher salt and coarsely cracked black pepper

1 pound (455 g) bone-in beef shanks, with the most marrow you can find

3 bay leaves, fresh or dried

1 medium yellow onion, peeled

2 medium Yukon Gold potatoes, peeled

8 ounces (225 g) baby white turnips or 1 large turnip, peeled

2 cloves garlic

1 large leek

1 ear corn, husk and silk removed

½ small head savoy cabbage or green cabbage

1 tablespoon fish sauce

6 medallions beef marrowbones, cut crosswise into 1½-inch (4 cm) pieces, soaked for 12 to 24 hours in brine (optional)

Steamed rice, for serving

Fill a large pot with 2.5 quarts (2.4 L) water. Salt and pepper the beef shanks and add them whole to the pot, along with the bay leaves. Cover and bring to a boil, then reduce the heat so that the liquid ripples without bubbling. Keep the lid on the pot. For the first 10 minutes of simmering, periodically lift the lid to check on the stock and skim off any foam that rises to the surface. Continue to simmer, skimming occasionally, for about 2 hours.

•

While the stew is simmering, chop the onion, potatoes, and turnips into 1½-inch (4 cm) pieces. Smash the garlic cloves and discard the skins. Cut the leek crosswise into 2-inch (5 cm) lengths, discard any tougher bits, and submerge in cold water to clean them; drain well. Cut each ear of corn crosswise into 1-inch (2.5 cm) wheels. Cut the half-head of cabbage into wedges, each about 1½ inches (4 cm) at the widest part, making sure to keep the core intact in each wedge.

→

NILAGA CONTINUED

After the stock has simmered for 2 hours, break apart the meat inside the pot by prodding it with a spoon; the meat should fall off the bones easily. Do not discard the bones, as the marrow will continue to melt into the broth. Season the broth with the fish sauce and 1 tablespoon kosher salt (or to taste), and check the texture: If the broth is too thick and syrupy, add a little water to loosen. Then add the onion, garlic, potatoes, and turnips and simmer for 20 minutes, or until the root vegetables begin to soften. If using marrowbone medallions, add them to the broth now. (If your pot isn't big enough to hold all the medallions, cook them in a separate, smaller pot with a ladling of the nilaga broth.) Add the leek, corn, and cabbage and let simmer for another 15 minutes.

•

To serve, ladle the stew over warm rice and be sure to give each bowl at least one piece of beef, potato, turnip, corn, and cabbage and a finish of coarsely ground pepper—plus, for special occasions, a bone medallion, for each diner to scoop out the buttery marrow.

BOLA-BOLA SOUP
BOH•lah BOH•lah
BEEF MEATBALL SOUP SERVES 2

his is not a traditional Filipino dish—I was inspired by Mexican sopa de albóndigas, which features small but hearty meatballs from a recipe with roots in sixth-century Spain, then under Islamic rule; the name comes from the Arabic al-bunduq, or hazelnut, a hint at the meatballs' size. Their Filipino counterpart, bola-bola, are good eaten straight, but if you have leftover meatballs on hand, try simmering them in this light, easy soup, with a last, bracing touch of lemon and lush drops of olive oil.

---

1 tablespoon olive oil, plus 1 tablespoon to finish

4 to 6 Bola-Bola (page 27), raw or cooked

1 quart (960 ml) chicken stock, store-bought or homemade (see headnote, Sinigang Roast Chicken, page 141)

2 teaspoons fish sauce

2 tablespoons barley or your favorite rice or other grain

4 or 5 leaves black kale, stems removed

¼ cup (13 g) coarsely chopped fresh parsley (including stems)

1 (1-inch/2.5 cm) piece fresh ginger, peeled and grated

2 wedges lemon

Coarsely cracked black pepper

Garlic Chips (page 197; optional)

Heat a 2-quart (2 L) saucepan over medium high. If using raw bola-bola, add 1 tablespoon of the olive oil, then add the raw bola-bola and brown for 2 to 3 minutes on each side.

•

Add the chicken stock, fish sauce, barley, and cooked bola-bola, if using. Cover and bring to a boil, then reduce the heat to a low simmer, so that the cooking liquid just trembles at the surface. With the lid on the pan, simmer for about 30 minutes, until the barley has softened and bloomed.

•

Tear the kale into small pieces, then add to the pan and stir. Replace the lid and let simmer for another 5 minutes. Lift the lid and stir in the parsley and grated ginger.

•

Divide the soup between two bowls. Squeeze one lemon wedge over each serving, then toss the wedge into the bowl. (I like the bitterness and the sting of lemon oil from the rind.)

•

Finish with a drizzle of nice olive oil, black pepper, and garlic chips, if you have them.

When I was first working in New York and broke all the time, this stew saved me—it was cheap to make and super-nourishing. Back then, I biked everywhere because it was free, and in the summer my friends and I would ride to the beach, 14 miles (22.5 km) round trip, and come back after hours of swimming, cold and ravenous. I'd work up a huge pot with mineral-rich whole green mung beans, which don't need to be soaked before cooking. (You can use hulled, split mung beans, too, known as moong dal in Indian cuisine.) Instead of adding spinach like my mom, I'd put in collard greens, which were cheaper and yielded more volume, so I could feed a crowd. Collards take longer to cook, but in a stew, that doesn't matter.

MUNGGO *mung* • GOH
MUNG BEAN STEW WITH PORK
AND WILTED GREENS SERVES 6

1 tablespoon olive oil, plus extra for finishing

8 ounces (225 g) pork shoulder, trimmed and cut into 1-inch (2.5 cm) pieces

Kosher salt and coarsely cracked black pepper

3 garlic cloves, peeled and coarsely chopped, about 1½ tablespoons

1 medium yellow onion, cut into ½-inch (12 mm) pieces

7 ounces (200 g) dried mung beans

1 medium tomato

8 ounces (225 g) spinach, collards (tough ribs discarded), or stewing greens of your choice, washed and dried

8 ounces (225 g) okra

1 small bitter melon (about 7 ounces/200 g)

4 ounces (115 g) any size shrimp, shelled, deveined, and coarsely chopped (optional)

2 tablespoons fish sauce

Steamed rice, for serving

1 ounce (28 g) chicharrón (fried pork rind), crushed, for serving

Garlic Chips (page 197; optional)

Set a large stockpot over high heat and add the olive oil. Add the diced pork shoulder, season generously with salt and some pepper, and brown, stirring intermittently to get a nice hard sear on the pork, about 5 minutes. This searing releases and concentrates the pork's juices, bringing depth of flavor to the broth.

•

Add the garlic, onion, and mung beans to the pot and stir. Add 2 quarts (2 L) water to cover, then put a lid on the pot and bring it to a boil. Reduce the heat to medium low and let the liquid simmer with the lid on.

•

While the beans are cooking, chop the tomatoes into ¾-inch (2 cm) dice. Roughly chop the greens and slice the okra into thin coins.

•

Slice the bitter melon in half, then trim off and discard the hard ends. Using a teaspoon, scoop out and discard the pith and seeds, then slice each half in half again. Cut the quarters crosswise into ½-inch (12 mm) pieces.

•

When the stew has been cooking for 1½ hours, test for doneness. The mung beans should be completely broken down, so that you can no longer distinguish their individual shapes, and you should be able to shred the pork easily with a spoon. Add the tomatoes, greens, bitter melon, and shrimp, if using, then replace the lid and continue to braise for another 15 to 20 minutes, until the greens and bitter melon are tender.

•

Just before serving, season the stew with the fish sauce and salt to taste, then swirl in the coins of okra, which are so thin, they'll cook right away.

•

Ladle a generous scoop—the stew should be thick but still soupy—in a bowl over warm rice. Repeat with the remaining bowls. Finish each serving with coarsely ground pepper and a fistful of crushed chicharrón and garlic chips, for a crackle in every spoonful.

Sometimes you don't appreciate the true glory of a dish until you eat it in its perfect context. On my first visit to the Philippines, at age twenty, I wandered through a tall grassy field one morning in my dad's home province of Batangas, and whatever was growing there gave me an allergic reaction bad enough that I was rushed to the emergency room. Back at the house where I was staying, I woke from antihistamine-induced grogginess to a hot bowl of chicken tinola. I'd eaten many versions of this soup in my childhood, but never like this. With each spoonful, I could feel it returning me to myself.

As folk medicine, tinola shares kinship with Korean samgyetang, heady with ginseng, and Chinese herbal chicken soup, steeped with goji berries and jujubes. Part of the dish's restorative power lies in the fragrance of lemongrass, garlic, and ginger. The chayote (a type of squash) offers juicy bursts—green papaya, winter melon, or white daikon would do the same trick. In Batangas, the soup is finished with chile pepper leaves or mineral-rich malunggay (moringa) leaves, a plant that has become coveted in the West as a superfood, in powdered form; I often swap in watercress, which is more readily available fresh in the United States, and sometimes add freshly grated or ground turmeric at the end, for extra power.

TINOLA *tee•NOH•lah*
CHICKEN SOUP WITH GINGER
AND MORINGA LEAVES SERVES 6

2 stalks lemongrass, cut into 3-inch (7.5 cm) pieces

1 (5-inch/12-cm) piece fresh ginger, peeled, plus more for finishing

6 cloves garlic, not peeled

1 chicken (3½ pounds/1.6 kg)

Kosher salt

3 bay leaves, fresh or dried

1 large yellow onion, cut into 2-inch (5 cm) dice

2 chayote or green papaya (about 2 pounds/ 910 g), peeled and cut into 2-inch (5 cm) dice

1 bunch moringa or pepper leaves (fresh or frozen), or watercress, rinsed and dried, ½ inch (12 mm) of the stems trimmed and discarded

2 tablespoons fish sauce

Coarsely cracked black pepper

2 tablespoons grated fresh turmeric or 1 tablespoon ground turmeric (optional)

Using a mallet, pestle, or small heavy-bottomed saucepan, smash each piece of lemongrass several times to release the fragrance and oil. Set aside. Do the same with the ginger and garlic, discarding the garlic skins.

•

Season the chicken, including the cavity, with salt. (Remove giblets from the cavity, if present, and save for future use.) Then stuff the cavity with the bay leaves, smashed lemongrass, and ginger. This seasons the chicken from the inside and stows the aromatics so they don't float out into the stew.

•

Put the chicken in a large Dutch oven or stockpot. Surround it with the garlic, onion, and chayote. Add enough water to just cover the chicken, about 2 quarts (2 L). With the lid on, bring to a boil over high, then reduce the heat so that the liquid ripples without bubbling. Replace the lid. If the liquid sputters, leave the lid slightly ajar but keep checking to make sure that not too much water is evaporating, so there is still enough to keep the chicken submerged.

•

After about 1½ hours, the legs and thighs should pull away easily from the rest of the chicken, a sign that the meat is tender. This is a rustic dish, so there's no need to shred the meat or remove the bones or skin; when you use a spoon to serve the soup, the meat will fall off the bones naturally, and you're meant to eat the skin, which has a lovely slippery, chewy texture.

•

Add moringa leaves to the broth and season with the fish sauce, a generous amount of pepper, and freshly grated ginger, all to taste. For a boost of flavor and anti-inflammatory power, stir in the turmeric.

•

Ladle from the pot into individual bowls and serve.

*I*t's fun for me, as a chef, to go off-book with a recipe and experiment. But with my lola Josefina's dishes, I often find that I like the way she did it best. Of all her dishes, this is the one I've kept the closest to the original. At first I tried it with sweet potato noodles (good, but too slippery), then thin rice noodles (really good, but still not quite right). Finally I had to concede that Lola knew what she was doing using sotanghon, skinny translucent noodles made from mung bean starch, also known as glass, crystal, or cellophane noodles. They have just enough slide, and quickly soak up the broth's flavors.

The wood ear mushrooms, sometimes labeled black fungus, should be chewy and firm, in contrast to the soft poached chicken, the juicy shallow crunch of the water chestnuts, and the slick sotanghon. As for the meatballs, you could make them bigger, but the smaller they are, the quicker they cook, so they're more tender, the better for slurping up along with the noodles.

CHICKEN SOTANGHON SOUP
soh • tahng • HAWN
CHICKEN SOUP WITH GLASS NOODLES AND PORK–SCALLION MEATBALLS SERVES 4

8 ounces (225 g) ground pork

1½ teaspoons soy sauce

½ teaspoon coarsely cracked black pepper, plus more for garnish

½ small red onion, finely minced

1 bunch scallions, trimmed and finely minced

2 large eggs, beaten

1 (8-ounce/226 g) can water chestnuts, coarsely chopped

6 cloves garlic, smashed and peeled

1 large yellow onion, cut into 1-inch (2.5 cm) chunks

1 large carrot, cut into 1 by ½-inch (2.5 cm by 12 mm) chunks

3 bay leaves, fresh or dried

1 cup (30 g) dried wood ear mushrooms, broken up into ¾-inch (2 cm) pieces

4 quarts (3.8 L) chicken stock, store-bought or homemade (see headnote, Sinigang Roast Chicken, page 141)

8 ounces (225 g) chicken breast

3 ounces (88 g) glass noodles (see headnote)

Kosher salt and fish sauce

In a large mixing bowl, using your hands, combine the ground pork, soy sauce, black pepper, red onion, half of the minced scallions (save the other half for garnish), eggs, and water chestnuts. Mix until the ingredients are just melded together; if you overwork the mixture, the meatballs will have more of a bouncy texture, and we're aiming for tenderness. Roll the ground pork mixture into 12 meatballs, each about 1 inch (2.5 cm) in diameter, and set aside. (If they're a little loose, you can put them in the refrigerator to firm up before dropping them in the soup.)

•

In a large stockpot, combine the garlic, onion, carrot, bay leaves, mushrooms, chicken stock, and chicken breast. Bring to a boil, then reduce the heat to a simmer. After 10 to 12 minutes, depending on the thickness of the chicken breast, check for doneness: The chicken should feel firm and spring back at the touch. While the soup continues to simmer, remove the chicken and transfer to a plate. Once cool, shred the chicken into ½-inch-wide (12 mm) strands.

•

After the soup has cooked for a total of 20 to 25 minutes and the carrots and onions have just softened, add the glass noodles and gently slip the meatballs into the simmering broth. Cook the noodles and meatballs in the broth for another 8 minutes. Stir in the shredded chicken breast, then remove from the heat.

•

Ladle into bowls, making sure each bowl has three meatballs and some of each of the ingredients. Season with salt and fish sauce, then garnish with the reserved minced scallion and a couple extra cracks of black pepper.

We had an electric stove when I was growing up, and my mom used to put eggplant right on top of the glowing red coils and pinch the stems to turn them. I helped by peeling off the charred skin, mashing the flesh, and dipping it in egg. The result was a kind of omelet, typically layered with ground beef. My mom liked to fry the eggs hard, until they were speckled brown, with crispy lace at the edges.

The version I make now is almost vegetarian—save for a seasoning of fish sauce—and inspired by Tito Elpie, the father of my sister Astrid's husband, Daniel. (Astrid and Daniel live in the house that I grew up in, a five-minute drive from where my parents live now and fifteen minutes from Daniel's parents; when I'm in town, that's where we all hang out.) Tito Elpie lets the eggplant blacken over high heat on an outdoor charcoal grill, until the flesh goes creamy, then cooks the eggs gently so they come out creamy, too. It's simple and luxurious at once.

TITO ELPIE'S TORTANG TALONG
TORE • tung tah • LONG
CHARRED EGGPLANT OMELET

SERVES 4 AS A SIDE DISH AND 2 AS A MAIN COURSE

2 small Japanese eggplants, about 4 inches (10 cm) long; if larger, prick all over with a fork

2 large eggs

1 teaspoon fish sauce or Vegan "Fish Sauce" (page 181), plus more to taste

Flaky sea salt

2 tablespoons olive oil

Banana ketchup, store-bought or homemade (page 167), or tomato ketchup, for serving

Set two stovetop burners on high heat and lay one eggplant directly on each burner. Let one side of the eggplant sear and blacken for 1 minute, then turn, using tongs. Repeat every minute for about 5 minutes total (longer if using larger eggplants), until the skin is charred and the eggplant is steaming from cracks in the skin. The flesh should yield under light pressure. Remove from the burners and lay on a plate to rest. (Alternatively, you could broil the eggplant in the oven on a tray on the top rack for 15 minutes, flipping the eggplant halfway through the cooking time.)

•

In a small bowl, crack the eggs and add the fish sauce and a pinch of salt. Beat until fully combined. Transfer to a flat-bottomed bowl or rimmed plate that is large enough to fit a whole eggplant.

•

After the eggplant has cooled just enough for you to touch it, use the tips of your fingers to peel off the charred skin. Discard the skins but leave the tops of the eggplant attached. Using a fork, gently press down on each eggplant, flattening it to ½ inch (12 mm). Lightly splash each eggplant with a few drops of the fish sauce and season with salt on both sides.

•

Heat a large sauté pan over medium high and add the olive oil once hot. Using a fork and spatula, pick up one eggplant, quickly dip it into the egg mixture, and put in the sauté pan. Pour a tablespoon or two of the egg mixture onto the eggplant so it slightly pools over the sides. Fry for about 2 minutes on each side and transfer to a plate. Repeat with the remaining eggplant.

•

Finish with flakes of sea salt and serve immediately with banana ketchup.

You don't need a lot of seasonings when ingredients are fresh. So this dish is intentionally simple, the better to showcase the natural bounty. Each vegetable plays a necessary role, from the long beans, crunchy and squeaking, to the bitter melon with its grown-up bite. There's not too much of any one thing, so you can appreciate and anticipate each part.

All it takes to draw out the flavors is a little garlic, salt, and above all bagoong—a satisfyingly funky paste of fermented shrimp or fish, which you can find at an Asian market or make yourself (page 169). Bagoong may be oily or dry, toasted or raw, bright pink and briny or dark brown and slightly sweet. For this recipe, I like it pink, with larger formations of salt crystals.

Pinakbet comes from the Ilocos region in the northern Philippines, but it's adored by all, so much so that when people call it pakbet, I think of it as an affectionate nickname. (No one I've consulted has been able to say for sure where that alternate name actually comes from—reminding me of the many layers and depths to our cooking traditions, spread across more than seven thousand islands.)

PINAKBET *pee • nahk • BEHT*
VEGETABLES STEWED IN FERMENTED SHRIMP PASTE

SERVES 4 TO 6

1 tablespoon canola or other neutral oil

6 cloves garlic, peeled and coarsely chopped

1½ tablespoons tomato paste

2½ tablespoons (37.5 ml) homemade Bagoong (page 169) or, if store-bought, preferably the lighter, pink variety

2 very ripe tomatoes, halved, then each half cut into quarters

1 large yellow onion, halved, then each half cut into quarters

5 ounces (140 g) kabocha squash, peeled and cut into 2-inch (5 cm) chunks

¾ tablespoon kosher salt

8 ounces (225 g) okra, ends trimmed

4 ounces (115 g) long beans, cut into 2-inch (5 cm) pieces

1 Japanese eggplant, cut into 1-inch (2.5 cm) pieces

½ bitter melon, halved lengthwise, seeds removed, and cut into ½-inch (12 mm) half-moons

Steamed rice, for serving

In a large pot, heat the oil on medium high; when it's the right temperature, it should shimmer. Add the garlic and cook, stirring, for about 3 minutes, until softened. Add the tomato paste and cook, stirring, for 2 minutes, as the paste darkens to a deep rust-red. Add the bagoong and cook, stirring for 2 minutes, releasing the shrimp paste's deep, nutty, briny fragrance.

●

Add the tomatoes and their juices and stir for 3 minutes, deglazing the pan by scraping and lifting the browned bits from the bottom and sides, to give the liquid extra flavor. Add the onions, squash, salt, and 1 cup (240 ml) water and continue to cook over medium high for about 10 minutes, with the occasional stir, until the vegetables start to soften and the sauce becomes glossy and thick.

●

Add the okra, long beans, eggplant, and bitter melon, and cook over medium high for 5 minutes, stirring occasionally. Reduce the heat to medium low and cook for another 15 to 20 minutes, continuing to stir, until the squash and other vegetables are yielding but still offer some resistance and the long beans are floppy.

●

Serve immediately over rice, or set it on a buffet—this is a dish that's just as good whether it's hot or at room temperature.

ow this is luxury: mineral-rich gabi, or taro leaves, shaped like hearts and cooked down with creamy coconut milk and searing chiles, the signatures of the Bicol region of the Philippines. Taro leaves can be hard to find in the United States; some Filipino groceries sell them pre-packaged and labeled "dried laing," but that yields a different flavor and texture. You can try ordering them shipped frozen from Hawai'i, where they're known as lu'au leaves, or substitute other hardy dark greens, like collards or black kale.

If you do end up using taro leaves, be sure to cook them thoroughly, as they're embedded with microscopic, needle-shaped crystals of calcium oxalate that can make your throat sting. Once, lost in thought, I sampled a pinch raw, and it felt like I'd swallowed a tiny cactus. To neutralize the crystals, some swear by hanging the leaves to dry before cooking. I just recommend not over-stirring the pot.

I forego the usual pork or shrimp added to bulk up the dish, preferring to layer on more coconut in the form of coconut oil and Latik (crunchy toasted coconut-milk curds, page 193), which you can make at home. (Latik is typically reserved for desserts but brings a wonderfully unexpected savory-sweet note here.) Or skip the latik and just use store-bought coconut oil—it'll still be delicious. At the end, fold in some squash blossoms, when in season, or scatter with edible flowers for a touch of color.

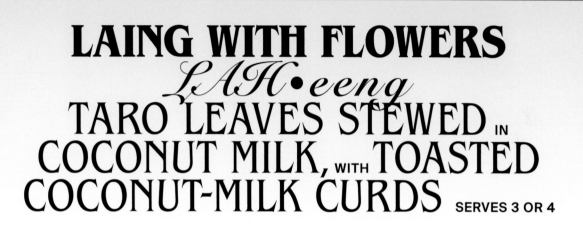

LAING WITH FLOWERS
LAH•eeng
TARO LEAVES STEWED IN COCONUT MILK, WITH TOASTED COCONUT-MILK CURDS SERVES 3 OR 4

2 tablespoons coconut oil, store-bought or home-made (page 193)

1 teaspoon red chile flakes

1 small onion, cut in half then lengthwise into ¼-inch (6 mm) slices

5 cloves garlic, smashed and peeled

1 (1-inch/2.5 cm) piece fresh ginger, peeled and minced

1 whole fresh chile, such as serrano, cayenne, or red Fresno

1 cup (240 ml) unsweetened, full-fat coconut milk

Fish sauce or homemade Vegan "Fish Sauce" (page 181)

1 pound (455 g) your choice of greens (taro or cassava leaves, collards, or black kale), tough stems removed, leaves cut into 1-inch (2.5 cm) pieces

Squash blossoms or edible flowers (optional)

2 tablespoons Latik (page 193; optional)

Bagoong, store-bought or homemade (page 169; optional)

Heat a large sauté pan over medium high. Add the coconut oil, red chile flakes, onion, garlic, ginger, and chile, and cook while stirring for about 3 minutes.
•
Add the coconut milk and fish sauce, stir, then add the greens and combine. Stew for about 20 minutes, stirring intermittently, until the greens are cooked through, darkened in color and tender (taste to be sure!), and the coconut milk has thickened and turned glossy but still pools at the bottom of the pan, like a loose gravy.
•

Transfer to a platter. If using the optional garnishes, fold in the squash blossoms or scatter the edible flowers and latik on top. Serve right away, with a side of bagoong, or refrigerate for up to 4 days and reheat.

Ampalaya, or bitter melon, is beautiful: green, bumpy, and vaguely reptilian, like an embryonic dragon. True to its name, it's profoundly bitter. When I was growing up, it definitely seemed like food for adults. Still, I had fun preparing it, running my fingers over its rough Braille, cutting it in half lengthwise and then scooping out the white pith and seeds, or shaving it super-thin on a mandoline and adding salt to make a pickle (page 183).

It was Chinese food that taught me to *like* the taste of bitter melon. It trained my palate. I started to understand what bitterness does for dishes, activating the tongue to better recognize all the different flavors at play.

Here the bitterness is juxtaposed with bright, juicy tomato and creamy scrambled egg. When a recipe calls for only a few ingredients, each one counts and you want them at the peak of freshness. (We're used to this kind of attention to detail in Italian cooking, and Filipino cuisine is no different.) Use good eggs and good tomatoes and this dish is a revelation. Serve it with sliced cucumbers or Lacto-Fermented Green Mango (page 189)—tucked in the bowls or on the side—and Bagoong (page 169), for an extra lift.

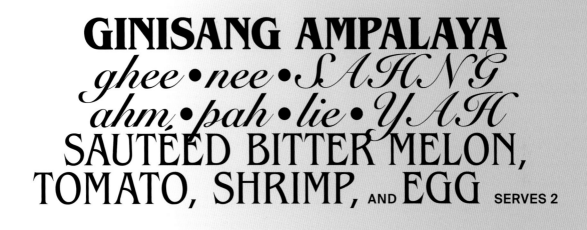

GINISANG AMPALAYA
*ghee • nee • SAHNG
ahm • pah • lie • YAH*
SAUTÉED BITTER MELON, TOMATO, SHRIMP, AND EGG   SERVES 2

¼ bitter melon (2 ounces/55 g), ends removed, deseeded and cut into half rings

Kosher salt

2 teaspoons olive oil

1 clove garlic, smashed into a few pieces

½ red onion, cut in half then cut lengthwise into ¼-inch (6 mm) slices

4 ounces (115 g) shrimp, shelled, deveined, and cut in half or, if small, leave whole (optional)

1 small, very ripe tomato, cut into 1-inch (2.5 cm) chunks, with any juice from the cutting board reserved

1 large egg

Fish sauce or Vegan "Fish Sauce" (page 181) to taste

Steamed rice, for serving

Finely minced chives, for garnish

In a small bowl, combine the bitter melon and a couple pinches of salt; this will draw out some of the bitterness. Set aside while you cut the rest of the vegetables.

•

In a small sauté pan, heat the olive oil on medium high. Add the garlic and onion, then reduce the heat and sauté on medium low for about 2 minutes, until softened. Rinse the bitter melon and squeeze out any excess water with your hands. Add the shrimp, if using, and bitter melon to the pan, stir, then add the tomato chunks and juices from the cutting board. Let soften in the pan for about 1 minute. The juices of the tomato should start to pour out, and the shrimp should start to turn firm and pink.

•

Whisk the egg with the fish sauce or vegan "fish sauce," then drizzle into the pan. Stir once, then turn off the heat, but keep the pan on the burner. Continue stirring with a rubber spatula until the egg is just beginning to set; it will form small curds but still be very saucy with the tomato juices.

•

Divide into two bowls over rice and garnish with the chives.

Rice WITH EVERYTHING

That scent: I'd know it anywhere. It's the smell of home, of rice steaming in the cooker, warm mounds of it dug out with a paddle, always the first thing on the plate. As kids, we'd smash grains between our fingers and use them to paste together the bodies of paper airplanes. Stray grains would spill on the floor and catch on the bottoms of our socks, picking up lint and turning brittle.

For Filipinos, rice is never just a steady backdrop—it shapes the meal, as the cultural historian Doreen Gamboa Fernandez has written; its calming earthiness allows for and invites the ardencies of salt and sour and the throb of fermented, sea-deep funk. Rice is so fundamental to our lives, our ancestors even etched its image on their bodies: angular lines evoking rice stalks near harvest, bent from the weight of the grain, or triangles with stripes like sheaves of drying stalks bound together after reaping, as illustrated in *Filipino Tattoos: Ancient to Modern*, by the traditional tattoo artist Lane Wilcken. In one of the early Spanish colonial dictionaries that attempted to record indigenous Filipino speech, 201 words related to rice appear, ones for each stage of its existence, from planting to eating. At harvest time, farmers cut the stalks swiftly but gently, so as not to scare the spirits who inhabited and protected the fields.

We are not the only culture to revere rice, of course, and each has its own way to cook it. Some shun rice cookers and insist on the stovetop, for greater control—like driving stick instead of automatic—but when you're feeding a big family and need rice in bulk and always at the ready, you don't mess around. I offer guidance on the stove below, but a good rice cooker will save you time and vexation. As a young cook, I used to pride myself on getting by with as few gadgets as possible, until I finally broke down and got a Zojirushi (the Ferrari of rice cookers!). It's a serious investment but worth it for a lifetime of eating rice every day.

As for what type of rice to cook: My general preference is short-grain, although I grew up eating mostly jasmine, which my family bought in fifty-pound bags that we poured into a plastic dispenser; you pressed a button for the amount you wanted and it came out, pre-measured, in a little drawer. These days, I change up my grains a lot. Right now I like mixing together 1½ cups (285 g) sushi or brown rice with ¼ cup (45 g) red or white quinoa and ¼ cup (50 g) black rice. But if you're aiming to make fried rice, you want something more neutral, so plain white short-grain or jasmine works best.

In traditional Filipino tattoos, rice motifs include panyat (top), drying bundles of rice stalks, and pang-ti-i', stalks just before harvest, symbolizing abundance.

How to cook rice:

Put the rice in the rice cooker pot (or a pot for cooking on the stove). Add cool water and wash the rice, working over the kitchen sink, swirling and shaking the pot and then pouring out the water, being careful not to lose any grains. Wash three times or until the rinse water is more clear than cloudy. On the final rinse, discard as much rinse water as possible, then flatten the rice by shaking the pot from side to side. Hold your hand over the top of the pot as a visual check to make sure that the rice is in an even layer.

•

Add the recommended amount of water, then dip your middle finger into the water, perpendicular to the surface of the rice and barely touching the grains. The water's height should come to just above the first knuckle. Measure by looking at the inside of your finger, not the knucle side. (We call this the finger trick.)

•

If using a rice cooker, follow the manufacturer's instructions. Some rice cookers automatically include a final 15-minute period of rest time; if not, when the machine signals that the rice is done, let it sit untouched for another 15 minutes.

•

If cooking the rice on a stovetop, cover with a tight-fitting lid and bring the rice to a boil. As soon as it starts boiling, reduce the heat to a simmer on the lowest setting. When the water has completely evaporated—after 20 to 25 minutes—turn off the heat and let the pot sit on the still-warm burner, covered and untouched, for another 15 minutes; the rice will continue to cook. It's very important not to remove the lid, otherwise you'll lose the precious steam needed for the rice to cook evenly.

•

Fluff and serve warm—it's so good right out of the pot, sometimes I eat the first bites of it straight, with nothing else.

Rice is always (see "Rice with Everything," page 70). But noodles—our pancit—are a necessity, too, and you can't have a proper feast without both, if not multiple versions of each. There's no real hierarchy of dishes in Filipino cooking, so don't think of these as sides or mains, but part of the pageantry. They make the table complete.

RICE AND

NOODLES

Plain rice is elemental, the backdrop to almost every dish. Garlic fried rice is the treat. It's one of the building blocks of silog, our version of a full breakfast–although by breakfast I mean a meal that can be eaten all day. (The name silog is a mash-up of sinangag, Tagalog for garlic fried rice, and itlog, egg; see Breakfast and Silogs, page 118.) This recipe is straightforward: all the ingredients are in the title. In Philippine folklore, garlic gives you protection against aswang, supernatural shapeshifters, so I guess it's good that I make my fried rice even more garlicky with garlic oil and a fistful of garlic chips at the end.

To dress it up, try a variation inspired by one of my favorite maki sushi combinations, ume-shiso: After coating the rice with the garlic butter, add one umeboshi (Japanese salted plum) to the pan and smash it into a paste. (Or you can just add a squeeze of store-bought ume paste.) When the ume is thoroughly mixed in, transfer the rice to a plate and top it with three shiso leaves cut into wispy ribbons, followed by Garlic Chips (page 197). The sour ume and bright, fragrant shiso balance the richness of the garlic butter.

GARLIC BUTTER FRIED RICE

SERVES 4

3 tablespoons (45 ml) garlic oil, store-bought or homemade (page 198), or canola or another neutral oil

6 cloves garlic, peeled and finely minced

3 tablespoons (40 g) butter

3 cups (615 g) steamed rice, warm or cold

Kosher salt

Garlic Chips (page 197; optional)

In a wok or a large skillet, heat the garlic or neutral oil on medium high. Add the minced garlic and sauté for about 2 minutes, until softened and light golden brown. Slip in the butter, and, as soon as it melts, add the rice. Turn the heat to high and mix thoroughly until well combined and hot.

●

Season with salt and a sprinkling of garlic chips, if using (please do!).

I grew up with a eucalyptus tree in the backyard, one of the Bay Area's legions of blue gum eucalyptus, gnarled, hardy, and nourished by fog. The plant is not native to the state, which is a source of some controversy today; its seeds were tucked into envelopes and carried over the sea by Australian gold-hunters in the mid-nineteenth century. Nevertheless, its scent–cool and clean, with hints of pine, mint, and honey–always says to me: California. In the kitchen, bay leaves are perhaps the closest approximation to that fragrance. Here rice is steeped with crushed dried bay leaves as it cooks, then adorned with dill, bright and grassy, and fresh bay leaves, giving off a soothing waft of menthol. I call it "spa" rice because when you lift the lid off the rice cooker, the perfumed steam feels like a facial, reminding me of unwinding in a eucalyptus-scented Turkish hammam. It's light yet indulgent, gilded with butter and Soy-Cured Egg Yolks (page 173).

BAY LEAF SPA RICE

SERVES 4 TO 6

5 dried bay leaves plus fresh bay leaves, for garnish

1 pinch kosher salt, plus more to taste

1½ cups (285 g) uncooked jasmine rice

2 tablespoons butter

5 sprigs fresh dill, coarsely chopped

4 to 6 Soy-Cured Egg Yolks and eggshells (page 173)

In a spice grinder, combine the bay leaves and salt. Crumble the bay leaves with your fingertips, then pulse and blend until the mixture becomes a fine powder. Use your fingertips or a clean dry pastry brush to remove the powder from your spice grinder.

•

Wash the rice (see How to Cook Rice, page 71) and submerge in 1¼ cups water. Add the bay-leaf salt to the water. Cook the rice and let rest for 15 minutes (see How to Cook Rice, page 71).

•

Add the butter and fluff the grains. Transfer to a serving platter and sprinkle the dill over the rice.

•

Dimple the rice with an eggshell to create little wells. Make sure there is one yolk per person. Drain the yolks of curing liquid and present them in egg-shells, nestled in the wells in the rice and surrounded by fresh bay leaves.

During the COVID-19 pandemic, I was marooned for a few months in the Cayman Islands—how lucky!—and, thanks to my friend and fellow chef Gerardo Gonzales, found a second home at the Palm Heights hotel. The crispy coconut rice at Tillie's, the hotel restaurant, inspired me to try my own version, with the addition of pandan leaves, an indigenous ingredient in the Philippines.

The taste of pandan (known as screw pine in the West) is difficult to describe: delicate, grassy, and floral at once, as much scent as flavor, and almost translucent, if such a word applies—like water left to steep in a bamboo cup. You might find it in the frozen goods section of an Asian supermarket, and if not, you could try a different aromatic, tipping in turmeric or a tea bag's worth of chamomile.

The secret to this dish is the crackly crust at the bottom where the rice is almost scorched, flipped over to display in all its dark glory. In the Philippines, this is called tutong, but it goes by many names across the world: tahdig in Iran, xoon in Senegal, nurungji in Korea, concón in the Dominican Republic, socarrat in Spain. For a vegan version, swap out the Greek yogurt for coconut-milk yogurt or an extra 2 tablespoons of coconut oil, to help get that smoky crunch.

CRISPY PANDAN COCONUT RICE

SERVES 4

2 pandan leaves

1 cup (190 g) uncooked jasmine rice

½ teaspoon kosher salt

¾ cup (180 ml) unsweetened, full-fat coconut milk

2 tablespoons Greek yogurt

2 tablespoons coconut oil, store-bought or home-made (page 193)

1 cup (40 to 55 g) loosely packed mixed herbs: finely minced scallion, mint, cilantro, and dill

1 wedge lemon, for juice

Splash olive oil

Flaky sea salt

Fill a 2-quart (2 L) saucepan with 1 quart (960 ml) water and set to boil.

•

Pour ½ cup (120 ml) water into a blender. Using kitchen shears, cut the pandan leaves into 1-inch (2.5 cm) pieces over the blender so they drop right into the water. Blend into a smooth puree, about 2 minutes.

•

Once the water on the stove is boiling, add the rice and salt to the pan. Take the blender pitcher of pandan water and pour it through a small fine-mesh strainer directly into the boiling water. Use a spoon to press down on the pandan pulp to squeeze out every drop of pandan water into the pan.

•

Lower the heat to medium high and continue cooking for 12 minutes, stirring occasionally. Carefully taste a few grains of rice. The outside will be tender, but the center should still have a little bit of resistance, like pasta al dente. Drain the rice in a fine-mesh strainer, then spread it over a tray to rest for 20 minutes, or until cool.

•

In a small mixing bowl, combine the cooled pandan rice with the coconut milk and stir until melded. Scoop one-third of the mixture into another small bowl. Add the yogurt to the second bowl and stir to thoroughly combine.

•

Heat a small nonstick pan or saucepan over medium high. Once hot, add the coconut oil, swirl the pan, then add the yogurt-rice mixture from the second bowl. With a spoon, flatten the yogurt rice into an even layer. Then add the remaining rice from the first bowl and flatten. Put a lid on the pot and let steam on medium high for 15 minutes.

→

CRISPY PANDAN COCONUT RICE CONTINUED

Remove the lid to release the steam and continue to cook for another 5 minutes. The bottom and edges of the rice should be crackling, releasing a nutty fragrance from caramelizing and crisping at the bottom of the pan.

•

Turn off the heat and use a serving plate to cover the pan. With one hand on the back of the plate and one holding the pot, steady yourself, then carefully but in one swift motion invert the pan, so that the rice falls onto the plate intact, with its deep golden crust on top.

•

Combine the herb mix in a bowl with the lemon juice, olive oil, and a pinch of flaky sea salt. Toss with your fingers, then scatter over the crispy rice. Serve immediately.

DINUGUAN BLOOD RICE
dee • noo • goo • AHN   SERVES 4

The classic pork blood stew Dinuguan (page 31) is often served with tender little steamed rice cakes called puto, a perfect match of earthy and sweet. It's a staple of merienda (page 96), our ritual of mid-morning and mid-afternoon snacks. Here the iron-rich flavors of dinuguan are infused directly into rice, balanced by some of the warming and faintly sweet spices—cinnamon, cloves—found in black pudding, which I used to buy at chip shops in Glasgow when I was a college exchange student. Slice into black pudding and you reveal constellations of fat, mimicked in this dish with optional scattered nubs of lardo.

You could present this as a side, or reserve it for stuffing Sinigang Roast Chicken (page 141)—add 2 cups' worth to the cavity before putting the chicken in the oven—or, if there's a celebration coming up and you have a couple days to devote to cooking, roll it up into Porchetta Bellychon (page 159).

½ whole star anise

1 teaspoon whole cloves

½ teaspoon whole black peppercorns

½ teaspoon fennel seeds

¼ teaspoon ground cinnamon

2 dried bay leaves

1 teaspoon kosher salt, plus more to taste

2 cups (400 g) uncooked sushi rice

½ yellow onion, finely minced

2 cloves garlic, peeled and finely minced

1 (1½-inch/4 cm) piece fresh ginger, peeled and finely minced

2 tablespoons unsalted butter

1 cup (240 ml) pork blood

1¾ ounces (50 g) lardo or cured pork fat, cut into ¼-inch (6 mm) cubes (optional)

In a mortar or spice grinder, combine the anise, cloves, black peppercorns, fennel seeds, cinnamon, dried bay leaves, and salt and grind to a fine powder.

•

Wash the rice (see How to Cook Rice, page 71) and submerge in 2 cups (480 ml) water. Add the ground spices, onion, garlic, and ginger to the water and stir with your fingers, then gently shake the pot to distribute and flatten the rice. Cook the rice and let it rest (see How to Cook Rice, page 71).

•

With the rice still in the pot and piping hot, pour in the pork blood, butter, and lardo, if using. Working quickly, fluff the rice so that the blood and fat are distributed evenly.

•

Put the lid back on the pot and let the rice rest for about 5 minutes on the rice cooker's "keep warm" setting or on the same stovetop burner, but turned off. The heat of the rice will gently cook the blood and help integrate the flavors.

•

Serve immediately, or store in an airtight container in the refrigerator for up to 5 days, or in the freezer for up to a month.

The word pancit comes from the Hokkien for convenience food—a reference to the ready-to-go noodles sold on the street by migrant Chinese vendors under colonial rule, who were called panciteros, a fantastic mash-up of Spanish and Hokkien. Today pancit is an entire genre of noodle dishes, and of all of them, palabok is the richest. The sauce is as thick as an Italian ragù, with strands of chicken slowly disintegrating into a gravy lush from liquid chicken fat, and stained reddish-gold by achuete (annatto). It comes to the table in layers, unmixed, with a pageantry of hard-boiled eggs, poached shrimp, garlic chips, and a crispy rubble of chicharrón.

Traditionally, the recipe calls for boiling shrimp heads and shells, crushing the heads to squeeze out all the juice, and then straining the broth through a sieve. Here I use chicken stock, made fresh—a handy byproduct of cooking the chicken—but if you want to go the extra mile, save the shrimp shells after cleaning and toast them in a 300°F (150°C) oven for about 45 minutes, until dried out and crispy, then pulverize them in a coffee grinder, into a fine powder. You can add this shrimp-shell dust at the same time as the achuete powder to give a briny boost and extra depth to the sauce.

PANCIT PALABOK
pan • SEET pah • LAH • bok
RICE NOODLES WITH SAFFRON-SCENTED CHICKEN GRAVY SERVES 5 OR 6

1 pound (455 g) bone-in, skin-on chicken breasts, split

1 pound (455 g) bone-in, skin-on chicken thighs

Kosher salt

8 ounces (225 g) small shrimp (51/60 count per pound), shelled and deveined

3 large eggs

1½ tablespoons canola or other neutral oil

1½ tablespoons achuete powder (also known as annatto)

1 large yellow onion, finely minced

4 stalks celery, finely minced

1 head garlic (7 to 8 cloves), peeled and finely minced

Fish sauce, as needed

½ teaspoon coarsely cracked black pepper, plus more for finishing

Banana leaves (see headnote for Suman, page 229), fresh or frozen, for lining serving dish (optional)

8 to 9 ounces (225 to 255 g) rice vermicelli (ideally about the thickness of spaghetti), cooked per package instructions

1 bunch scallions, thinly sliced

1 ounce (28 g) chicharrón, crushed

A few tablespoons Minced Fried Garlic (page 198) or store-bought fried garlic

3 calamansi (see headnote for Pulpy Salty Citrus Soda, page 271), halved, or lemons, cut into wedges, seeds removed

A couple more tips: Skim some of the chicken fat off the poaching liquid to use in lieu of oil when you start the mirepoix of celery and onions. And save the chicken skin after poaching to make your own version of chicharrón, dropping it in hot oil in the fryer or laying it in a nonstick pan over low heat to let the fat render, then raising the heat until it crisps.

Put the chicken breasts and thighs in a large pot. Cover with about 1 quart (960 ml) water, so that the chicken is fully submerged. Add enough salt to make the water taste like the ocean and bring to a boil over high heat. Reduce the heat to medium low and simmer for about 40 minutes, until the meat is cooked through and can be easily pulled off the bone.
•

Transfer the chicken to a bowl to cool and reserve the cooking liquid, or chicken stock, for later in the recipe. Once the chicken is cool enough to handle, remove and discard the skin. Tear the chicken into bite-size pieces and then shred those pieces into thin strands. Discard the bones.
→

PANCIT PALABOK
CONTINUED

In a medium saucepan, bring 2 cups water and 1½ teaspoons salt to a boil. Prepare an ice bath in a large bowl. Add the shrimp to the boiling water and cook for about 2 minutes, until just pink and tender. Pour into a colander to strain, then quickly transfer the shrimp to the ice bath and let rest for 2 minutes, or until chilled. Strain the shrimp again, return to the bowl, and refrigerate until use.

•

Rinse out the saucepan and fill with 2 cups (480 ml) water. Add ½ teaspoon salt and bring to a boil. Carefully slip the eggs into the boiling water, one at a time, then reduce the heat to low and gently simmer for 9 minutes. While the eggs are simmering, prepare an ice bath in a large bowl. Transfer the eggs to the ice bath and let cool. Drain, then peel and slice crosswise into thin rounds. Set aside.

•

In a large saucepan, heat the oil over high until it shimmers. Add the achuete powder and stir for about 1 minute, until dark and fragrant. Add the onion, celery, garlic, and 1½ teaspoons salt, and cook, stirring occasionally, for about 8 minutes, until softened. Deglaze by adding 2 cups (480 ml) of the reserved chicken stock and scraping any browned bits from the sides and bottom of the pan.

•

Add the shredded chicken and simmer for about 30 minutes, occasionally mashing the chicken with a whisk to encourage more shredding and increasing the mashing toward the end, until the strands disintegrate into fine hairs and the sauce thickens. Season with fish sauce and the pepper.

•

Line a large baking dish with banana leaves, if using. Arrange the cooked noodles in the dish and top with the warm chicken mixture, spreading it evenly. Follow with most of the sliced scallions—saving a few—and then alternate rows of the sliced hard-boiled eggs and the shrimp, squeezing about half a calamansi or a wedge of lemon over the surface. Scatter a crunchy mix of the chicharrón and minced fried garlic over the top, then finish with a few more sliced scallions and a crack of pepper.

•

Serve with the remaining calamansi halves or lemon wedges on the side, for diners to dress the noodles as they wish.

In the Philippines, fish balls are a street snack—we call them tusok-tusok, or poke-poke—skewered and deep-fried. My dad used to bring home packs of them frozen, to pop in the fryer and then slake with different sauces. I learned to love them in broth by eating pho, ordering the Pho Dac Biet #1 at one of San Jose's many Vietnamese restaurants, which came with everything: bouncy fish balls, tripe, braised beef tendon with the texture of a warm Haribo gummy bear, and flimsy sheets of sirloin slipped in raw and still ruby-hearted in the bowl, slowly cooking in the heat of the broth.

Then I went to Singapore and the German curator Ute Meta Bauer took me to Hua Bee, a kopitiam (coffee shop) that dates back to the 1940s. It was my introduction to mee pok—wide, chewy egg noodles primed with fermented shrimp paste and pulverized chile, and meant to be dipped in a bowl of clean broth that arrived loaded with more types of fish balls than I'd ever seen, from little sausages to a shaggy orb wrapped in a sheet of fish paste, so it looked like a wonton. Sweat beaded on my skin and it felt as if the liquid inside my body was becoming one with the broth. I finally understood the Asian tradition of eating spicy food and hot soup on a sweltering day.

The fermented shrimp paste on the noodles reminded me of bagoong, so I decided to try making my own version. This recipe is my homage to mee pok, with flavors that are distinctly Filipino. Look for fresh egg noodles or ramen noodles at an Asian market, along with Chinese chile crisp.

DRY SPICY BAGOONG NOODLES WITH FISH BALLS IN BROTH
bah•goh•AWNG SERVES 2

2 fillets (10 ounces/280 g) mackerel or your favorite oily or white fish, bones and skin removed

Kosher salt

1 quart (960 ml) chicken stock, store-bought or home-made (see headnote, Sinigang Roast Chicken, page 141)

1 (2-inch/5 cm) piece fresh ginger, peeled and smashed

3 scallions, 2 left whole and 1 finely chopped for garnish

2 cloves garlic, smashed and peeled

1 shiitake mushroom

1 teaspoon soy sauce

2 teaspoons fish sauce

8 ounces (225 g) fresh wide egg noodles or fresh ramen noodles

2 tablespoons bagoong, store-bought or homemade (page 169)

2 tablespoons Chinese chile crisp or Indonesian sambal oelek

Cilantro, coarsely chopped including stems, for garnish

Cut the fish into a small dice, add a pinch of salt, and pulse in a food processor until smooth. If you do not have a food processor, chop the fish and salt together into a paste. Transfer to a bowl and refrigerate.

•

Pour the chicken stock into a 2-quart (2 L) stockpot and add the ginger, whole scallions, garlic, and shiitake. Bring to a boil, then simmer for about 30 minutes. Strain, discard the seasonings, and return the liquid to the stockpot on the stove to simmer over low heat. Season the broth with the soy sauce and fish sauce.

•

Take the cold fish paste from the refrigerator. Using a small ice cream scoop or round measuring spoon, scoop out a ball of the paste, then transfer it to a teaspoon. Pass the ball back and forth between the scoop and the teaspoon until it's nice and round, then drop it directly into the simmering broth. Repeat with the rest of the paste; you should have enough for about 10 fish balls. Keep the fish balls poaching in the broth while you prepare the noodles, stirring once to ensure they cook evenly.

•

In a 3-quart (2.8 L) stockpot, bring about 2 quarts (2 L) water up to a boil. Fluff the noodles to untangle and drop them into the water to cook for about 2 minutes. Using a strainer, transfer the noodles to a mixing bowl, and dress with the bagoong and chile crisp until the noodles look glossy. Use a couple tablespoons of water to keep the noodles moist and help distribute the dressing evenly.

•

Transfer the noodles to two bowls and garnish with some of the cilantro and scallion. Take two more bowls and divide the broth between them, giving each a few fish balls, and garnish with the remaining cilantro and scallion. To serve, give each diner a bowl of noodles and a bowl of broth, for dipping and slurping together.

There is no Filipino party without pancit, great trays of it on the table, sturdy enough to sit out all day and still be delicious on the fifth helping. Everyone has their favorite kind of noodle, and some dishes mix two at once, for a tangle of textures: miki (egg), canton (wheat), sotanghon (mung bean starch—see Chicken Sotanghon Soup, page 61), and bihon, rice noodles so skinny they're also known as rice sticks. I like to substitute bihon camote, which are made with sweet potato starch and fantastically chewy; they turn this dish into a cousin of Korean japchae.

Consider this recipe a sketch for you to fill out as you wish. For the sweet potato noodles, you can go wide or narrow, ribbons or vermicelli, depending on your taste. Calamansi is the traditional seasoning citrus, but difficult to find in the United States (though worth searching for), and lemon works fine to bring the necessary sting. And just like with Chinese chow mein, you can toss in your favorite protein or vegetable—chicken poached and pulled into obliging strands, whorls of shrimp, scarlet lap cheong (sausage), bouncy wood ear mushrooms, carrots holding their crunch—or skip the meat and swap in Vegan "Fish Sauce" (page 181) to make it wholly vegetarian.

PANCIT BIHON CAMOTE
pahn • SEET BEE • hawn kah • MOH • teh
STIR-FRIED SWEET POTATO NOODLES WITH PORK BELLY, BLACK PEPPER, AND RED CABBAGE SERVES 4

5 ounces (140 g) dried sweet potato noodles

3 scallions, trimmed

2 teaspoons olive oil

4 ounces (115 g) pork belly, cut into bite-size pieces

Kosher salt

2 ounces (60 g) snap peas, cut in half at a very hard bias

½ red onion, cut lengthwise into ¼-inch (6 mm) slices

4 ounces (140 g) red cabbage (about one-eighth small head), cut into ¼-inch (6 mm) slices

1 tablespoon soy sauce

1 tablespoon fish sauce

4 calamansi, 2 for juice, 2 for garnish, or 1 lemon, half for juice, half for garnish

1 teaspoon coarsely cracked black pepper, plus more for garnishing

1 cup (90 g) bean sprouts

3 tablespoons (15 g) Minced Fried Garlic (page 198)

In a shallow baking dish, cover the dried sweet potato noodles with water. Allow the noodles to soak for about 45 minutes.

•

Using a sharp knife, cut the scallions very thin at a 45-degree angle (a bias cut). Submerge the scallions in a bowl of ice water. They will begin to curl and lose a little of their sharp bite.

•

Fill a large stockpot with water halfway, cover, and bring to a boil. Put the noodles in the pot and cook for about 5 minutes, then strain in a colander and set aside. Heat a large sauté pan over medium high. Add the olive oil, then the pork belly, and season with salt. Sear for about 2 minutes, turning the meat a couple times.

•

Add the snap peas, red onion, and cabbage and toss to combine. Turn off the heat but keep the pan on the burner. Add the cooked noodles from the colander, the soy sauce, fish sauce, the juice of 2 calamansi or half a lemon, and black pepper, and toss for about 1 minute, until the noodles are evenly seasoned.

•

Add the bean sprouts and give the noodles a few final tosses, then transfer to a serving platter. Cut the remaining calamansi or lemon half into 4 wedges and arrange them around the circumference of the plate. Drain the soaked scallions to garnish the noodles, along with minced fried garlic and a few extra fresh cracks of black pepper.

This could just as well be called Italian pancit. It's essentially Bolognese, transformed by bouncy hot dogs—which some Westerners might find sacrilegious—and a tiny shock of sweetness, and famously paired with fried chicken in the Chickenjoy and Jolly Spaghetti combo at Jollibee, a chain that rules the fast-food market in the Philippines, more popular than McDonald's and steadily opening outposts across the United States. (To make your own combo, inspired by another beloved Filipino chain, see Max's Style Fried Chicken, page 35.)

For this version, I take a cue from the Italian chef Marcella Hazan: Instead of adding straight-up sugar or Banana Ketchup (page 167), I put in a lot more onion, carrot, and celery, teasing out sweetness from the vegetables themselves. (Feel free to chop the vegetables in a food processor as a shortcut.) Nutmeg brings another shade

and layer, while the wine mellows and deepens the sauce. It's worth spending an extra dollar or two to get top-quality tomato paste and canned tomatoes preserved at the height of summer, locking in that peak flavor.

Spaghetti is the classic pasta of choice, but I sometimes use oversized tubes like paccheri or mezze maniche, for texture. I cut the hot dogs into rounds as thin as nickels, because I love how the edges curl up as they cook and make little teacups, which look like orecchiette and helpfully catch drops of sauce.

For kids, you could make octopus hot dogs, each cut with eight "legs," or skewer hunks of hot dog on sticks of dried spaghetti, then boil them—the noodles will look like they're snaking through the meat. Or flip the dish around and make the hot dog the star, tucked in a warm bun with the finished spaghetti heaped on top (see the special bonus recipe on the next page).

FILIPINO SPAGHETTI
FILIPINO BOLOGNESE WITH
HOT DOG COINS

MAKES ENOUGH SAUCE FOR 2 BATCHES, SERVING 4 EACH

5 tablespoons (75 ml) olive oil

4 tablespoons (½ stick/55 g) salted or unsalted butter

1 teaspoon coarsely cracked black pepper

1 teaspoon red pepper flakes

2 large yellow onions, finely minced (4 cups/500 g)

2 cloves garlic, peeled and finely minced

4 large carrots, finely minced (2 cups/280 g)

3 stalks celery, finely minced (1 cup/100 g)

1 pound (455 g) ground beef

1 teaspoon kosher salt

1 cup (240 ml) milk

Dash nutmeg

3 bay leaves, fresh or dried

1 cup white cooking wine

1½ cups (360 ml) canned crushed tomatoes

2 tablespoons tomato paste

1 box (16 ounces/455 g) spaghetti

2 hot dogs, cut crosswise into coins as thin as a nickel

Fistful of fresh parsley, coarsely chopped

Parmesan, freshly Microplaned or grated

cheddar, freshly Microplaned or grated

Heat a saucepan over medium. Add 3 tablespoons of the olive oil, then 3 tablespoons (40 g) of the butter and let melt. Increase the heat to medium high and add the black pepper and red pepper flakes. Stir, then add the onions and garlic, which will immediately start to sweat. Drop the heat to medium and cook, stirring for about 7 minutes, until the onions soften and turn translucent. Add the carrots and celery and continue cooking while stirring for another 7 minutes.

•

Add the ground beef and salt and cook while stirring for another 5 minutes. Add the milk, nutmeg, and bay leaves, and cook, stirring occasionally, for 10 to 15 minutes; as the milk reduces, it creates a thick glossy sauce that coats the beef. Add the wine and cook for another 10 to 15 minutes.

→

FILIPINO SPAGHETTI CONTINUED

Add the canned crushed tomatoes and tomato paste, increase the heat to medium high, and bring the sauce to a boil. Once it's boiling, turn down the heat to a low simmer, and continue cooking for 1 to 1½ hours, letting the sauce grow more concentrated, until it's thick, rich, and almost sticky. Check on the sauce every so often to make sure it still has enough liquid and isn't on the verge of burning. If it's thickening too quickly, drop the heat and add a few tablespoons of water.

•

This sweet Bolognese can be served within several days or frozen for up to a month.

•

When you're ready to serve, cook the spaghetti according to the package instructions in ocean-salty water. Taste a strand of pasta about 10 minutes into cooking; when it's al dente—slightly chewy—it's ready.

•

Strain the pasta in a colander over a mug, to catch and reserve the pasta water. (A mug is good because it's built for heat and has a helpful handle.)

•

Heat a 2-quart (2 L) saucepan, then add 2 tablespoons of the remaining olive oil. Fry the hot dog coins on medium high for about 2 minutes, until the edges start to caramelize, shrink, and turn inwards, making little cup shapes.

•

Add about half the Bolognese—reserving the rest for a future meal—and stir and simmer with the hot dogs for another minute.

•

Add the cooked pasta to the pan and toss with the Bolognese. Add the last tablespoon of butter, a pinch of Parmesan, and a few glugs of the cooking water to loosen the sauce. Drop the heat to medium low and continue to toss until well mixed.

•

Divide among four bowls. Finish each serving with some parsley, cheddar, and more Parmesan, to taste.

Special Bonus: FILIPINO SPAGHETTI HOT DOGS SERVES 4

Filipino Spaghetti, minus hot dogs
4 hot dogs, grilled, pan-fried, or boiled
4 hot dog buns, toasted
Cheddar, freshly Microplaned or grated
Parmesan, freshly Microplaned or grated
Fistful of fresh parsley, coarsely chopped
½ small white onion, ¼-inch (6 mm) dice

Make the Filipino Spaghetti, minus the hot dogs. After tossing in the final pat of butter and Parmesan, take a tongs' worth of the pasta and drape it over a hot dog in a warm bun. Finish with cheddar, more Parmesan, parsley, and onion. Repeat with the remaining hot dogs and buns. Serve immediately.

Ito Ako (THIS IS ME*)

FOR SARAH DULCE (DOLLY) SANTIAGO DIMAYUGA

Top far left: My great-grandparents Francisco Santiago and Concepcion (Conching) Ocampo on their wedding day. Top left: My great-grandfather's commemorative stamp. Middle: My great-grandfather. Bottom left: A kundiman concert. Right: Sheet music of my great-grandfather's works.

My first music was kundiman, love songs with doom written in their bones. Early nineteenth-century versions were heartbroken serenades on guitar, in a waltz-like simple triple meter, with the verses shifting from a minor key to its parallel major as if to suggest uplift, but only as an impossible dream. (The name is believed to be a collapsing of the refrain "kung hindi man," which means "if not"—if you don't love me back; if it isn't meant to be.) Later they became songs of protest, expressing secret fealty to the motherland under Spanish and later American occupation.

I used to think, lovingly, that there was something campy about these songs. But that's wrong: camp, as the cultural critic Susan Sontag wrote, is exaggeration and artifice, and the kundiman is in dead earnest. The

singers put it all on the line, defiant, daring you to feel something. My great-grandfather Francisco Santiago saw this open-hearted, nigh-fatalistic devotion as heroic, and in the early twentieth century he transformed the genre from a folk art into a more operatic form. Today he's remembered as "the father of kundiman," and in 1989 his face appeared on a "Great Filipinos" commemorative stamp set, which my mom keeps in a gilt frame.

My mom has fame of her own: In the early 1970s she toured the world with Bayanihan, the Philippine national folk dance troupe. (The word bayanihan comes from bayan, community, and translates as "working together toward the common good.") She was the opening act, playing the kulintang, small brass gongs with little knobs at the top, laid out horizontally on a

*Or, as the meme goes, "It me."

Mom at age 19 in a formal Filipiniana gown with butterfly sleeves, handing out programs before a Bayanihan performance at the Cultural Center of the Philippines.

bamboo frame and struck like drums. To show off her skills, she would spin the sticks between notes, cross her arms, even reorganize the gongs mid-song. Back in Manila, the troupe performed every weekend for tourists, who shrieked when they were brought onstage to try the tinikling, dancing between bamboo poles that, if you stepped wrong, cracked mercilessly against the ankles.

I inherited a love of music, but not so much the talent. I started piano lessons late, as a teenager, and at my first (and thankfully last) recital, after the youngest students had played their easy beginner pieces, my teacher introduced me as "a descendant of the father of kundiman!" Seats squeaked; a murmur ran through the crowd. I sat down, red-faced, and proceeded to plonk my way through "Scampering Squirrels" just like the little kids before me.

I got another shot at family tradition through our school's Filipino club. Everybody wanted to join; so many students showed up for meetings, I couldn't see who was at the back of the room. It didn't matter if you were actually Filipino. We hosted rehearsals for Philippine Cultural Night at my house, forty kids dancing at a time, one group on the lawn, one in the driveway, two in the street, while my mom sewed our costumes, gently adjusted choreography, and fed us.

Above all, everybody wanted the lead in the singkil, a folk dance in which diwatas (forest spirits) play a prank on a Maranao princess, causing a small earthquake, so that she has to bob among the shuddering rocks—symbolized on stage by four crossed bamboo poles that clack open and shut at her heels, as in the tinikling. All the while she blithely twirls fans in both hands, nodding in her gold headdress, shaking her slippers with bells on, never looking down. They gave the role to me, out of reverence for my mom. I was terrible, awkward and uncertain, concentrating so hard on the steps that I lost sight of the larger moment.

Still, I had learned enough piano to be able to play my favorite No Doubt songs on keyboards with my band, Love Bubbles. We took the stage on Philippine Cultural Night, sometime after the singkil. The crowd roared and I was myself again, somehow finding all the right notes.

Left: Me at 17 with my friends performing the singkil for Philippine Cultural Night, in costumes my mom sewed for us.
Bottom middle: Me later that year at the Vans Warped Tour.
Top middle and right: Mom in Bayanihan in the 1970s.

Ancestral WHISPER

I love the word susurrus because it sounds like what it is: a murmur, a rustle, a whisper. It makes me think of the quiet persistence of my ancestors and how much of my family history survives only in spoken form. Our recipes were rarely written down, and only piecemeal, so they've come to me riddled with ellipses and approximations. Sometimes my lola and my titas forgot to mention a particular ingredient because, well, of course you need *that*, wasn't it obvious?

For them, cooking was a matter of feel, adjusting for minute changes in weather, what was in the cupboard, their own passing whims. That's how I cook, too. You add, subtract, make and fix mistakes, take chances, improvise, all the while trusting your intuition to get it right. And what is intuition, really, but collective memory—all those voices still rustling over time?

While I was writing this book, a stranger reached out to me on Instagram, saying that they wanted to give a special knife to their partner, a non-binary chef of Black and Asian heritage who saw cooking as a way to connect with the past. They asked if I could suggest an inscription for the sheath. I carried the request in my mind for a week, thinking about medieval times when knights would name their swords, and then it came to me: Ancestral Whisper—that little shush with each stroke of the knife, like a murmured message, a gift of breath.

Mealtime is just a social construct. Merienda is what you eat in between, mid-morning or mid-afternoon—why not both?—and anywhere: in the street or at home; while sipping a soft drink, fizzy and ice-cold; or sun-bright calamansi juice; or sweet-sweet sago't gulaman, water swirled with brown sugar syrup, tapioca pearls, and cubes of jelly. (Or tea if you're being fancy.) To know a culture is to know its snacks, and Filipinos are serious about these tiny and not-so-tiny bites, so much so that it can be hard to tell where snacking ends and a meal begins. All of the recipes here can and should be mixed and matched, in any way you like.

MERIENDA

meh•ree•
Y&N•dah

These fritters are intentionally shaggy, a deep-fried thatch of seafood and vegetables, each ingredient distinct and legible through the batter. I make mine ultra-crispy with rice flour, cornstarch, and cornmeal. It's fun to leave the heads of the shrimp on, so they can poke out of the batter, like creatures draped in finery—or else use baby shrimp, if you can get them. (Following tradition, I use shrimp still in their shells, for extra crunch.)

There are a lot of flavors and textures: a little chewiness from squid tentacles and, in a nod to Italian fritto misto, layers of herbs and thin slices of lemon fried with the pith and rind still attached, bringing a lovely hint of bitterness. Feel free to add other favorite vegetables or small sardines or sprats. Typically ukoy is served with Suka at Bawang (page 177), but I find it's a bit too strong here, and recommend just lemon wedges on the side, so you can taste everything.

UKOY *OOH•koi*
SEAFOOD AND VEGETABLE FRITTERS MAKES 8 FRITTERS

1 (7-ounce/200 g) medium sweet potato, peeled

1 large (3½ ounce/100 g) carrot

½ red onion, cut into ½-inch-thick (12 mm) strips

8 pieces squid, cleaned, with body cut into 1-inch (2.5 cm) rings and tentacles left whole

2 lemons, rinsed

1 bunch fresh cilantro (including stems), cut very coarsely

½ ounce (2.5 g) fresh Thai basil leaves

¾ cup (96 g) cornstarch

½ cup (60 g) rice flour

⅓ cup (60 g) fine cornmeal

¾ cup (180 ml) cold light lager or club soda

2 teaspoons fish sauce

4 cups (960 ml) canola or other neutral oil

8 pieces head-on shrimp, each about 2 to 3 inches (5 to 8 cm) long

Using a mandoline, cut the sweet potato and carrot into matchsticks ⅛ inch (3 mm) wide. Transfer to a large mixing bowl and add the red onion strips and squid.

•

Cut 1 lemon in half lengthwise. Reserve one half for serving. Take the other half, trim off the ends, and cut into ⅛-inch-thick (3 mm) half-moons. Remove and discard the seeds, but keep the peel and pith. Add the half-moons, peel and pith included, to the mixing bowl with the vegetables and squid. Add the cilantro and Thai basil, and fluff the mixture together.

•

In a separate mixing bowl, whisk together the cornstarch, rice flour, and cornmeal, breaking down any lumps. Add the lager and fish sauce, and stir to combine.

•

Heat the oil in a 3-quart (2.8 L) saucepan over medium high, until it reaches around 350°F (175°C).

→

Take a fistful of the ukoy mixture, being sure to grab some of each of the ingredients, and put it in a small mixing bowl. You'll need enough of the mixture to make fritters the size of baseballs. Add 1 head-on shrimp to the bowl. Using a small ladle, scoop about ¼ cup (60 ml) of the corn-starch batter and lightly coat the vegetable mixture. I like to tuck the single shrimp in the center of the mixture, so its head and whiskers stick out, as if it were wrapped up in a puffy coat.

•

Carefully slip the battered nest of ingredients from the bowl into the hot oil. Fry until crispy, 2 to 3 minutes. Using a slotted spoon or spider, scoop the fried ukoy out of the oil and let drain on a paper-towel-lined plate. Sprinkle with a little kosher salt to season, and make sure to skim any fragments of ukoy left behind in the fryer oil, so that no burnt bits stick to the next fritter.

•

Repeat until you've made about 8 ukoy. Cut the remaining lemon and reserved half-lemon into wedges and discard the seeds. Serve the ukoy immediately, while hot, with the lemon wedges for squeezing.

FRIED GARLIC PEANUT

MAKES 1 CUP (160 G)

This is street food in the Philippines, heaped high in shallow bamboo baskets and handed over in little oil-stained paper bags; and bar food, eaten by the fistful to reawaken your thirst; and all-day food, reported to boost brain function, even more so with the antioxidant-rich skins left on. It's as much garlic as peanut, with some recipes demanding a whole head. The two ingredients are fried separately—it's good to have Garlic Chips (page 197) ready to go—then tumbled together; I take the extra step of frying the peanuts in garlic oil reserved from making the chips. Sometimes I toss in aromatics like makrut lime leaves or fennel seed in the last 30 seconds of frying, or dust the cooled peanuts in vinegar powder, for a smack of salt-and-vinegar. You can easily double or triple the recipe, and still be surprised at how soon it's all gone.

1 cup (240 ml) garlic oil, store-bought or home-made (page 198), or canola or other neutral oil
1 cup (160 g) raw red-skin peanuts
Kosher salt
2 tablespoons Garlic Chips (page 197)

Pour the oil into a 1-quart (960 ml) saucepan and heat over medium high to about 325°F (165°C). Once at temperature, add the peanuts and fry, stirring occasionally, for 3 minutes, or until the peanuts have darkened a couple shades and the bubbles in the oil have slowed.

•

Drain on a paper-towel-lined plate. Season with salt while still warm; the heat will help the salt cling to the peanuts. As the nuts rest, they'll turn darker. When cool enough to handle, toss with the garlic chips and serve, or store in an airtight container at room temperature for up to 3 months.

ike Andean cancha and American corn nuts, cornick is hominy—corn that's been nixtamalized, the outer hulls loosened and dissolved while the kernels soften and swell—dried to near husks, then bronzed in the fryer to a primal crunch. It was popularized in the 1980s in the Ilocos region, sold by street vendors and sari-sari stores in cellophane packets; now there's an entire snack industry devoted to it. My version is a salute to Boy Bawang brand garlic-flavor cornick: I drop the desiccated hominy in hot garlic oil, then toss the crisped kernels with Garlic Chips (page 197). You need a double dose of garlic to match the potency of the original, because in the Philippines, indigenous bawang (garlic) is smaller but punchier than its foreign counterparts. (You fry the pea-sized cloves skin and all—the skin is so thin, it's edible.)

You can use white or yellow hominy, canned or dry—just know that dry hominy turns out craggier. And if using dry hominy, you'll need to soak it overnight, then boil it in salted water until tender, about one-and-a-half to two hours, before popping it in the oven to dehydrate. One 16-ounce (454 g) bag yields around 3 pounds (1.3 kg).

Have fun with it—treat cornick like popcorn and try out unexpected seasonings, like a crushed cube of chicken bouillon or a dusting of nutritional yeast. This can be spicy or skew a little sweet. I eat it by the fistful, ideally with a garlic chip in every other bite, while sipping an ice-cold lager.

GARLIC CORNICK

MAKES 4 TO 6 CUPS (220 TO 330 G)

4 cans (15 ounces/430 g) white or yellow hominy

3 tablespoons (45 ml) olive oil

1 cup (240 ml) garlic oil, store-bought or homemade (page 198), otherwise canola or
another neutral oil

Kosher salt

3 tablespoons (15 g) Garlic Chips (page 197)

Preheat the oven to 275°F (135°C).

•

Rinse the hominy in a colander under cold water and let drain.

•

Divide the hominy evenly between two sheet trays. Add a little olive oil to each heap of hominy and combine with your hands or a large spoon. Put the trays on separate racks in the preheated oven and dehydrate the corn for 3 hours. Every 30 minutes or so, give each tray a good shake to mix the kernels and make sure they are drying evenly, and rotate the trays between racks.

•

After 3 hours or more, the kernels will have shrunk to 40 percent of their original size. You'll know that they're completely dry and ready to fry when they look translucent, like nubs of shrunken, wrinkly plastic corn. Allow the hominy to cool on the trays while you set up the fryer.

•

On the stove, set a 1-quart (960 ml) saucepan over medium high and heat the garlic oil, if using, or the neutral oil. Carefully tip in about a quarter of the dehydrated corn. The kernels will puff up in less than a minute, all at about the same time, the way they do when you make popcorn. (The oil may smoke a little.) Scoop out the puffed cornicks with a fine-mesh strainer and let them cool and drain on a plate lined with paper towels. While they're warm, sprinkle a little salt over them; the warmth will make the salt stick.

•

Repeat with more batches of the same size, or save some of the dehydrated corn for another time. Once you've fried as many as you wish, toss them with garlic chips. Serve immediately or store in an airtight container at room temperature for up to a week.

eat pies are ancient: Before the empanadas of Galicia there were the sanbusaj of ninth-century Persia, heralded in poetry. They took on many names as they traveled the world. Our version came from the Spanish by way of Latin America, one end of the empire reaching out to the other, and like our compatriots in Latin America, we made them ours. My family used to buy these by the tray for parties; they're sturdy enough to last all day and delicious whether minutes out of the fryer, so hot they might burn your tongue, or settled down to room temperature. This is Lola's recipe—I've hardly messed with it. Ground beef is simply browned with garlic, onions, tomato paste for umami, a splash of soy sauce and oyster sauce for brine, and raisins, which grow fat from soaking up the juices. It's then tucked inside a buttery dough that, once fried, flakes on cue.

BEEF EMPANADAS

MAKES 20 EMPANADAS

FOR THE EMPANADA DOUGH:

2¼ cups (280 g) all-purpose flour, plus more as needed

2 teaspoons kosher salt

½ cup (1 stick/115 g) cold unsalted butter, diced

1 large egg

2 tablespoons milk

1 tablespoon white vinegar

⅓ cup (75 ml) ice water

FOR THE FILLING:

2 teaspoons canola or other neutral oil

2 teaspoons tomato paste

½ small yellow onion, finely chopped

½ small green bell pepper, cut into ¼-inch (6 mm) cubes

½ small red bell pepper, cut into ¼-inch (6 mm) cubes

2 cloves garlic, peeled and finely minced

1 teaspoon kosher salt

½ teaspoon coarsely cracked black pepper

¼ medium russet potato, peeled and cut into ⅜-inch (1 cm) cubes

2 tablespoons brown raisins

6 ounces (170 g) ground beef

2 teaspoons oyster sauce

1½ teaspoons soy sauce

¼ cup (60 ml) chicken stock, store-bought or homemade (see headnote, Sinigang Roast Chicken, page 141)

1 bottle (48 ounces/1.4 L) canola or other neutral oil, for frying

Prepare the empanada dough:

In a large bowl, combine the flour and 1½ teaspoons of the salt. Add the butter and merge it with the flour using your hands or a food processor, integrating until sandy in texture.

●

In a medium bowl, use a fork to beat the egg with the milk and the remaining ½ teaspoon salt. Whisk in the vinegar and ice water. Add the egg mixture to the flour mixture and beat with a fork to meld into a dough.

●

Dust flour over a work surface. Lay the dough on top. Press and fold the dough onto itself a few times with the palms of your hands. Being careful not to overwork, split the dough in half and shape it into two equal logs; they should look like small sausages, 1½ to 2 inches (4 to 5 cm) thick. Roll the logs up in plastic wrap and refrigerate for about 1 hour, until firm.

●

Prepare the filling:

In a large skillet, heat the canola oil over medium high. When the oil shimmers, add the tomato paste and stir frequently for about 3 minutes as it darkens. Add the onion, bell peppers, garlic, salt, and black pepper. Cook, stirring occasionally for about 5 minutes, until slightly softened.

→

Add the potato and raisins and cook, stirring for 8 to 10 minutes, until the mixture starts to caramelize. Drop the heat to medium and cook for about another 5 minutes, stirring occasionally, until the potatoes are fork-tender and the raisins have swelled with the cooking juices.

•

Add the beef. Return the heat to medium high and cook for about 10 minutes, stirring occasionally, until the beef is browned and juicy. Stir in the oyster sauce and soy sauce until coated, then stir in the chicken stock. (The mixture should be glossy but not overtly wet; if too wet, cook for another 5 minutes or so to reduce the amount of liquid.) Transfer to a sheet pan and smooth into a thin, even layer. Refrigerate for at least 20 minutes so that the mixture has a chance to cool, allowing the juices to settle and lacquer the beef mixture.

•

To shape the dough, fill a small bowl with flour, for dusting. Remove one log of dough from the refrigerator and cut it in half crosswise, then cut each half crosswise into 10 equal pieces that look like thick coins. Dust flour over the work surface. Using your thumb and forefinger, gently round the edges of each coin of dough, then press lightly against the work surface to flatten. Switch to a rolling pin and roll out each coin to make a 4½-inch (11 cm) disk. Lightly dust the disks with flour and stack them on a plate or transfer to a parchment-lined baking sheet. Chill in the refrigerator until you are ready to assemble the empanadas, since the dough is easier to work with when it's cool. Repeat with the second log.

•

To assemble: Fill a small bowl with cool water, to help in sealing the empanadas. Put about 1½ tablespoons of the meat filling at the center of each disk of dough, leaving at least a ½-inch (12 mm) border around the filling. Using a brush or your finger, wet the edges of the dough with the water. Take the edge closest to you and fold upward and over the filling, making a half-moon shape and eliminating as much air as possible by gently patting and pressing the empanada. Crimp the edges with the tines of a fork to seal.

•

(At this point, you can freeze the uncooked empanadas on a baking sheet lined with wax paper. Once frozen, transfer to a zip-top bag and store for up to a month. When it's time to cook them, don't let them thaw; take them directly from the freezer to the fryer, as described in the next step, and cook for 5 to 6 minutes.)

•

In a large, heavy Dutch oven or pot, heat about 2 inches (5 cm) of the canola oil over medium high until it reaches 365°F (185°C). Fry the empanadas in batches of 4 to 5 depending on the size of your pot, making sure not to crowd the pan. (Overcrowding would cause the oil temperature to drop, making the empanadas soggy.) Turn frequently for 4 to 5 minutes, until the empanadas start to bob; they should be crisp and golden brown, with the pastry and meat cooked through. Transfer to a baking sheet lined with paper towels, arranging them in an even, spaced-out layer—they're so hot at this point, they're steaming, and you don't want that steam to dampen the other empanadas and make them lose their crispness.

•

Cool for a few minutes. (The filling is too hot to eat straight out of the fryer.) Serve warm.

*L*umpia are descendants of spring rolls, their name taken from the Hokkien spoken by early traders from southeastern China. They are party food, made for a crowd and often *by* one: As kids, we'd mob the kitchen counter and clash spoons as we reached for the bowl of filling, before carefully rolling up the delicate skins and sliding them into the waiting hot oil. Some might come filled with ubod, the crunchy heart cut from a coconut palm, or long green finger chiles stuffed with pork and cheese—we call this "dynamite"—or sugared bananas, for dessert (see Salted Caramelized Turon with Mochi, page 221); others

are left "fresh" and unfried, the wrapper as spongy as a crepe, or even served "naked," with no wrapper at all, just a heap of fillings. This is the classic version, given the honorific Shanghai in a nod to its Chinese origins: skinny golden cigarillos with crackly skins, packed with meat, juices seething.

Don't work too hard—you can dice the vegetables very roughly, then throw them in a food processor to get them minced fine. Be gentle with the lumpia skins when you peel them apart, although it's not the end of the world if they tear; you can hide the rips when you roll them up. Once deep-fried, they taste best with a sweet-sour daub of Banana Ketchup (page 167).

LUMPIA SHANGHAI
LOOM•pee•yah MAKES 20 LUMPIA

1 medium carrot, peeled then coarsely grated on
   a box grater
½ medium yellow onion, finely minced
½ (8-ounce/225 g) can water chestnuts, drained
   then finely minced
1 stalk celery, finely minced
3 cloves garlic, peeled and finely minced
2 large eggs, 1 separated into yolk and white
1½ teaspoons fish sauce
2½ teaspoons kosher salt
8 ounces (225 g) ground pork
8 ounces (225 g) ground beef
¾ teaspoon coarsely ground black pepper
20 lumpia or spring-roll wrappers (8 by 8
   inches/20 by 20 cm each), thawed if frozen
Canola or other neutral oil
Banana ketchup, store-bought or homemade
   (page 167), for serving

In a large bowl, combine the carrot, onion, water chestnuts, celery, garlic, 1 whole egg and 1 separated egg yolk, the fish sauce, and ½ teaspoon of the salt. Mix with a spoon until well blended. Add the pork, beef, black pepper, and remaining 2 teaspoons salt. Using your hands, gently mix until the ingredients are evenly distributed, being careful not to overwork the meat mixture—otherwise it will turn tough when cooked.

•

In a small bowl, whisk about 3 tablespoons (45 ml) water with the remaining egg white.

•

Take a stack of thawed lumpia skins and slowly peel one off the top, using your fingertips and pulling two corners at a time so they don't rip. (If you do get any rips, it's not a big deal; just arrange the lumpia skin so the rips are closest to you, and they will get rolled up into the lumpia.) Drape a damp paper towel over the remaining skins so they don't dry out.

•

Lay a lumpia wrapper on a work surface with 1 corner closest to you, so it makes a diamond shape. Put 3 tablespoons (40 g) of the meat filling in the center of the wrapper and spread it out to make a log 7 inches (17 cm) long, reaching from the left corner of the wrapper toward the right; there should be a ½-inch (12 mm) margin of wrapper left open at either end.

→

LUMPIA SHANGHAI
CONTINUED

Lift up the bottom corner of the lumpia wrapper and fold it up and over the filling; make sure there's no air between the filling and the wrapper. Bring the left and right wrapper corners toward the center, pulling and folding them tightly over the filling. Brush the remaining upper triangle of the wrapper with the egg-white wash, the way you'd moisten the flap of an envelope. Then roll the log away from you toward the top corner and seal the wrapper closed.

•

Repeat with the filling and each lumpia wrapper.
In a deep pot, add enough oil to reach 3 inches (7.5 cm) in height. Heat over medium high until about 350°F (175°C). Working in small batches, add 5 lumpia at a time and cook for 3 to 4 minutes, rotating frequently and separating as needed, until golden brown. Transfer to a large baking sheet lined with paper towels and let cool while you fry the remaining lumpia.

•

(You can also freeze uncooked lumpia on a baking sheet lined with wax paper. Once frozen, transfer to a zip-top bag and store for up to a month. When it's time to cook them, don't let them thaw; take them directly from the freezer to the fryer and cook for 4 to 5 minutes.)

•

Serve the lumpia whole or cut in half crosswise, with banana ketchup for dipping. For a crowd, you can cook the lumpia an hour or two ahead, let rest at room temperature, then reheat in a 350°F (175°C) oven for 10 minutes.

In the Philippines, this is pulutan, bar food, but I ate it as a kid going to the Turo-Turo (page 16), where the squid rings and tentacles somehow stayed crunchy all day, even though they were fried in big batches and stocked in hotel pans on the steam table. I loved the texture—a little crackle, a little chew—especially paired with the velvet of Munggo (page 57) and the sour thrill of Sinigang (page 47). Here, milk in the marinade keeps the calamari tender, and equal amounts of cornstarch and flour give it a crispy armor. Baby squid is my favorite for this if you can find it: one bite, with all the arms and tentacles!

CRISPY FRIED CALAMARI

SERVES 4

½ cup (65 g) cornstarch

½ cup (65 g) all-purpose flour

½ teaspoon baking soda

¼ teaspoon garlic powder

¼ teaspoon coarsely cracked black pepper

1 pound squid, 5 inches (12 cm) long or smaller, cleaned and cut into ¾-inch (2 cm) pieces

1 cup (240 ml) milk or buttermilk

1 teaspoon fish sauce

4 cups (960 ml) canola or other neutral oil, for frying

Kosher salt, for finishing

1 whole lemon, cut into wedges, seeds removed, for serving

Suka at Bawang (page 177), for serving

In a mixing bowl, combine the cornstarch, flour, baking soda, garlic powder, and pepper. Whisk together the batter, breaking down any lumps.

•

Put the cleaned squid in another bowl and add the milk and fish sauce, using your hands to combine. Dredge each piece of calamari in the flour mixture, careful to get between all the arms and tentacles and inside the rings. Arrange the dredged calamari on a tray in a single layer, lying flat.

•

Line another tray with paper towels. Add the oil to a 3-quart (2.8 L) stockpot and heat over medium high until it reaches 365°F (185°C). Fry the calamari in small batches, 1 to 2 minutes per batch, making sure there's enough space in the pot for each piece to evenly fry. (If the fryer is too crowded, the calamari will steam and get soggy.) Once the calamari is golden, firm, and crisp, transfer the batch to the paper-towel-lined tray to drain and season with a little salt while warm. Repeat with the remaining batches.

•

Serve immediately with the lemon wedges and suka at bawang.

On day trips to San Francisco, a forty-minute drive from our house in San Jose, we'd swing by Chinatown and double-park our Aerostar van in a sleepy alley while my mom waited in line at the bakery to pick up two large pink boxes of baozi, or pork buns—what we call siopao. Sometimes us younger kids would tag along with an older brother or sister to the back door of the fortune-cookie factory and sneak in to watch the assembly line: hundreds of hot round steel plates turning, each given a squeeze of loose batter before they clapped shut. A spit of steam and a flat bronzed cookie would appear, to be plucked by workers who quickly pinched them into shape. We'd buy a dozen with fortunes and another dozen discards, broken cookies left flat and unfolded, just to eat, alongside our siopao.

We are indebted to the Chinese for this snack, and in particular to Ma Mon Luk, who came to the Philippines after World War I and sold chicken noodle soup on the street until he had enough money to open his own restaurant, which is famous to this day for its siopao. Traditionally the buns are steamed on squares of parchment, but I suggest a natural base–banana or bamboo leaves or corn husks (the kind used for tamales), washed and cut into 3-inch (7.5 cm) squares–to lend a bit of extra flavor.

I like to stuff the buns with tocino, our version of char siu (Chinese barbecued pork). You follow the same recipe, but chop the tocino into nubs before frying and pour a little more of the marinade liquid into the pan for a sweet, binding glaze. You can also take classic pork adobo and reduce the sauce, discard the bay leaves, and gently shred the meat. Or mix some seasoned ground pork, your favorite aromatics, a few tablespoons of strong broth or liquid, chopped Chinese sausage, and a piece of Salted Egg (page 190). Have fun with the fillings–just make sure they're juicy!

SIOPAO *shee•OH•pow*
STEAMED BUNS MAKES ABOUT 10 BUNS

2½ cups (315 g) all-purpose flour

1 teaspoon active dry yeast

1 teaspoon sugar

1 tablespoon canola or other neutral oil or shortening

1 cup (100 ml) lukewarm water

1½ cups chilled filling of your choice: Tocino (page 123), Pork Adobo (page 23), or improvise

10 (3 by 3-inch/7.5 by 7.5 cm) squares cut out of fresh or frozen banana leaves (see headnote for Suman, page 229) or parchment

In a medium bowl, whisk together the flour, yeast, and sugar for a few seconds to remove any lumps. Pour the oil and water into a bowl—no need to stir or whisk—and slowly drizzle into the flour mixture. With a small rubber spatula, mix to make a dough. Tip the dough onto a clean countertop and knead for about 10 minutes, until the dough ball feels very smooth.

•

Return the dough ball to the mixing bowl and cover with a damp kitchen towel. Set the bowl someplace warm (but not hot), near the stove or in an oven or dryer that has been heated and shut off, or outside on a temperate day, between 75°F and 82°F (24°C to 28°C). Allow the dough to rest and double in size; this should take 45 minutes to 1½ hours, depending on the warmth of the resting location.

•

Once the dough has doubled, knead it a few times until it reverts to its original size. Roll the dough into a cylinder, then cut the cylinder in half and cut each half into 5 even disks.

→

SIOPAO CONTINUED

Using a rolling pin, roll one disk into a flat round about ¼ inch (6 mm) thick and 4 to 5 inches (10 to 12 cm) wide. (Cover the remaining disks with the damp kitchen towel until needed.) Put about 1½ tablespoons filling in the center of the disk. Take the bottom edge of the disk and pull it up over the filling, then do the same with the adjacent edge of dough, pinching the dough together in the center to make a pleat. Repeat 7 to 8 times all around the circumference of the disk, until the filling is covered. Twist the final pinch so it looks like a swirl.

•

Put each filled siopao on a square of banana leaf or parchment and cover with another damp kitchen towel. Repeat with the remaining dough disks, making sure that the towel covers all the siopao, with enough space between them for the dough's final rise.

•

Once all the buns have been filled, rest under the towel for another 15 minutes. While the dough is rising, prepare a large saucepan with a steamer inset and about 1 inch (2.5 cm) of water underneath. Cover and bring to a boil over high heat.

•

Remove the lid and gently transfer 3 to 5 siopao, each with its banana-leaf or parchment square attached, to the steamer, leaving 1 inch (2.5 cm) of space between the siopao and the sides of the pan. Replace the lid. Steam for about 20 minutes, then repeat with the remaining siopao. (The number of batches depends on the size of your steamer.) Serve warm, or store in an airtight container in the refrigerator for a few days or in the freezer for up to a month and then steam as described above to reheat, about 7 minutes from the refrigerator and 15 minutes from the freezer.

KINILAW *kee•nee•ℒAO*
RAW FISH SERVES 2

Kinilaw is one of the earliest forms of Filipino cooking: the freshest of fish immersed ever so briefly in vinegar, emerging neither raw nor cooked but transfigured by sourness. The cultural historian Doreen Gamboa Fernandez describes an even more primal kinilaw in her 1998 essay collection *Tikim*: live fish flopped in the bottom of a boat, swiftly deboned, and simply rinsed in the surrounding sea for a touch of salt. Here I rely on salt and lime juice as a souring agent, to bring firmness to the fish's flesh, and add creamy and cooling elements of avocado and coconut jelly (the delicate meat scooped out of a young coconut).

For this recipe, I like a light, tender fish—red snapper, halibut, flounder, sole—but the potent oiliness of mackerel has its own allure. You can see the kinship between kinilaw and ceviche, each an indigenous tradition that predates the arrival of the Spanish and their escabèche. As a Californian dedicated to trawling marisquerías (seafood restaurants), I always long for tostadas when I eat kinilaw; they turn a snack into a meal.

---

3 ounces (85 g) fresh red snapper, cut into ½-inch (12 mm) dice
Juice of 2 limes
1 fresh Thai chile or chile of your choice, minced and added to taste
¼ red onion, finely minced
Kosher salt
½ avocado, cut into ½-inch (12 mm) dice
3 ounces (85 g) coconut jelly (fresh young coconut meat, in bite-size pieces), plus 2 tablespoons of its coconut water
Coarsely chopped fresh cilantro, plus stems for garnish

In a small mixing bowl, combine the red snapper, lime juice, chile, red onion, and a couple pinches salt. The lime will start to cure and firm the fish, while the seasonings imprint their flavor.

•

This dish is best made all at once, from start to finish, and eaten right away, but if you want to do some advance preparation, you can season the fish as just described up to 30 minutes before serving. When ready to eat, add the diced avocado, coconut jelly, coconut water, and chopped cilantro, and gently fold to combine, so the avocado pieces retain their shape but release a little fat, adding just enough creaminess to coat and lightly bind together the kinilaw. Top with the cilantro stems and serve immediately, adding more salt to taste as you wish.

Extra Value

FOR ALAN DIMAYUGA

Dad in front of one of his McDonald's branches.

*E*very family has its legends. When my dad was young, he ran with a rebellious crowd. To keep him out of trouble, his parents packed him off to Europe, where he hitchhiked his way to the Netherlands and landed a job as a pageboy at the Philippine Embassy at the Hague. That's where fate found him, in the summer of 1971, when my mom appeared in a bevy of gold-ankleted dancers, on tour with the Bayanihan national folk troupe (see page 93). He was tasked with showing them around town. Stars fell from the sky.

They got married a few years later and moved to northern California, home to one of the country's largest Filipino communities, including both recent arrivals and those born in America, some of them descendants of the migrant farmworkers who started settling here a century ago. (We've been around a long time.) My mom found administrative work at IBM while my dad rose up the ranks at McDonald's, ultimately managing eight stores.

MCDONALD'S

While the McDonald's on Landess Ave. may not compete with more elegant establishments, manager Alan Dimayuga knows his restaurant is a good value. McDonald's has moved forward with the times, adding leaner sandwiches and healthier items to their menu and permanently instituting value meals, a complete breakfast, lunch, or dinner for less than $3.50. With a renewed commitment to customer satisfaction, cleanliness, community service, and fast and friendly service, no other place can compare.

A newspaper clipping highlighting Dad's introduction of value meals.

Top left: Dad watching Mom dance at the Hague in the Netherlands, when they had just met.

Top right: Dad with my nephew Max, 2021.

Bottom left: Me at age 8, with a pony outside one of Dad's McDonald's branches.

Bottom right: Dad receiving an award for his work.

In 1991, he got the idea to put up posters, lit from behind like in a marquee—glam shots of burgers, sodas, and fries, grouped together instead of isolated on separate menus, and in numbered sets, so customers could place orders faster. Higher-ups scolded him for this departure from corporate standards, and then looked at the data and realized that his approach had shaved off at least eight seconds per purchase, boosting profits. Not long after, the company officially introduced the Extra Value Meal; according to the *New York Times*, in the program's first year of existence, sales went up by 6 percent. ("So you invented the set meal?" I asked my dad years later, in wonder. He laughed and said, "Yeah.")

My dad received a commendation for his idea, but no further reward. He didn't complain; he loved his job. Then, when I was in seventh grade, he came home late one night from work and while making dinner for himself had a sudden, violent cough. It triggered a headache so severe, my mother took him to the hospital. He'd had a brain aneurysm. Just like that, after eighteen years, his career at McDonald's was over.

When I told him my dream of becoming a cook, he was worried at first. The industry's not glamorous, he said. It can be brutal. But I'd seen the joy his work brought him, no matter how tough it was, and the affection he'd lavished on each McDonald's under his care. He was an innovator, and I wanted to be one, too, experimenting with ingredients and finding ways to make familiar dishes surprising and new.

He still talks fondly about those days. And I remember how cool it was, when I was a kid, to have a dad who worked at McDonald's and all the Happy Meal toys you could ever want. Sometimes, en route to the night shift, he'd drop by school with my special order: that slightly squashed burger still warm in wax paper, with extra pickles, Sprite, a strawberry milkshake, and fries—Super Sized, so I could share with all my friends.

Silog, a portmanteau of sinangag (garlic fried rice) and itlog (egg, typically fried sunny-side up), is an entire genre of breakfast, although it can really be eaten all day. Almost any cured meat can be slotted into the format, from Tapa, jerky-like beef (page 121), and Tocino, somewhere between Western bacon and Chinese char siu (page 123), to Corned Beef (page 129) and Homemade Spam (page 131)–always matched with pickles and vegetable sides, to temper the richness: Salted Bitter Melon (page 185), Lacto-Fermented Green Mango (page 189), Atsara (page 183), crunchy cucumber, and juicy wedges of tomato. For a sweeter start, there's Champorado (page 135), chocolate rice porridge–although this too is typically given a savory finish of crispy dried salted fish, shredded and scattered or laid whole on top, delicate bones, head, tail, and all.

BREAKFAST

AND SILOGS
see LOHGS

Some trace the word tapa to the Spanish tradition of small plates and snacks, others to the Sanskrit word for heat. Whatever the etymology, the dish's origins go back to pre-colonial traditions of preserving meat (beef, carabao, deer, boar) by leaving it out to dry in the sun. In the 1980s, Vivian Del Rosario, an enterprising cook in Quezon City, came up with tapsilog as a slangy name for the combination of tapa, sinangag (garlic fried rice), and itlog (egg), selling it as a cheap set meal to jeepney drivers out of a cafeteria in the corner of a parking lot–making it the first official silog (see Breakfast and Silogs, page 118).

To make tapa, I use sirloin, a tender cut, and simply cure it with salt in the refrigerator overnight, for a little chewiness and fervor. It helps to cut the meat as thin as you can; some cooks pound the slices with a mallet to get them even thinner. Quickly fried, the panels of beef turn out like mini-steaks, generously salted and peppered, needing nothing more.

TAPA *TAH•pah*
AIR-DRIED CURED BEEF SERVES 2

8 ounces (225 g) beef sirloin

Kosher salt and coarsely cracked black pepper

4 tablespoons (60 ml) olive oil

Garlic Butter Fried Rice (page 75) or steamed
    rice, for serving

2 large eggs, any way you like, for serving

Your favorite pickles and vegetable sides (see
    Breakfast and Silogs, page 118), for serving

Freeze the beef in its packaging (butcher paper or plastic wrap is fine) for about 1 hour, or until the meat is partially frozen and firm. Remove from the packaging and slice into thin, even slices about ¼ inch (6 mm) thick. Generously salt and pepper both sides. Arrange on a plate and keep uncovered in the refrigerator overnight to dry out and cure before frying.

●

The next day, heat a frying pan over medium high. Add 2 tablespoons of the olive oil and fry half the batch. Cook the beef on each side for about 1½ minutes or until browned. Set aside on a plate and cook the second batch with the remaining oil.

●

Serve immediately with rice, eggs (if frying or scrambling, cook them in the same pan for a beefy flavor), and any of your favorite pickles and vegetable sides (pictured here: Salted Bitter Melon, page 185; pickled chiles from Suka at Bawang, page 177; and fresh tomato).

ocino is bacon in Spanish, but our version is closer to Chinese char siu, sweet with a throb of sour, and redder, verging on incarnadine. The sweetness has a dark side, like Vietnamese nước màu, caramel brought perilously close to burning. Its origins lie in Pampanga (where my mom grew up) and a long tradition of fermenting pork with salt and rice (burong babi)—and later with sugar (pindang babi)—to preserve it in the heat. In 1967, a Kapampangan elementary-school teacher named Lolita O. Hizon improvised her own pindang recipe to make use of a neighbor's excess pork. She called it tocino, and when local butchers started clamoring for it, she pawned her jewelry to build a bigger kitchen and what would become a nationwide brand, Pampanga's Best.

As made here, the distinctive crimson color of the tocino comes from achuete (annatto) and cranberry juice. (You could also add a tablespoon of strong hibiscus tea.) The cranberry brings extra acid to boost the action of the vinegar, and the rice flour binds the marinade to the meat, so flavor finds its way to every cranny. I suggest pork shoulder but you can never go wrong with a fattier cut like belly.

TOCINO *toh • SEE • noh*
SWEET CURED FRIED PORK SERVES 4

2 cloves garlic, peeled and finely minced or Microplaned

1 teaspoon fresh ginger, peeled and finely grated or minced

½ small beet, finely grated or Microplaned

⅓ cup (50 g) light brown sugar

1 teaspoon kosher salt

1 teaspoon fish sauce

½ teaspoon finely ground black pepper

2 teaspoons rice flour

¼ teaspoon achuete powder (also known as annatto)

2 tablespoons cranberry juice

1 tablespoon rice vinegar

2 teaspoons soy sauce

1 pound (455 g) pork shoulder, sliced ¼-inch (6 mm) thick

Garlic Butter Fried Rice (page 75) or steamed rice, for serving

4 large eggs, any way you like, for serving

Your favorite pickles and vegetable sides (see Breakfast and Silogs, page 118), for serving

In a small mixing bowl, mix together the garlic, ginger, beet, sugar, salt, fish sauce, pepper, flour, achuete powder, cranberry juice, vinegar, and soy sauce.

•

Arrange the pork slices in a zip-top bag or small container. Pour the marinade over the pork and lightly massage it so the marinade coats each slice. Marinate in the refrigerator for at least 12 hours or overnight.

•

Remove the pork from the container, leaving behind any excess marinade. Heat a nonstick frying pan over medium high, then add a few pork slices, making sure that there's at least ½ inch (12 mm) of space between them. Pour in a few tablespoons of water plus some of the marinade, strained through a fine-mesh strainer, to help steam and render the fat; by the time the liquid evaporates, there'll be enough liquid fat to crisp and brown the meat.

•

Watch the pan closely. The sugars in the marinade will begin to caramelize and lacquer the meat. Turn each pork slice over once every 1 or 2 minutes, collecting any caramel. Each batch will take about 8 minutes total cooking time. When the pork slices are a deep, dark brown on both sides, transfer the meat to a plate. Repeat with the remaining pork.

•

Let cool, then serve with warm rice, eggs, and any of your favorite pickles and vegetable sides (pictured here: Lacto-Fermented Green Mango, page 189; pickled chiles from Suka at Bawang, page 177; and fresh tomato).

This was my favorite cured meat when I was a kid: a chubby little sausage, sticky-sweet from the juices caramelizing in the pan, each bite dunked into suka at bawang and followed by a mouthful of hot rice. Two links were just enough. Longganisa is a cousin to chorizo and has countless preparations; I put brown sugar and soy sauce in mine, a union of salt and sweet. You get some sting from the garlic vinegar, and paprika brings a hint of smoke. I like the snap of a sausage casing, but you can easily make this without, just rolling the ground pork into short, fat cylinders, like the stubbed-out ends of cigars.

LONGGANISA
lawng • gah • NEE • sah
FILIPINO-STYLE CHORIZO
MAKES ABOUT 16 LINKS

1 pound (455 g) ground pork

½ pound (225 g) pork shoulder, ¼-inch (6 mm) dice, fat included

1½ heads garlic (4½ ounces/75 g), finely minced

⅓ cup (75 g) packed brown sugar

2 teaspoons soy sauce

2 teaspoons salt

2 tablespoons Suka at Bawang (page 117) or apple cider vinegar, plus more for serving

2 teaspoons coarsely cracked black pepper

2 teaspoons paprika

5 feet (1.5 m) pork sausage casing, 1 inch (2.5 cm) in diameter (optional)

Garlic Butter Fried Rice (page 75) or steamed rice, for serving

Eggs, any way you like, for serving

Your favorite pickles and vegetable sides (see Breakfast and Silogs, page 118), for serving

Put the ground pork, diced pork, garlic, sugar, soy sauce, salt, suka at bawang, pepper, and paprika in a large mixing bowl and combine using clean hands, until just melded. Be sure not to overwork the mixture; otherwise the meat will have a bouncy texture once cooked.

•

If you are making caseless sausages, roll the meat into short, fat cylinders, 1 inch (2.5 cm) thick and about 2 inches (5 cm) long, weighing about 1½ ounces (40 g) each. Arrange on a plate or in a food-safe container and store in the refrigerator for the seasoning to marinate the meat overnight.

•

If using a sausage casing, first submerge the casing in a bowl of cold water and rinse carefully, so it doesn't get tangled on itself. Drain and refill the bowl with fresh water. Press the water gently through the inside of the casing, to flush out any remaining salt. Then place one end of the casing over the tube side of a funnel and double-knot the other end. Push the meat mixture through the funnel and into the casing with the handle of a wooden spoon. Once the casing is filled, press it at 2-inch (5 cm) intervals, twist to make individual links, then tie off the open end. (If you tie off the end first, it can create too much pressure and cause the links to burst when you twist.) Store in the refrigerator overnight, then cut the links with scissors and prick the sausages before cooking.

•

The next day, heat a nonstick frying pan to medium high. Add the longganisa and just enough water to pool at the bottom of the pan, then cover with a lid and let steam for about 2 minutes if caseless and 3 minutes if cased. Remove the lid and flip the sausages. Keep frying and flipping until the juices render and begin to caramelize and coat each sausage, another 5 minutes if caseless and 7 minutes if cased.

•

Serve with rice, eggs, lots of suka at bawang, and any of your favorite pickles and vegetable sides (pictured here: Atsara, page 183, and pickled chiles from Suka at Bawang, page 177).

In the wild, bangus, or milkfish, is silver and shimmery as a disco ball. An oily fish, it's often deboned, butterflied, and plunged in a tangy marinade, then fried whole and served splayed open to show off its creamy fatty belly, which is so rich, I ration it out to myself, spooning it up between other bites. Because milkfish is hard to get in the United States, I use sardines or sprats (with the guts, gills, and scales removed). Mackerel or other oily silver fish work, too—try to find ones that aren't too big, so you can keep the belly intact when cooking. Leave the head and frilly tail on: With the smaller fish you can eat them whole, and with the larger ones, just break off the crunchy bits.

MARINATED SILVER FISH

SERVES 2

4 ounces (125 g) any small silver fish, such as
    sardines, cleaned
3 cloves garlic, peeled and thinly sliced
Coarsely cracked black pepper
¼ teaspoon kosher salt
½ cup (120 ml) Suka at Bawang (page 177) or apple
    cider vinegar, plus more for serving
1 fresh serrano or Thai chile, sliced (optional)
¼ cup (60 ml) canola or other neutral oil
Garlic Butter Fried Rice (page 75) or steamed
    rice, for serving
2 large eggs, any way you like, for serving
Your favorite pickles and vegetable sides (see
    Breakfast and Silogs, page 118), for serving

In a small zip-top bag, combine the silver fish, garlic, pepper, salt, vinegar, and chile if using. The fish should be entirely submerged in the marinade. Seal the bag, making sure to remove as much air as possible. For smaller fish, marinate for 2 hours; for larger ones, up to 8.

•

Remove the fish from the marinade and pat dry with paper towels. Heat a small sauté pan over medium high. Add the oil, and once it's shimmering, slip the fish in the pan. Fry smaller fish for about 4 minutes and larger fish for about 6, flipping halfway through. (Depending on their size, you may need to fry them in batches, no more than three at a time.) When the fish are crispy and golden brown, remove and drain on a plate lined with paper towels.

•

Serve with rice, eggs, suka at bawang, and any of your favorite pickles and vegetable sides (pictured here: Lacto-Fermented Green Mango, page 189, and cucumber).

Corned beef is humble and glorious. It was one of the canned goods brought to the Philippines in the early twentieth century by American colonialists who didn't trust local ingredients; what the Americans saw as mundane necessity, the Filipinos found exotic and learned to make irresistible.

As a kid, I ate it for breakfast, hashed and crisped, next to the requisite rice and sunny-side-up egg. So when I got to New York I was ready to fall in love with Jewish deli food and the mammoth sandwiches at Katz's on the Lower East Side. That's the neighborhood that arguably made corned beef an American tradition in the first place: Kosher butchers sold it to their Irish immigrant neighbors as a substitute for the heavily salted Irish bacon they missed from back home. To this day my go-to order at any New York City diner is corned beef, eggs, and grits (which is like rice, only in porridge form).

CORNED BEEF

SERVES 4 TO 5

¼ cup (60 ml) canola or other neutral oil

2 medium russet potatoes, cut into ½-inch (12 mm) dice

1 medium onion, cut into ½-inch (12 mm) dice

2 cloves garlic, peeled and coarsely chopped

Coarsely cracked black pepper

1 medium ripe tomato, cut into ½-inch (12 mm) dice

1 can (12 ounces/340 g) corned beef

Garlic Butter Fried Rice (page 75) or steamed rice, for serving

4 or 5 large eggs, any way you like, for serving

Your favorite pickles and vegetable sides (see Breakfast and Silogs, page 118), for serving

Heat a large sauté pan over medium high. Add the oil, and when it shimmers, add the potatoes and fry for about 7 minutes, stirring occasionally, until golden and slightly crispy. Transfer to a plate lined with paper towels and set aside to rest.

•

Discard all but 1 tablespoon of the remaining oil in the pan. Add the onion, garlic, and pepper, and cook while stirring for about 4 minutes, until the onions are translucent.

•

Add the tomato and corned beef. Using the back of a large wooden spoon, break up the corned beef so that it's loose. Cook for another 4 minutes, or until the corned beef is hot. Add the fried potatoes to the corned-beef mixture in the pan and combine to make the corned-beef juices seep into the potatoes.

•

Serve immediately with warm rice, eggs, and any of your favorite pickles and vegetable sides.

•

Optional (and really nice when reheating leftovers): Take the corned-beef mixture (without the potatoes) and form it into thick patties around 4 to 5 inches (10 to 12 cm) wide and 3 to 4 inches (7.5 to 10 cm) high. Sear the patties in a nonstick skillet over medium high for 3 to 4 minutes, until the corned beef takes on a dark brown crust. Flip the patty and repeat on the other side. Serve as above.

There are nearly two hundred distinct languages in the Philippines, and most folks speak more than one and sometimes five or more—which may explain in part why we love to play with words and mint new ones, whether through repetition (see Bola-Bola, page 27), mash-ups (see Breakfast and Silogs, page 118), or tadbalik, rearranging syllables and letters (baliktad means "reverse"), a legacy of anti-colonial fighters from the Philippine Revolution of 1896-98 that's still used in modern slang.

So perhaps it's inevitable that we would embrace Spam, a collision of spiced pork and ham. It was introduced to the world by the American company Hormel in 1937, just in time to feed the troops, who at the peak of World War II ate some 15 million cans a week. In the hunger that followed the devastation of war, Filipinos had to turn to surplus army rations. We've been eating Spam ever since.

I always loved peeling back the lid of that iconic blue oblong tin and frying slices until crispy. Then, on New Year's Eve in 2018, I flew to Hawai'i, invited by friends from the QTPOC dance-party collectives Bubble_T and Papi Juice who'd grown up there. Every day we found a new hiking trail, then sprawled out on the beach, and almost always someone brought along a plastic-wrapped Spam musubi, picked up at 7-Eleven: Spam fried to a sheen atop a slab of rice dusted with furikake, all trussed together by nori—Hawai'i's own onigiri.

It inspired me to try making my own version of Spam. My recipe is more pork shoulder than ham, because of the higher fat content. I bind the meat together with a little cornstarch, then cook it "low and slow"—for a long time, at low heat. Feel free to take creative liberties and add aromatics, if you like flavored Spam. (One limited-edition version sold by Hormel in the Philippines comes seasoned like Tocino, page 123.)

I've made this with fancy chef tools, vacuum-sealing the meat and plopping it in a sous vide water bath at 155°F (68°C) for about 2 hours. But you can get a perfect loaf with just an oven. The key, after cooking, is to stack the loaf pans so they nest one in the other, then weigh them down overnight with an extra loaf pan or any canned goods you have on hand.

When it's ready, you can crisp slices with a little oil, adding a slosh of soy sauce and cane sugar to caramelize and cling. The loaves freeze nicely, so don't worry about making too much—it will last.

HOMEMADE SPAM

MAKES TWO LOAVES (8 BY 4-INCH / 20 BY 10 CM)

1½ pounds (680 g) ground pork shoulder

8 ounces (225 g) ham, diced into 1-inch (2.5 cm) chunks

2 teaspoons pink curing salt

1 tablespoon sugar

1 tablespoon cornstarch

1 tablespoon kosher salt

⅓ cup (75 ml) room temperature water

⅓ cup (75 ml) cold water

1 clove garlic, Microplaned or grated

½ red onion, Microplaned or grated

2 tablespoons canola or other neutral oil, for frying

Soy sauce, for frying (optional)

Cane sugar, for frying (optional)

Preheat the oven to 250°F (120°C).

•

When buying the ground pork shoulder at the butcher's or pre-packaged at the supermarket, ask or look for a medium-coarse grind with a ratio of 30 percent fat to meat. (20 percent works fine as well, but more fat yields more flavor when fried.)

•

Grind the diced ham in a food processor (or meat grinder if you have one at home) and pulse for about 1 minute, until the pieces are even.

•

In a large mixing bowl, whisk together the pink salt, sugar, cornstarch, kosher salt, and ⅓ cup (75 ml) room temperature water. Transfer the ground pork and ham to the bowl, then add the Microplaned garlic and onion and the cold water. Mix to combine.

→

Divide the meat mixture equally between two 8 by 4-inch (20 by 10 cm) loaf pans. Spread the mixture evenly and tap the bases of the pans on the counter to remove any air bubbles.

•

Arrange the loaf pans inside a large baking tin or casserole, and carefully pour hot water into the tin or casserole up to the half-way mark of the loaf pans. (You can use a measuring cup with a spout to pour the water in.) This is called a bain-marie or water bath: It allows the loaves to bake slowly and gently without the sides turning brown.

•

Set the baking tin or casserole in the oven and bake the loaves for about 3 hours, until their internal temperature, tested with a meat thermometer, reaches 155°F (70°C) and they feel firm to the touch.

•

While the baking tin/casserole is still in the oven, remove the loaf pans from the water bath—careful, as the water will be very hot—and transfer to a rack. Turn off the oven. (When cool, take out the baking tin/casserole and discard the water bath.)

•

Tip the loaf pans slightly over the sink to discard the cooking liquid, or pour it into a container to freeze and save for a future pork-based stew. While warm, cover each spam loaf with a generous piece of plastic wrap, directly touching the surface of the loaf and draping over the sides. Stack the pans so they are nested on top of each other. If you have a spare third loaf pan, put it on top of the stack to press and weigh down the loaves, or use any canned goods or a bottle of wine or olive oil—the weight helps the spam keep its shape. Cool overnight in the refrigerator.

•

The next day, take out the loaves, slice, and fry in a skillet with the canola oil until crisp, adding soy sauce and cane sugar to taste for caramelization, if you like. Transfer any remaining spam to the freezer and store for up to a month, or keep in your refrigerator but be sure to eat it within a week of cooking.

Mexican champurrado—a hot slurry of a drink, made with chocolate and masa harina (the corn flour used to make tortillas)—came to the Philippines around the same time as chocolate, in the late seventeenth century. In lieu of corn, we used rice (of course!) and turned it into porridge. Eating this, I now understand why my parents let me toss a spoonful of Nestlé Quik chocolate milk powder into my Quaker instant oats at breakfast. It made sense to them.

Note that champorado isn't necessarily sweet, unless you want it to be. Tablea, the chocolate used to make it, is raw cacao that's been fermented, roasted, and ground not smooth but left slightly grainy, with the barest dusting of sugar and a welcome note of bitterness. (No wonder, then, that the dish is often served with tuyo, small silver fish, salted, sun-dried, and crisped.) You can doctor it with sugar and milk like you would coffee; condensed milk makes the porridge sweeter, evaporated milk more savory. (I prefer the latter, and still remember a version I once made with evaporated goat's milk, for extra tang.) Either way, a finishing pinch of salt brings the flavors into focus.

CHAMPORADO
chahm•poh•RAH•doh
CHOCOLATE RICE PORRIDGE SERVES 2

Pinch kosher salt
2 tablets tablea (36 g), store-bought or home-made (page 205)
⅓ cup (70 g) glutinous ("sweet") rice or sushi rice
Flaky sea salt
Condensed milk or evaporated milk, or your milk of choice, to finish

In a 2-quart (2 L) saucepan, bring 2 cups (480 ml) water to a boil, then add the kosher salt and tablea, stirring to dissolve. Add the rice and stir. When the water comes to a boil again, drop the heat down to medium and cook, stirring occasionally, for about 25 minutes, until the grains have cooked through and the rice is as creamy as risotto.

•

Serve in two small bowls and finish with a filigree of flaky sea salt. Offer evaporated milk, condensed milk, or your favorite milk on the side, to add a splash or flood the bowl, as you wish.

Kamayan

Children of immigrants are sometimes called third-culture kids, because we have to make our own way, navigating the in-between. We inherit the traditions of our ancestors, but know them only secondhand, removed from their origins; and at the same time, we witness our parents' struggle to adapt to and stake a claim in a place that's alien to them but that we call home. This isn't a question of allegiance but of belonging: We don't always feel that we fit in, either in the country our parents came from or in the one where we were born.

In California, I grew up surrounded by fellow Filipinos, both immigrants and American-born. Still, there were traditions I never really understood, like kamayan, eating with your hands. It's an ancient practice that was scorned as savagery and discouraged by the Spanish colonialists who arrived in the sixteenth century, and even more so by the Americans after them, who took possession of the Philippines in 1898. But I didn't know any of that history when I was a kid.

Then, at age twenty, I finally had a chance to go to the Philippines. One day I hiked with friends to a swimming hole. We made a fire and our guide went to catch fish. Suddenly kamayan made sense to me: We were outdoors, it was hot, and we'd been sweating all day; why be dainty all of a sudden and set out forks and knives? In that moment, eating with my hands felt not primitive but primal and totally right.

Scenes from a kamayan at a cold spring in Boracay, the Philippines, 2007.

On the menu: grilled pork and fish.

These days, Filipino restaurants in the United States have started serving kamayan feasts inspired by the boodle fight, a military practice of feeding the troops at long tables cloaked in banana leaves and half-buried under mounds of food. Rice is mounded down the middle, sticky fistfuls for the plunder. You tear off strips of grilled meat, hot from the coals, and nab plump Longganisa (page 125) and crunchy batons of Lumpia (page 107). If it's a true celebration, there must be lechon, whole roasted suckling pig, burnished and gleaming, to be daubed with a tangy sauce of mashed livers (page 157).

There's too much to eat, but nothing will go to waste. Guests are always sent home with baon, a box of food to remember the festivities by. Lechon leftovers might wind up in paksiw, a vinegary stew; pots of Sinigang (page 47) and adobo (page 23); or sisig, a sizzling hash of jowls and ears. After a birthday kamayan a couple years ago at Maharlika in the East Village (now sadly shuttered), Ligaya's mom asked if she could pack up the remaining rice, saturated with juices from the roast, and the puzzle pieces of crackly skin—along with the pig's head. The ultimate baon!

If celebrations are defined in part by the extravagance of the food, half my life has been spent celebrating—everything from a clumsy first piano recital (see "Ito Ako," page 92) to a hundredth birthday (see Pork Bellychon, page 157). My family was always on the lookout for an excuse for a party, because it meant being together, everyone crowded into one house: aunties and uncles both official and unofficial, and cousins of such obscure lineage, I don't even know if we were really related, the family tree big enough to hold us all. My lola cooked for days, and we measured our lives in bites of Chicken Relleno (page 147) and Pastel de Lengua (page 153). Sometimes we didn't even need an excuse; we just celebrated our continuing, in this place far from what my elders once knew as home, in a country they had finally made their own.

A kamayan heaped with Bay Leaf Spa Rice (page 77), Soy-Cured Egg Yolks (page 173), fried whole fish and seasonal steamed prawns and crabs, Filipino Pork BBQ (page 41), Lumpia Shanghai (page 107), Croquettes (page 37), Porchetta Bellychon (page 159), Embutido (page 143), Atsara (page 183), Salted Bitter Melon (page 185), Suka at Bawang (page 177), and Lacto-Fermented Hot Sauce (page 175).

CELEBRATIONS

here's no shame in using premade seasonings, like bricks of Japanese curry roux or Maggi cubes in bright yellow foil. Some nights, my hard-working parents needed a shortcut, and they found it in a sinigang soup packet– typically a compound of tamarind, tomato, onion, and shrimp powders, laced with salt, citric acid, and a little sugar. (To make Sinigang from scratch, see page 47.) They used it as a spice rub, patting down a whole chicken, then popped it in our Imarflex turbo broiler, the must-have appliance from the Philippines back in the 1990s.

I take the shortcut, too, albeit with a few extra seasonings, and slip pre-blanched baby potatoes and onions under the chicken to soak up the drippings, cooking the sides right under the main course. For a richer meal—and to really wow guests—you can stuff the chicken with 2 cups (355 g) of fried rice, like Dinuguan Blood Rice (page 80), before putting it in the oven. Since you use only half the sinigang packet here, you've got more to play with: Give chicken wings a shake of it before and after deep-frying, or dust it over a bowl of buttered popcorn instead of salt.

And since you're already going to the trouble of roasting a whole chicken, why not make chicken stock? After dinner, drop the chicken carcass and any extraneous bones in a stockpot with the blanching liquid from the potatoes and onions. Throw in whatever vegetable scraps and aromatics you have on hand—carrot peelings and tops, onion, garlic, thyme, bay leaves, parsley stems—and let simmer on low for a couple hours, then strain into a 1-quart (960 ml) container and freeze for a future soup.

SINIGANG ROAST CHICKEN
sih • nee • GAHNG   SERVES 4

1 chicken (3½ pounds/1.6 kg)

1 pound (455 g) baby potatoes, 1½ inches (4 cm) long (creamy Yukon Golds, if possible), rinsed

2 small yellow onions, not peeled, rinsed

1 tablespoon kosher salt

1 tablespoon olive oil

3 dried bay leaves

1 tablespoon whole black peppercorns

½ (1.41-ounce/40 g) packet tamarind soup (sinigang sa sampalok) base

3 tablespoons (40 g) unsalted butter, melted

¼ bunch fresh parsley, stems and leaves, coarsely chopped

Rinse the chicken, then carefully pat dry using paper towels. (The drier the chicken is, the quicker the fat will render, ultimately yielding a crispier-skinned chicken.) Store the chicken on a plate with two fresh paper towels under it and let rest at room temperature.

•

Take a 2-quart (2 L) saucepan and add the potatoes and onions, whole. Cover with 1½ quarts (1.4 L) water and add the salt. Bring to a boil, then lower the heat slightly to a rippling simmer and cook uncovered for 12 to 15 minutes, until the potatoes are tender. Test the tenderness by gently pricking with a paring knife, which should slip into the potato without any resistance.

•

Preheat the oven to 425°F (220°C).

•

Strain the onions and potatoes using a colander set over a bowl to catch the cooking liquid, which will have a deep, dusky hue from the yellow onion skins. Return the cooking liquid to the pot and reserve to use later as a base for a simple stock.

•

Move the potatoes and onions to a large cutting board while still warm. Using a paring knife, carefully slice each whole onion in half without crushing the soft cooked flesh. Using the back of a clean, sturdy mug, glass, or hefty wooden spoon, gently press down on each potato to crush it a bit.

→

SINIGANG ROAST CHICKEN CONTINUED

Heat a large cast-iron skillet over high. Once hot, add the olive oil, then put the onion halves into the skillet, cut side down. Scatter the crushed potatoes among the onions, then drop the heat to medium high and cook for about 8 minutes. This will begin the caramelization of the onions and potatoes.

•

Using your fingertips, crumble the bay leaves into a spice grinder or mortar. Grind the leaves until they are as broken down as possible, then add the black peppercorns and grind coarsely. (They should not be ground into dust.) Add the sinigang base from the packet to the bay leaves and peppercorns, and loosely mix.

•

Give the chicken a final pat down to make sure it's as dry as possible. Dust every side of the chicken and inside its cavity with the sinigang spice mixture. Then put the chicken on top of the potatoes and onions in the skillet.

•

Drizzle the melted butter all over the chicken. Put the skillet on the middle rack in the preheated oven and roast for about 45 minutes. To check if the chicken is done, prick the thigh with a paring knife. If the juices run clear instead of rosy pink, remove the skillet and let rest on the stovetop for about 15 minutes; otherwise continue roasting in the oven for another 10 minutes and check again.

(Or insert an instant-read thermometer, if you have one: The temperature should reach 165°F/74°C.) When the chicken has rested, transfer it to a cutting board. In the skillet, strew the parsley over the remaining potatoes and onions. Give the pan a couple of shakes so that the parsley coats all the vegetables.

•

When carving and serving the chicken, make sure to give each diner some of the crispy skin, a few potatoes, and a halved onion, steamy and tender, with the cut side, now blackened and gilded, facing up.

At the start of my life in restaurants, I learned the art of terrines. I'd spend every Friday hunched at the counter like a jeweler, tweezing the veins out of lobes of foie gras, making enough to last the week. I was proud of my work; I was the only person at the restaurant who made them, getting paid less for a ten-hour shift than it would've cost diners to buy half a terrine, at $22 a slice. I had the mindset of a child of immigrants: I worked hard, because this was my opportunity.

Only later did I realize that, all along, my lola had been using the same techniques to make embutido, a pork and sausage stuffing akin to a French farce fine that can also stand on its own as a meal. You could call it meatloaf, which sounds humble—but so was pâté in its original form, before it was elevated to aristocrats' tables: a dish of frugality and convenience, using up leftover parts so that nothing went to waste. (As Anthony Bourdain once wrote, if you've made meatloaf, you're "halfway to being an ass-kicking, name-taking charcutier.")

And while embutido might look humble from the outside, cut in and its elegance is revealed: a cross-section of golden yolk, pork, gleams of pickle, plump raisins, and scarlet flecks of chorizo. (In Pampanga, where Lola grew up, the cooking juices that spill out of the meat would be jarred and sold separately, a sufficient glory unto themselves.) Lola was very strict about ingredients. Even when her memory started to fade, the first thing she'd say when she saw me was always, "Are you using chorizo de Bilbao?" (Yes, Lola.)

I like to make this as an elegant, round steamed torchon with the silky texture of a terrine, but at the end of the recipe you'll find a meatloaf-inspired variation that's easier to shape and baked in the oven so it's firmer, with a crust on top and a ketchup glaze. You can also save the raw meat mixture, unshaped, to stuff Chicken Relleno (page 147), Lola's real showstopper. One important note: I tried chopping the meat for texture, but whipping the ingredients in a food processor, the way Lola did it, makes everything meld better.

EMBUTIDO em•boo•TEE•doh
PORK GALANTINE WITH PICKLE, EGGS, AND CHEESE SERVES 6 TO 8

Kosher salt

9 large eggs

8 ounces (225 g) chorizo de Bilbao (3 links; I like the Marca El Rey brand)

6 tablespoons (¾ stick/85 g) unsalted butter, softened

¾ cup (70 g) finely grated Parmesan

¼ cup (40 g) bread-and-butter pickles, chopped into ¼-inch pieces

¼ cup (40 g) pitted green olives, chopped into ¼-inch pieces

¼ cup (35 g) brown raisins

4 cloves garlic, peeled and finely chopped

1 teaspoon coarsely cracked black pepper

1 pound (455 g) ground pork

FOR THE MEATLOAF VARIATION:

Nonstick vegetable oil spray

¼ cup (60 ml) banana ketchup, store-bought or homemade (page 167), or tomato ketchup

2 teaspoons Worcestershire sauce

Fill a large saucepan with 1 quart (960 ml) water, add a pinch of salt, and bring to a boil over high heat. Prepare an ice bath in a large bowl. Slip 6 of the eggs into the boiling water, one at a time, then reduce the heat to low and gently simmer for 9 minutes. Transfer the eggs to the ice bath and let cool. Drain, then peel, taking each egg and lightly cracking the wide bottom part first (where the air pocket is) for easier peeling; handle gently.

•

Roughly chop the chorizo, then transfer to a food processor. Give it a few quick pulses so it breaks down into small crumbs.

•

Put the chorizo, butter, Parmesan, pickles, olives, raisins, garlic, pepper, and 1 tablespoon salt in a large bowl. Stir until combined. Crack in the remaining 3 eggs. Add the pork and mix without using too much force—you don't want to pack the meat mixture too tightly, or else it will end up with a bouncy texture.

•

At this point, if you are planning to make Chicken Relleno (page 147), store the meat mixture in the refrigerator until ready to stuff the bird. Use any of the mixture left over from stuffing to make one torchon, following the directions below.

→

EMBUTIDO CONTINUED

Preheat the oven to 350°F (175°C).

•

To shape the meat into torchons, tear off 2 sheets of aluminum foil, each 15 inches (38 cm) long. Divide the meat mixture into 4 equal portions. Set one portion at the center of one sheet of foil and shape into a 3 by 10-inch (7.5 by 25 cm) rectangle. Lay 3 peeled hard-boiled eggs lengthwise along the top of the meat mixture, leaving about 1 inch (2.5 cm) open between each egg. (You want to leave space between the eggs so that they can each be fully enrobed in meat, which protects them from overcooking.) Put a second portion of the meat mixture over the first, tucking the meat between and around the eggs and flattening the top. Pat the mixture into the shape of a log, completely surrounding the eggs with meat, so they are no longer visible.

•

Arrange the foil sheet so that one of the longer edges is closest to you. Lift this edge and fold upward, completely covering the log, then roll the log toward the top edge of the foil. To seal the sides, start at one open end and fold the foil at an angle over the log. Continue with four more folds, clockwise around the circumference of the log.

Take the log, or torchon, and stand it upright, with the end you've just sealed now at the bottom. Repeat the folding process to seal the top, then press down gently to get rid of any air pockets.

•

Tear off a 16-inch (40.5 cm) length of plastic wrap. Set one torchon at the center of the wrap. Lift the edge of the wrap closest to you and fold upward, covering the torchon, then roll the torchon away from you toward the top edge of the wrap. Twist the excess plastic wrap tightly at both ends. Repeat with two more layers of plastic wrap, then after the third layer, use your dominant hand to pinch one twisted end of the torchon. With your other hand, roll the torchon on the surface toward you, keeping the twisted end pinched in your dominant hand; this will create the necessary tension to make the torchon into as compact a cylindrical shape as possible. Tie the twisted end into a knot, then twist and knot the other end tightly. Your final torchon should be roughly 2½ by 10 inches (6 by 25 cm), about the size of a salami.

•

If you're not reserving meat to stuff chicken relleno, repeat to make a second torchon.

•

Transfer the torchons to a large cast-iron pot or deep roasting pan. Cover completely with room temperature water. (The torchons will float.) Put the pot or pan on the middle rack of the preheated oven and cook for about 1 hour. (To check if the pork is done, insert a cake tester into a torchon, then touch the bottom of your lip with the cake tester: If it feels hot, the meat is cooked through. Repeat with the second torchon.) Transfer the torchons from the water to a cutting board and let rest for about 15 minutes, to cool and set. Unwrap both torchons, or just one and freeze the other for future use; it keeps for up to a month. Beautiful cooking juices will spill out of the meat—save them for serving. Cut each torchon into 10 (½-inch/12 mm) slices. Transfer the slices to a platter and drizzle with the reserved cooking juices. Just before serving, dust with flaky sea salt.

•

To make the meatloaf variation: After preheating the oven, line two 9 by 5-inch (23 by 12 cm) loaf pans with a sheet of foil each, leaving a 3-inch (7.5 cm) overhang on the long sides. Lightly coat with nonstick spray. Divide the meat mixture into 4 equal portions and put one quarter-portion in each pan, spreading it out evenly so it covers the bottom and touches the sides. Lay 3 peeled hard-boiled eggs lengthwise along the top of the meat mixture in one pan, leaving about ¾ inch (2 cm) open between

each egg. Put a second portion of the meat mixture over the first, tucking the meat between and around the eggs, so they're no longer visible, and flattening the top. Repeat with the second pan.

•

Mix the ketchup with the Worcestershire sauce in a small bowl. Spread over the top of each loaf.

•

Bake the loaves in the preheated oven for 55 to 70 minutes, until an instant-read thermometer inserted into several places—avoiding the eggs if possible—registers 155°F (70°C). Let cool for 15 minutes.

•

Transfer the embutidos to a platter and slice. Store leftovers in an airtight container in the refrigerator for 3 to 4 days or freeze for up to 3 months.

his is the dish that changed my life as a chef–that made me realize that Filipino cooking shares the same level of technique and precision we expect and revere in French cuisine. I learned how to make it from my lola Josefina (see "Listening to Lola," page 42) and served it as a large-format meal at Mission Chinese Food in New York, for $75 a platter.

I won't lie to you: This is hard labor. Somehow Lola could knock off three at a time for a party, using just a crummy old boning knife–an almost inconceivable feat for a home cook, once you get a load of the instructions. The prize at the end will be worship from all those you deem worthy enough to share it with.

At Mission, I used so-called Buddhist chickens, with the head and feet still attached. They came from a Chinese-run farm upstate and were bred to have big thighs, for more dark meat. But there's no need to go that far–just try to find a chicken at the butcher's that's 3 to 3½ pounds (1.4 to 1.6 kg), with perfect skin, no tears or rips. Often frozen whole chicken has been mishandled, so if you can find a fresh chicken, it will make a big difference. And then you can save the chicken bones to make stock (see the headnote for Sinigang Roast Chicken, page 141).

The chicken can be prepared and trussed ahead, then pulled out of the refrigerator about 30 minutes before putting it in the oven. You may present it immediately, but it's also fine to leave it out at room temperature as the centerpiece of a buffet, with the pan drippings on the side. Don't be insulted if people eat only one or two slices–it's that rich, and that means more to go around.

CHICKEN RELLENO
ray • YEHN • oh
WHOLE ROASTED CHICKEN STUFFED WITH EMBUTIDO

SERVES 10 TO 12

1 chicken (3½ pounds/1.6 kg)

Kosher salt

5 large eggs, cooked in boiling water for 7 minutes, then chilled in the refrigerator and peeled (store in water to retain shape)

1 pound (455 g) Embutido chorizo-pork mixture (page 143), unshaped and without the eggs, chilled in the refrigerator

2 tablespoons unsalted butter, softened at room temperature

1 tablespoon cold unsalted butter

Watercress, for garnish (optional)

Garlic Chips (page 197), for garnish (optional)

Flaky sea salt

Edible flowers, for garnish (optional)

Steamed rice, for serving

Debone the chicken: Rinse the chicken and pat dry with paper towels. Trim the excess fat–you're looking for yellowish blobs, typically near the open cavity–but don't cut the skin. Remove the giblets and any other offal from the cavity and save in the freezer for a future use.

•

On a cutting board, lay the chicken breast side down. (It's important that the chicken has been completely dried; otherwise, lay a paper towel on the cutting board so the chicken doesn't slide around.) Using a sharp boning knife or small paring knife–sharpness is key; a dull knife is more dangerous than a sharp one–cut a single vertical slit along the backbone, from neck to tail. Cut around the tail and keep it intact if you can.

→

CHICKEN RELLENO CONTINUED

Start pulling the skin and meat away from the rib cage. Use the tip of the knife to make small cuts where the meat is connected to the bones to help separate it.

•

When you get down to the thigh bones, use your hands to crack and bend the bones where the thigh joints meet the rib cage and the drumsticks. You want to dislodge these bones from the sockets. Then, using the tip of the knife, make small cuts in the thighs on either side of the cartilage at the joints. Once you can see the thigh bones, start cutting them away from the joints. Keep cutting until you can pull the bones out. Set aside. (These are the only bones you'll remove besides the rib cage; you'll keep the drumsticks and wings, so that the chicken appears whole again once sewed shut.)

•

While you are making all these cuts, be very careful not to prick the skin: It needs to be perfectly intact to hold the stuffing.

•

Turn the chicken on its side. Pull the breast meat away from the breast bone, making small cuts between meat and bone, until you reach the thin piece of cartilage at the center of the breast. Turn the chicken to the opposite side and repeat. Cut as close to the central piece of cartilage as you can, then carefully rip the meat and skin away. (It's okay if some meat is left behind.) Collect the bones and save them for stock.

•

Lay the chicken completely flat and locate the chicken tenders, two long strips hanging from the underside of the breast. Remove the tenders and save for stock.

•

Season both sides of the chicken liberally with the salt.

•

Stuff the chicken: Take a sewing needle and thread (any color will do—I like darker shades because they're easier to see). Measure out an arm's length of thread, then double it and pull through the eye. Triple tie a knot at the end of the thread, leaving 2 to 3 inches (5 to 7.5 cm) from the end to help you find it easily when it's time to remove it.

•

Line up the two sides of the cavity so they are as even as possible. Start sewing up the cavity at the tail end of the chicken, leaving at most ¼ inch (6 mm) of space between stitches. After sewing up the tail cavity, continue sewing around the tail and about two inches past it. Pull the thread taut and set the thread and needle aside.

•

Lay the chicken on the cutting board so that the open part is closest to you and the sewn tail end away from you. Take the loose embutido mixture from the refrigerator—it's easier to work with when still chilled—and gently pat it into the cavity, until there's a ¾-inch (2 cm) thick layer all around, covering both back and breast.

•

Make 2 indentations in the stuffing along the back and fill each indentation with an egg, arranged lengthwise where the backbone would be. Point the tips of the eggs toward the tail, to protect the yolks so they'll stay creamy and not overcook. Add more of the filling to cover the sides and tops of the eggs. Make sure not to press down too hard on the eggs, or they'll crack. (If one cracks, replace it with another egg.) The goal is to surround the eggs with the embutido mixture, spreading it as evenly as possible to protect the yolk from overcooking.

•

Once the 2 eggs are surrounded on three sides with the stuffing—leave the end of the egg nearest to you exposed, as that's where you'll place the final egg—you should have one-fourth to one-third of the embutido mixture left. While the chicken is flat, continue sewing up the cavity to the end of where the backbone would be. (There will still be an opening.)

•

Holding both drumsticks, gently lift the entire chicken. Shake it a few times to let the stuffing settle into place and to get rid of any air pockets in the cavity.

•

Finally, add the last egg, with the narrow side pointing toward you, and pat and cover the egg and fill the cavity with the last of the stuffing. (Note that although the recipe calls for 5 eggs, you will only use 3; the others are back-ups in case of breakage.) Sew the cavity closed. If at any point it looks like you're going to run out of thread, leave an excess of three inches after the last stitch, rethread the needle, and continue. Those three inches make it easier to locate the thread for removal after roasting.

•

The chicken will look a bit amorphous at this point, sitting sewn side up, with legs facing you.

•

Truss the chicken: This is the time to preheat the oven to 375°F (190°C).

→

Locate the wing tip and tuck it under the drumette, so that it doesn't burn later in roasting.

Take some butcher's twine and pull out a piece as long as your outstretched arms from fingertip to fingertip, about 4 to 5 feet (1.2 to 1.5 m). On one end tie a 1-inch (2.5 cm) loop, then thread the opposite end through the hole to begin the truss.

Flip the chicken around and over, so the sewing seam is now facing the cutting board and the legs are away from you. Run the trussing twine over the legs and pull so that it encircles the chicken right under the drumsticks. Center the loop in the twine so it sits between the drumsticks. The twine should be snug but not too tight; the flesh will bulge slightly. Now tie a knot on the loop to secure the first ring in the truss.

From your new knot, pull the twine about 1 to 1½ inches (2.5 to 4 cm) down. Use your finger to hold the twine down at that spot. Turn the twine at a 90-degree angle, then loop around the breast and back of the chicken to make the second ring. Pull the twine and tie a knot where the twine connects to the first ring.

Repeat this at least once more or twice, depending on the size of the chicken. Once you have three or four rings, pull the twine towards you and around the back of the chicken, until it meets the first knot. Pull to tighten and tie a knot.

Now pull the twine upwards, doubling back towards the drumsticks. Hold the drumsticks together, crossed. Tie the twine around them a couple times and then tie a knot. Trim any excess twine close to the knot. If you run out of twine at any point, simply add another foot or two (about 30 to 60 cm) of twine and tie square knots anywhere you left off.

Now you have a full trussed chicken, which will help it roast evenly, while bringing the shape back to the bird.

Roast the chicken: Transfer the chicken to a roasting pan with a rack or a sheet pan lined with a rack. Add 1 cup (240 ml) water to the pan for steaming.

Cover the chicken and the pan with aluminum foil, sealing tightly at the edges so the steam will circulate around the whole chicken. Roast for about 35 minutes, if your chicken is larger than 3 pounds (1.4 kg), add about 15 minutes per pound at this stage.

Remove the foil and reserve. Rub the chicken with the butter. Using a baster or large spoon, pour some of the drippings over the chicken as well—the drippings include spices from the embutido stuffing. Rotate the chicken and return it to the oven. Increase the temperature to 450°F (230°C). Roast the chicken for another 20 to 25 minutes, basting every 7 minutes and rotating, until the skin turns a deep, glossy brown. If you happen to have a blowtorch at home, you could even very lightly torch the skin when you take it out of the oven, basting between each pass of the torch.

Remove the pan from the oven. Loosely cover the chicken with the foil and let rest for about 20 minutes.

Carve the chicken: Transfer the chicken to a clean cutting board. Remove the roasting rack, and using a small rubber spatula, pour the cooking liquids and scrape the drippings into a small saucepan. (Adding a few tablespoons water or chicken stock can make it easier to scrape the pan.) If there is quite a bit of liquid left, reduce the sauce to a gravy while you carve the chicken.

Carefully tip the chicken over to locate the sewing thread. Pull out and discard.

Using kitchen shears, cut each ring of twine and the knot by the chicken legs. Discard the twine.

Using a slicing knife or longer sharp chef's knife, cut off the drumsticks and wings and set aside.

Starting from the front of the chicken, cut 1-inch (2.5 cm) slices, wiping the knife between each slice, since the egg yolk likes to stick to the knife.

Transfer each slice neatly to a serving platter, and arrange them resting on each other.

Garnish with fresh watercress around the chicken slices. Arrange the drumsticks and wings as they would appear on a whole chicken.

Melt 1 tablespoon cold butter in the pan gravy and stir to combine. Pour the gravy through a fine-mesh strainer, either directly over the chicken or in a gravy boat to serve on the side. Sprinkle some garlic chips, flaky salt, and edible flowers, if available, on the chicken.

Present with a serving fork and spoon warm rice on the side.

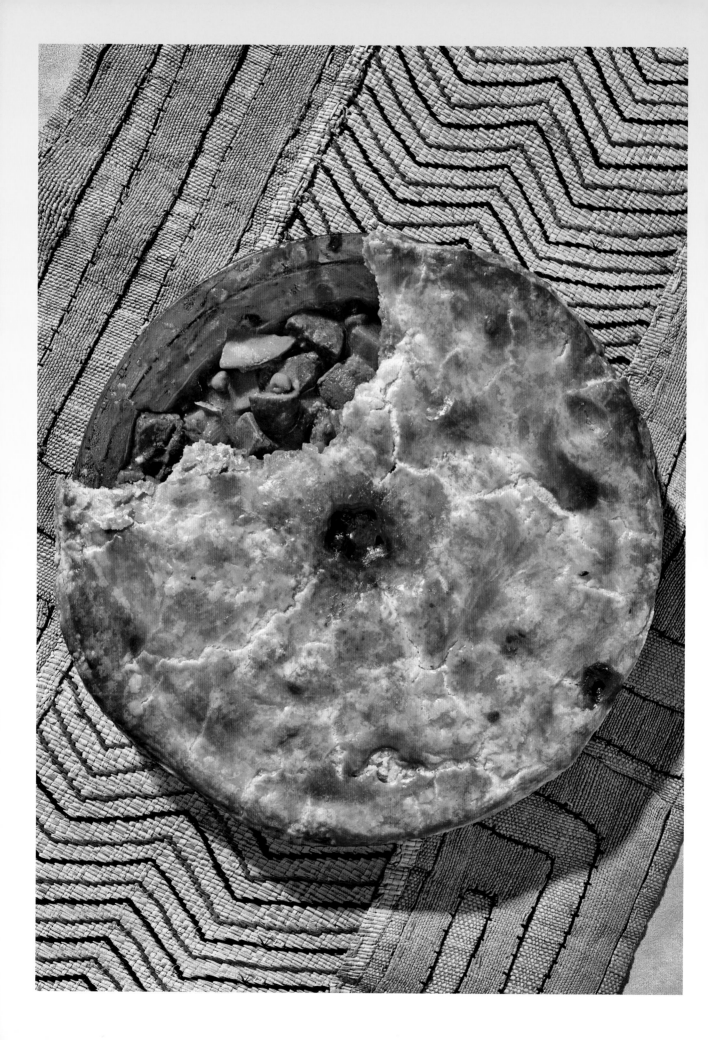

Ox tongue is decadence, fatty and rich. It has none of the mineral tang found in other offal, and when cooked right, it's all tenderness. Because it's typically sold whole, you can't really scale down this recipe, and the amount of labor involved–three days: I'm sorry!–means this is best saved for a party, where it will be the pièce de résistance. Although the dish looks rustic, the techniques that go into it are haute, with the kind of focus on minutiae that we typically associate with French chefs, like rinsing the potato slices to reduce their starch, which allows more of their moisture to evaporate in the frying pan, so they're crisp and better keep their shape in the sauce.

You can make this in a casserole or divide the crust and filling between two loaf pans or pie tins. I'm slightly obsessed with mushrooms, so I like making this in fall or winter and using whatever mushrooms are in season, or else I raid my stash of dried morels. Lola used cream of mushroom soup out of a can (which was delicious); my version has a darker, Creole-style roux, with yogurt for extra thickness and a little tang. I suggest making and freezing the crust in advance–up to 3 days before–then defrosting it overnight or 3 hours before you're ready to bake the pie. I often make it on the same day that I assemble the filling. One last tip from Lola: She always chilled the flour for the crust first, in the freezer.

PASTEL DE LENGUA
pas • TELL deh LEHNG • wah
OX TONGUE PIE IN MUSHROOM SAUCE SERVES 8

FOR THE OX TONGUE BRAISE:

2½ pounds (1.2 kg) ox tongue

½ cup (120 ml) vinegar (white, apple cider, rice, or any inexpensive vinegar)

1 tablespoon kosher salt

FOR THE AROMATIC BRAISING LIQUID:

1 large yellow onion, peeled

1 large carrot, peeled

8 cloves garlic, peeled and coarsely chopped

1 cup (240 ml) tomato sauce

Juice of 1 lemon

1 teaspoon whole cloves

3 bay leaves, fresh or dried

1 teaspoon whole black peppercorns

⅓ cup (75 ml) soy sauce

1 tablespoon kosher salt

2 chorizo de Bilbao (optional; I like the Marca El Rey brand)

FOR THE FILLING:

8 ounces (225 g) frozen peas

2 large Yukon Gold potatoes, peeled (about 1 pound/455 g)

⅓ cup (75 ml) olive oil

⅓ cup (75 ml) vegetable oil

1 large yellow onion, cut into 1½-inch (4 cm) chunks

2 large carrots, cut into 1-inch (2.5 cm) dice (about 5¼ ounces/150 g)

2 cloves garlic, peeled and minced

10 of your favorite mushrooms (I like to use cremini or porcini), cut into bite-size pieces

4 tablespoons (½ stick/55 g) salted or unsalted butter

⅓ cup (40 g) all-purpose flour

½ cup (115 g) Greek yogurt, chilled

1 recipe Flaky Piecrust (see Buko Hand Pie, page 245), plus additional flour for rolling

1 egg, for brushing

PASTEL DE LENGUA CONTINUED

Day 1: Braise the tongue.

Put the ox tongue in a 4-quart (3.8 L) stockpot and add the vinegar, salt, and 3 quarts (2.8 L) water. Bring to a boil, then reduce the heat to low for a slow bubbling simmer, and cover with a lid. Braise the tongue for 2 hours.

•

Using tongs, pick up the ox tongue to check the first stage of doneness. You should see a few bubbles on the skin of the tongue, air pockets where it's pulling away from the meat. (If you don't see any bubbles, simmer longer and check every 20 minutes.) Transfer the tongue to a plate to cool at room temperature for about 15 minutes, until the tongue is cool enough to handle. Discard the braising liquid and scrub the pot clean to reuse for the next step.

•

While you're waiting for the tongue to cool, prepare the aromatic braising liquid. Dice the onion and carrot into 1½-inch (4 cm) pieces. Put the onion, carrot, and garlic in the empty pot and add the tomato sauce, lemon juice, cloves, bay leaves, black peppercorns, soy sauce, 3 quarts (2.8 L) water, and the salt.

•

When the ox tongue is cool enough to handle, using clean hands, begin to peel away the outermost layer of the tongue, starting from the cut end. This rough skin should come off easily. It's okay if the skin tears, since it's easy to grab a new corner and keep going. When you've removed all the skin, discard it and return the peeled tongue to the pot. Bring the aromatic braising liquid to a boil, then reduce the heat to low for another slow simmer, and cover with a lid. After about 2 hours, add the chorizo de Bilbao, if using. Continue to simmer the tongue with the lid on for another hour. At this point the tongue will have been braising for a total of 5 hours and should be tender when pierced with a fork.

•

Remove the lid and let the braise cool on the stovetop for about an hour. Replace the lid and transfer the pot to the refrigerator. Let the tongue cool in the braising liquid in the pot overnight, to keep the meat juicy and tender.

•

Day 2: Assemble the filling and make the crust.

The next day, remove the tongue (and chorizo, if using) from the braising liquid with tongs, and let rest on a cutting board lined with paper towels to collect the leaking juices.

•

Position a fine-mesh metal sieve over a 2-quart (2 L) stockpot and pour the braising liquid and vegetables into the sieve. Using a small rubber spatula, press down on the softened vegetables, leaving behind and discarding the cloves, bay leaves, and peppercorns. Bring the stock to a boil, then lower to a simmer and reduce the liquid to about 3 or 4 cups (720 ml to 1 L), which will take about 30 minutes.

•

While your stock is reducing, return to the tongue and chorizo on the cutting board and discard the paper towels. Dice the tongue into even ½-inch (12 mm) cubes. Slice the chorizo in half lengthwise, then into ½-inch (12 mm) half-moons. Transfer the diced tongue and sliced chorizo to a large storage container and top with the frozen peas. Store uncovered in the freezer while you make the rest of the filling; you'll use the chilled meats and peas to speed-cool the filling later.

•

Wash the cutting board, then cut the potatoes into ½-inch (12 mm) by 2-inch (5 cm) rectangles, ½-inch (12 mm) thick. In a 4-quart (3.8 L) stockpot, heat the olive oil and vegetable oil over medium high until shimmering. Rinse the potato slices with cold water in a colander over the sink to remove some of their starch, and let drain. Once the oil is hot, add the potato slices and fry and rotate each piece with a slotted spoon until all sides have browned, 7 to 10 minutes. As the potatoes brown, transfer them to a plate lined with a paper towel—arrange them so they fill only half the plate and fold the towel so it covers them—and let rest. Discard all but 1 tablespoon of oil from the pot.

•

Raise the heat to medium high. Cook the onions, carrot, and garlic in the reserved oil for about 4 minutes, until softened. Toss in the mushrooms and cook for another 2 minutes. Transfer the softened vegetables to the uncovered part of the plate holding the potatoes.

•

Returning to the same pot, add the butter and reduce the heat to medium. Melt the butter, then add the flour. Using a whisk, make a tight, stiff roux that's light to medium brown (as opposed to loose and pale) by mixing the flour and butter together continuously, until the paste turns a deep golden-brown color, about 3 minutes. While the roux is hot, add the braising liquid from the smaller pot. The liquid should have reduced to 3 to 4 cups (720 to 960 ml); if it's reduced a little too much, just top it off with some water.

•

When you add the liquid to the roux, the sauce will thicken into a gravy very quickly, so keep whisking for about 2 minutes. After the sauce thickens, turn off the heat, and while the pot is still on the burner, add the chilled Greek yogurt and whisk to combine. Switch to a rubber spatula and add the diced tongue, chorizo, and peas from the freezer followed by the potatoes and cooked vegetables. Gently fold to combine. This will cool the sauce significantly, so you can transfer the mixture to your baking dishes of choice: a casserole, two pie pans, or two loaf tins. Cover with plastic wrap and cool overnight in the refrigerator.

•

Next, make the crust (see Buko Hand Pie, page 245). Prepare the flaky pie crust dough up to the point of adding the ice water and rolling and scraping. Instead of shaping the dough into two logs, roll it into a single cylinder, then flatten into a disk about 1-inch (2.5 cm) thick. Cover the disk with plastic wrap and refrigerate for at least 2 hours or overnight.

•

Day 3: Bake. Preheat the oven to 400°F (200°C).

•

Unwrap the refrigerated disk of dough and lay it on a floured work surface. Working quickly while the dough is cold and best to handle, dust a rolling pin and the top of the dough with flour. If using a single casserole dish, roll out the dough into a large rectangle; if using two pie pans or two loaf tins, cut the disk in two and roll out into two circles or two rectangles. In each case, the resulting sheet of dough should be ¼-inch (6 mm) thick, sized to fit each dish with 1 to 2 inches (2.5 to 5 cm) of extra dough all around the perimeter.

•

If you'd like to cut a decorative pattern in the dough—a lattice top, say, or a single braid down the middle—do so now. Using a bench scraper, gently lay the dough over the top of the baking dish. (If using two dishes, keep the second dish and sheet of dough in the refrigerator while you work on the first, to keep them as cold as possible.) Trim any excess overhang with scissors, leaving at least a ½-inch (12 mm) margin beyond the rim of the pan. With your fingertips, gently press the dough along the pan's perimeter, tucking and pinching it to the underside of the rim. You can stop there, or use the tines of a fork to press and crimp the edges of the dough. Prick the surface with a fork in a few places or cut a ¾-inch (2 cm) hole in the center to let a little steam escape while baking. Repeat with the second dish and sheet of dough, if using.

•

You've made it to the end! Whisk the egg in a small bowl, and using a pastry brush, gently paint the entire surface of the dough.

•

Tent the edges of the crust with foil, so they don't burn, and put the dish or dishes in the oven. Bake for 30 to 45 minutes, until deep golden brown. Once the center of the crust is brown, 20 to 30 minutes into baking, remove the aluminum foil shield from the edges so they too can brown. (Because everyone's oven is different, you may need to raise the temperature early in the baking, then reduce it, so the edges and center attain the same color.) You will know the pie is done by the evenly bronzed crust and the bubbling up of the meat sauce inside.

•

If you've baked two pies or loaves and want to save one for later, wrap it tightly in plastic wrap or put it inside a zip-top freezer bag with the air pressed out before sealing, then store it in the freezer for up to 3 months.

he Fil-Am poet Sarah Gambito once wrote what I think was the best description of lechon ever: "When God was Filipino / he put a pig and fire together and called it porkissimo." Lechon is the golden fulcrum, the point around which the most lavish Filipino feasts revolve: a whole roasted suckling pig, the skin fragile and shiny as lacquer and all crackle. It is a declaration: This is a party. Nothing less would do for Lola's hundredth birthday. Traditionally, it's made by skewering the pig on a bamboo spit and turning it for hours over hot coals, strategically arranged not directly under the pig but along the sides, so that the drippings don't make the flames flare up and scorch the meat.

This isn't a practical setup for most home cooks, so here's a tip: Since the first part of the pig to disappear off the table is always the belly, you can just make bellychon—lechon minus all the other parts, with the same shattering skin—and everyone will be happy. The skin bubbles and blisters, and at the end you carefully peel it off in one gleaming sheet, to be cracked into shards and strewn over the lush slabs of pork.

PORK BELLYCHON
CRISPY OVEN-ROASTED PORK BELLY SERVES 8

1 piece (4 to 5 pounds/1.8 to 2.3 kg) boneless pork belly, skin-on

Kosher salt

1 tablespoon canola or other neutral oil

4 bottles (12 ounces/360 ml each) hard apple cider

2 tablespoons honey

1 cup (240 ml) Suka at Bawang (page 177), including whole chiles

Steamed white rice, for serving

Season the pork belly generously with salt. Set skin side up on a wire rack nestled inside a rimmed baking sheet. Chill for at least 12 hours and up to 2 days.

•

Preheat the oven to 350°F (175°C). Pour 4 cups (960 ml) water into the baking sheet that holds the pork. Rub the pork skin with the oil and season with more salt. Roast in the oven for 1½ to 1¾ hours, checking on it periodically and adding more water to the pan as needed, until the skin is golden brown and an instant-read thermometer inserted into the thickest part of the pork registers 195°F to 200°F.

•

In a large saucepan, bring the hard cider and honey to a boil. Reduce the heat to a low simmer and cook for 30 to 45 minutes, until very syrupy.

•

Raise the oven temperature to 450°F (230°C). Continue to roast the pork for 15 to 20 minutes, until the skin puffs up, brown, crispy, and bubbled. (Add a few more splashes of water to the baking sheet if the juices are scorching.) Transfer the rack with the pork to a cutting board; let rest 20 minutes. Pour out the fat from the baking sheet and add ½ cup (120 ml) water. Scrape up the browned bits. (Return the baking sheet to the oven for a few minutes if needed to help loosen the browned bits.) Stir the browned bits into the cider mixture.

•

Remove the skin from the pork, using the tip of a paring knife and starting in a corner where the skin is already peeling away from the meat; the whole skin should come off in one piece with a little help. Slice the pork lengthwise into strips 2 inches (5 cm) wide, then crosswise into pieces ½ inch (12 mm) thick. Transfer to a platter and drizzle with the cider mixture. Break the skin into large pieces and scatter on top. Scoop a few whole chiles out of the suka at bawang and lay them around the pork.

•

Serve with warm rice and the suka at bawang.

he first time I went to the Cayman Islands, I was struck by the number of Filipino migrant workers. The Filipino diaspora is everywhere, which is comforting, but also a reminder of how many people in the Philippines have to leave their homes to find work abroad and send money back to support their families. So I invited the community to a dinner at the Palm Heights hotel, where my friend, mentee, and fellow Fil-Am chef Silver Cousler and I made a porchetta-style version of lechon (see Pork Bellychon, page 157), stuffed with Dinuguan Blood Rice (page 80), to soak up all the pork drippings, and roasted over a fire pit.

To recreate this at home, I suggest using half a pig belly, roughly 5 pounds (2.3 kg)—although for a bigger party, you can buy the whole belly, cut it in half, and double the recipe, roasting both sides. For the stuffing, you can substitute any fried rice (such as Garlic Butter Fried Rice, page 75) or even plain leftover jasmine or sticky rice. As an unabashed garlic lover, I like to poke whole cloves into the stuffing, so you get creamy, sweet bites of caramelized garlic. The slow-cook method gives you plenty of time to hang out with guests; the meat stays in the oven for 3 to 4 hours, and only in the last hour or so requires occasional visits for extra care in basting the pork in its own fat. The reveal and presentation make it all worthwhile: With each slice you're guaranteed to get crackly skin, tender meat, and luscious fat.

PORCHETTA BELLYCHON
ROLLED AND STUFFED
CRISPY PORK BELLY SERVES 8 TO 10

1 piece (5 pounds/2.3 kg) boneless pork belly, skin-on

Kosher salt, to season

5 bay leaves, fresh or dried

3 pieces lemongrass, tough ends discarded, finely minced

1 tablespoon whole black peppercorns

2 heads (2 ounces/60 g) garlic, peeled

2 cups Dinuguan Blood Rice (page 80)

Suka at Bawang (page 177) or apple cider vinegar, for serving

Your favorite hot sauce, for serving (optional)

Pork Liver Sauce (page 195), for serving (optional)

To prepare the pork belly:
The night before cooking or up to 3 days ahead, lay the pork belly skin side down on a cutting board. Score the meat by cutting diagonal lines, 1½ inches (4 cm) apart, across the entire fleshy part of the belly. Cut to a depth of about halfway through the thickness of the pork. Then cut diagonally across those lines, the same distance apart and the same depth, to make a crosshatch/diamond pattern.
●

Generously salt the pork belly, making sure to season both the skin and inside the cuts. In a blender, combine the bay leaves, lemongrass, peppercorns, half the peeled garlic cloves, and ¼ cup (60 ml) water. Puree until smooth, about 1 minute.
●

Scrape the marinade out of the blender directly onto the scored side of the belly. Massage the marinade into the belly and between the scored cuts. Push the remaining garlic cloves into the cuts, staggering them across the center of the belly, leaving a 3-inch (7.5 cm) perimeter at the edges, to ensure that the garlic gets completely rolled into the porchetta shape.
→

PORCHETTA BELLYCHON CONTINUED

Using your hands, spread the dinuguan blood rice in an even layer on the cut side of the pork belly. Press the grains into the scored cuts of the belly.

•

Cut eight lengths of butcher's twine, 16 inches (40.5 cm) long, and set aside. (You may not use them all, but it's good to have that many on hand.) Starting at the narrow end of the pork belly, roll the meat as tightly as you can, into the shape of a log. Holding the rolled belly together with one hand, use the other hand to slip a piece of twine around the center of the rolled belly, then tie it—again, as tight as you can—with a square knot.

•

Add another piece of twine 1 inch (2.5 cm) away from the center tie. Pull as tight as possible and tie. Repeat on the other side of the center tie and continue with the remaining pieces of twine, alternating sides and keeping 1 inch (2.5 cm) between them, until the entire log has been trussed. (It's okay if some of the rice spills out as you roll the log.) The goal is to create a neat cylinder, so that the meat roasts evenly in its long cooking process.

•

Trim any excess string and store the porchetta seam side down on a rack and tray. This will let the marinade penetrate the thick cut of meat while the salt dries out the skin, the better for crisping. Ideally you would have this air-drying in your fridge for up to 3 days.

•

6 to 7 hours before serving: The day you're ready to cook the porchetta, take it out of the refrigerator and let it rest on its rack and tray on the counter for an hour or two before roasting, so it can come up to room temperature. (A large piece of meat that has been chilling in the refrigerator is much colder at the center than on the surface, which means it won't cook evenly.) Preheat the oven to 300°F (150°C).

•

When the porchetta has reached room temperature, put it into the oven on the middle rack. Once enough fat has collected at the bottom of the tray, 1½ to 2 hours into the cooking time, gently take the tray out of the oven, moving carefully so the fat won't splatter, and rest it on a sturdy surface like a stovetop. (Close the oven door so you don't lose heat.) Using a basting bulb or brush or a large spoon, coat the skin with liquid fat, which will help make it nice and crispy. Then return the porchetta to the oven. Repeat this process every half hour or so.

•

When the porchetta has been roasting for about 3 hours, use a paring knife to test the doneness of the meat. After passing through the skin, the knife should be able to slip into the flesh smoothly, meeting little resistance. The meat may take as long as 4 hours to fully cook, so check every 15 minutes in the last hour.

•

If you're cooking from start to finish, just leave the porchetta in the oven. If you're preparing in advance of guests arriving, take the porchetta out to keep it warm (near the stove is good). Then make a tent of aluminum foil and put it over the roasted meat. When ready, return to the oven and move onto the next step to crisp the skin.

•

Crank up the temperature to 500°F (260°C). In 15 to 20 minutes, rotating halfway through, the skin should bubble and puff, taking on a light burnished bronze.

•

Once the skin has crisped, remove the porchetta and let rest for about 15 minutes. (If you cut it too soon, the juices will run out of the meat.) Using kitchen shears, cut off the twine. Then transfer the porchetta to a cutting board, seam side up, and use a very sharp chef's knife or large serrated knife to cut it into slices. A ½ inch (12 mm) slice per serving is fine. (Or you can just cut bespoke slices as your guests wish.)

•

Serve with suka at bawang—a splash helps cut through the fat—your favorite hot sauce, and pork liver sauce, for more contours of flavor.

Ferment

(TALKING WITH DR. ARIELLE JOHNSON)

I grew up on sourness and funk—that's how you eat in a Filipino home—so it was probably inevitable that as a young cook I started experimenting with fermentation. My apartment became a mini-lab: I cultivated kombucha scobies ("scoby" is an acronym for symbiotic culture of bacteria and yeast), sprouted koji (Aspergillus oryzae mold) on rice, and incubated natto (fermented soybeans) at the lowest setting of my toaster oven. Then, in 2014, I had a chance to visit the restaurant Noma in Copenhagen, Denmark, where I bonded with Dr. Arielle Johnson, a flavor scientist and co-founder of the Noma Fermentation Lab, a playground of culinary R&D.

Arielle is my people: We geek out together, whether over the fermentation boxes that she designed and we set up at the MIT Media Lab or the special-event dinners where we've made miso out of unexpected ingredients, from turmeric and Meyer lemon to sandalwood and vetiver, botanicals more commonly used in perfume. Since fermentation is a big part of what gives Filipino cooking its depth and character, I asked her to help give a little background here on the chemical reactions taking place as coconut water and sugar fizz into Coconut Vinegar (page 179) and tiny shrimp packed in salt break down into Bagoong (page 169). She took some time to share her expertise.

Arielle at the Murakamijyu honten workshop in Kyoto, Japan, fermenting kabu turnips into suguki, a type of tsukemono.

Arielle and me at the 2018 MAD Symposium in Copenhagen, Denmark, presenting "I thought the future of food would be cooler (but it still can be)."

Flavors are generally born outside the kitchen, on the farm and in the wild; we're just lucky enough to harvest and lay claim to them. To create our own flavors—beyond simply capturing, juxtaposing, and deepening these naturally occurring ones—cooks in the West have historically deployed heat to break down the sugars in fruit and vegetables or woody matter in wood and bring on the nutty richness of caramelization and the seductive depth of smoke and char, or to cause a concatenation of chemical reactions (collectively called the Maillard reaction) between proteins and simple sugars, the kind that give maltiness to a loaf of bread and a dark crust to a steak.

But there is another way to transform ingredients, drawn from the invisible in the air and on every surface around us. Fermentation requires as little as a bit of salt or simply a sealed vessel, plus time for those unseen microorganisms to convert carbohydrates into lactic acid (as in yogurt, kimchi, and Lacto-Fermented Green Mango, page 189) or alcohol (as in wine and beer), or alcohol and then acetic acid (as in Homemade Coconut Vinegar, page 179). The ancients knew these techniques, and they were probably known for thousands of years before there was any writing system to record them; hardscrabble settlers on the American frontier relied on them to make the land's bounty last through bitter winters; and cooks in the East have always considered them integral tools in the kitchen, delivering a profundity and range of flavors that could otherwise never be achieved.

Today, even as the freshness, seasonality, and purity of ingredients are celebrated, more and more chefs are turning to fermentation, which champions the opposite: age, decay, a faint whiff of rot. Think of it not as a dichotomy, but an openness to actualizing every kind of flavor potential available. The reward is, of course, new flavors—although they are, properly

The flavor scientist Dr. Arielle Johnson.

speaking, old flavors, long familiar to our ancestors from the greater part of human history before refrigeration, and literally old, teased out over time. Still, some authorities look askance at the idea of microbes having their way with food. If you work at a restaurant, you may find it difficult to convince the Health Department that you can ferment safely, even though billions of people have done it for millennia. Regulations, intended to be a fail-safe for the lowest and most irresponsible common denominator, often demand the eradication of all living bacteria, good or bad.

I look at microorganisms as partners, not enemies. You have to know their boundaries and your own, and figure out if that's something you can both work with. When you add enough salt to a culture, only certain bacteria—fortunately, the ones we want—can tolerate it; the rest quietly die off (or are killed by the preferred bacteria's alcohols or acids, in an unseen microbe war), and thus do no harm. Our job is to shape an environment in which the bacteria we can coax into a détente (what we might rather human-centrically call "good bacteria") can thrive, a cool, dark place with enough sugars to eat and limited exposure to oxygen. In exchange, they give us flavor: incredibly deep, sour, and funky. It's a collaboration.

I don't think it's a coincidence that we use the same word, *culture*, for our traditions, values, and social structures—how we identify ourselves as humans—and for the microbes we watch over and encourage to grow. (I know it's not, because the Latin root of both senses of the word is *colere*: to tend, guard, and cultivate.) It's an interesting analogy, reminding us that we have to tend and take care of our human culture, too: collaborating with microbes to make delicious flavors or with other humans on a shared sense of identity and purpose are both a diligent process. They're not going to happen without our active effort.

In Filipino cooking, condiments aren't afterthoughts but ingredients in and of themselves. They're part of a distinct culinary ethos, as the cultural historian Doreen Gamboa Fernandez has noted, one that rejects the myth of the chef as "sole authority" and invites the diner to take part in the making of a meal, so that "the creation is communal." Food arrives at the table essentially unfinished, awaiting the final touch: yours. Add a touch of sour Green Mango (page 189), briny Bagoong (page 169), or Salted Egg (page 190) with its dark orange-red yolk like the last gasp of sunset, and you make almost any dish taste Filipino.

PANTRY, SIDES, CONDIMENTS,

AND
SAWSAWAN

Before ketchup, there was ke-tsiap, a pickled fish sauce deployed centuries ago in southern China. It made its way to Malaysia and then England, where British voyagers tried to recreate it with the likes of anchovies, mushrooms, oysters, and beer. (Worcestershire is a cousin.) Americans added tomatoes in the early nineteenth century, and by the 1870s this was the standard recipe, codified by the industrialist Henry J. Heinz, whose recipes upped the proportions of vinegar and sugar so bottles would last longer.

The Filipino innovation: bananas, thanks to the early-twentieth-century chemist and World War II hero Maria Orosa, who devoted her life to championing native ingredients. Under the Japanese occupation, she was deputized as a captain in the guerilla resistance and saved countless lives by smuggling a soybean powder of her own invention to prisoners of war who were starving in concentration camps. With tomatoes scarce, she turned to the country's abundant bananas to make ketchup.

In the spirit of ongoing experimentation, I've crossed banana ketchup and pepper jelly, a staple of the American South, with a nod toward nam jim, a Thai sweet-sour-salty-hot dipping sauce. On my first try, I braised the chiles in simple syrup, then realized that you get all the sugar you need from the bananas. (But feel free to add a little sugar at the end to suit your own taste.)

I still have a soft spot for Jufran, the most famous Filipino brand of banana ketchup, applied liberally to everything from Fried Chicken (page 35) and Lumpia (page 107) to Pork BBQ (page 41). The version below can be swapped in anytime you find yourself reaching for Heinz.

SPICY BANANA KETCHUP

MAKES 2 CUPS (480 ML)

1 tablespoon olive oil

½ cup (65 g) minced white onion

2 cloves garlic, smashed, peeled, and minced

2 fresh red Fresno or cayenne chiles, finely minced

1½ teaspoons kosher salt

3 ounces (85 g) tomato paste

2 very ripe small bananas, peeled and broken into 2-inch (5 cm) chunks, frozen overnight then thawed

3 tablespoons apple cider vinegar

Raw cane sugar (optional)

Heat the olive oil in a sauté pan over high. Reduce to medium high, add the onion, garlic, chiles, and salt, and cook, stirring for 3 minutes, or until the onion and garlic are translucent. Reduce to medium low and cook for about 20 minutes, stirring occasionally, until soft. Stir in the tomato paste and cook for another 5 minutes.

•

Add the thawed banana chunks. The bananas should be brown and almost syrupy in texture. Stir in 1 cup (240 ml) water. Simmer over low heat with the lid on—the thick sauce becomes molten hot and can splatter—for another 20 minutes, uncovering and stirring every now and then.

•

Take the pan off the heat, remove the lid, and let the sauce sit at room temperature for 10 to 15 minutes, until cooled. Using a blender or immersion blender, puree the sauce until smooth. Stir in the vinegar (and sugar to taste, if you wish).

•

This keeps in the refrigerator in a covered jar for 2 to 3 weeks.

Bagoong is a distillate of the deep sea: tiny krill or fish laid out in the sun, then crushed, packed with salt in open clay pots, and left alone for weeks and in some places for up to two years, slowly turning into a thick paste with the heady funk of ancient things. It's essentially salt—actually, better than salt—and you can deploy it as such. Use it as an ingredient in Pinakbet (page 65) and Dry Spicy Bagoong Noodles (page 85); a condiment with Laing (page 67) and Ginisang Ampalaya (page 69); or a dip for green mango. Or experiment with it as a flavoring agent like miso or fish sauce, to boost the umami of a dish.

To make bagoong at home, I first tried rehydrating dried krill—disaster!—then settled on the freshest, smallest, best-quality shrimp I could find. Since the fermentation takes time, while you wait, buy bagoong at a Filipino grocery or online. You'll want to explore the varieties, shading from hot pink to chocolate brown, some closer to liquid and others almost crumbly. Keep in mind that this recipe is for bagoong alamang, unapologetically briny; order bagoong guisado and it'll be sweet, caramelized from a turn in the pan.

BAGOONG *bah•goh•AWNG*
FERMENTED SHRIMP PASTE

MAKES 1 TO 2 CUPS (280 TO 560 G), DEPENDING ON EVAPORATION

1½ pounds (680 g) fresh best-quality extra-small shrimp, 61/70 count per pound (larger sizes can work, too), shelled and deveined

2 tablespoons kosher salt

Rinse the shrimp and pat dry with paper towels. Using a sharp knife, chop the shrimp into a chunky paste, with the largest pieces about ¼ inch (6 mm). Transfer to a large bowl, add the salt, and combine with clean hands to distribute evenly.

•

Pack the mixture into a clean glass jar and lay a small square of plastic wrap directly on top of the shrimp inside the vessel (in lieu of a lid), in order to limit exposure to the air. Fill a sandwich-size zip-top bag with about 1 cup (240 ml) of room temperature water, seal, and put on top of the plastic wrap to weigh down the mixture. Using tape, label the jar with the start date, so you can keep track of how long it ferments.

•

Store in a slightly warm place where the contents will not be disturbed, like a cupboard above the refrigerator or under the sink. Be warned that the smell will be strong; if it's too much, you can put the entire jar in a large plastic bag and seal it partway (but not completely).

•

Depending on how warm your kitchen is, fermentation could take 1 to 1½ months or 2 to 3. Check the contents of the jar every week or so. You'll observe the salt slowly "cooking" the shrimp, which will start to turn pink after the first two weeks and slowly get pinker. You can stir the paste with a clean spoon, then pack it down again to continue to ferment.

•

The bagoong is ready when the paste is firm in texture and as pink as cooked shrimp. Remove the water-filled bag and plastic wrap, cover with an airtight lid, and then put in the refrigerator to store for up to 2 months.

In Pampanga, where my mom grew up, tagilo—known elsewhere in the country as burong hipon—is the vital sawsawan (dipping sauce): rice and shrimp or fish fermented for 3 to 7 days, depending on the temperature of the room, until deeply salty-sour. It has a whiff of rot, but so does fine aged cheese, and once you get past that (or embrace it!), the taste is sublime.

Be sure not to use warm rice. If just cooked, let it cool for a few hours; better yet, repurpose leftovers. I like making this with shrimp—it's even better if you can get them live—but small oily silver fish like sprats, herring, and sardines work well, too, if fresh. Once fermented, tagilo keeps in the refrigerator, ready to be cooked to order. (One-half cup is good for four people.) Serve it with simply prepared dishes like steamed or fried fish (as pictured here) or gently seasoned vegetables, or with green mango or okra as crudités.

TAGILO *tah•GHEE•loh*
FERMENTED SHRIMP AND RICE CONDIMENT

MAKES 1½ CUPS (315 G), FOR 3 BATCHES, SERVING 4 EACH

FOR THE FERMENT:

4½ ounces (130 g) fresh best-quality extra-small shrimp, 61/70 count per pound (larger sizes can work, too), shelled, deveined, and cut into ½-inch (12 mm) pieces

2 tablespoons kosher salt

1½ cups (215 g) cooked jasmine rice, room temperature or cold

FOR COOKING:

2 tablespoons canola or other neutral oil

3 cloves garlic, smashed, peeled, and finely minced

1 cup (125 g) finely minced white onion

1 large tomato, finely chopped

In a large mixing bowl, combine the diced shrimp and salt, and massage with clean hands. Add the cooked rice to the salted shrimp and continue to mix with your hands until thoroughly combined.

•

Pack the rice and shrimp mixture into a 3-cup (720 ml) sterilized jar or plastic food-safe container. Use a small square of plastic wrap to press against the top of the packed mixture. Screw on the lid and store in a cool, undisturbed place for 3 to 7 days, until the rice and shrimp mixture has broken down and gives off a soured smell. You should now store the jar in the refrigerator. (It should keep for up to 3 months.)

•

When you're ready to serve, heat a large sauté pan over medium high. Add the oil and when it's hot, add the garlic and onion. Cook while stirring for about 5 minutes, until softened, then add the tomato and cook for another 10 minutes. Add ½ cup (105 g) of the fermented rice and shrimp mixture to make one batch and save the rest for future batches. Depending on how much liquid the tomato and onion release, you may want to add about ½ cup (120 ml) water to the mixture as it cooks. It should achieve the texture of a loose risotto.

•

Serve the condiment warm or at room temperature.

This quick cure yields a creamy, wobbling yolk, amber and nearly translucent, like an ancient sun. Although this recipe comes from Japan, not the Philippines, the flavors match our love of pickling and fermenting, as well as our fondness—you've probably picked up on this by now—for eggs in all forms, whether fried sunny-side-up for Breakfast and Silogs (page 118) or submerged in brine for a few weeks (page 190). I like these yolks best at the two-hour mark, when their texture is at the perfect mid-point between liquid gold and custard; they get firmer and saltier the longer they cure. Add them as a finishing touch to noodles, pasta, or rice with pickles for a simple breakfast—or any dish you'd like to gild with a rich, salty topping. They're especially good nestled in the warmth of Arroz Caldo (page 51).

SOY-CURED EGG YOLKS

MAKES 6 EGG YOLKS

6 large eggs
2 tablespoons soy sauce

Save an egg carton to hold the cured eggs.

•

Take an egg and tap the top third of the shell against a sharp corner of your work surface. When it cracks, pop off the top and pour the egg into one palm over a bowl. (Keep the shell.) Let the egg white slip through your fingertips into the bowl while the egg yolk remains cupped in your palm.

•

Gently slide the yolk back into the shell and top it with 1 teaspoon soy sauce. Swirl the yolk in its shell so that the soy sauce slides around and under it, leaving no part of the yolk unstained. Transfer the yolk in its shell to the egg carton, setting it upright.

•

Repeat with the remaining eggs, one by one. Set aside to cure at room temperature for 2 to 3 hours.

•

(You can discard the egg whites or mix them with water to make an egg wash for sealing Lumpia Shanghai, page 107, or add to Garlic Butter Fried Rice, page 75, giving them a quick scramble in the pan just before you drop in the rice.)

•

Before using, tip the egg yolks into a slotted spoon and discard the curing sauce.

I love the straightforward, bracing smack of a vinegar pickle, but I find that lacto-fermentation yields more layers of flavor. All it requires is salt and time. In this recipe, you dissolve salt in water to make a brine, then submerge a pound of chiles and leave them alone for a while. The beneficial lactic acid bacteria that occur naturally in fruit and vegetables—and that live in your gut, keeping everything on keel and fending off disease—start to break down the sugars in the chiles and transform them into lactic acid, which in turn acts as a preserving agent and lends a thrilling sourness that underscores the heat.

Because no "cooking" is involved, the chiles retain their fruitiness, especially if plucked in summer, when they're at their height. Do add other seasonings as you wish: a strip of white onion, a grated clove of garlic, your favorite spices. I like to use red Fresno chiles for their balance of hot and sweet; they're plump and juicy and have a good ratio of fruit to seeds. But you can substitute mellower or stronger ones. (Thai chiles, if you dare!)

LACTO-FERMENTED HOT SAUCE

MAKES 2 CUPS (480 ML)

1 pound (455 g) whole fresh red Fresno chiles or
    your favorite red chiles
1½ teaspoons kosher salt

Combine the chiles, salt, and ½ cup (120 ml) water in a blender and pulse until smooth. Transfer to a plastic container or jar. Instead of covering with a lid, lay a small piece of plastic wrap directly over the top of the container, to limit exposure to the air. Using tape, label with the start date, so you can keep track of how long it ferments.

•

Store in a cool, dark place where the chiles will not be disturbed. Let ferment for 5 to 7 days; the timing will depend on the natural sweetness of the chiles and the temperature of the storage area. As it ferments, the sauce will bubble slightly and turn sour. After the fourth day, stir and taste, then decide whether to let it ferment another day or two. Keep tasting each day until it's as funky as you wish.

•

When you think it's ready, transfer to a clean bottle or jar and store in your refrigerator. It should be good for up to 3 months—longer than it takes to use it all.

In my house, when we got partway through a new bottle of vinegar, my parents would slip garlic and chiles down the neck. This was our suka at bawang, a nice slap of a sauce that we used to douse Longganisa (page 125), Tocino (page 123), Pork BBQ (page 41), and fried fish. If a piece of garlic or chile popped out, I'd eat it straight.

When it was chile season, the process went in reverse: Take an empty bottle, stuff it with chiles and garlic, then fill it—and keep refilling it—with vinegar. Over time, the chiles lost heat, but the suka got deeper in flavor. I called this T.J. Maxx vinegar because it reminded me of the pretty infused oils that seemed to stand permanently on the store's shelves, forlorn, as if no one ever bought them.

Please add as much garlic and chile as you want—in the Philippines, I've seen 12-ounce soda bottles filled to the brim. I suggest Thai and serrano chiles, but really, any will do. Try swapping in this suka in lieu of regular vinegar in other recipes, to get an extra punch of flavor. And keep a lookout for interesting bottles: The one I use is blue and shaped like a pyramid, from a really cheap shōchū I got at a 7-Eleven in Hokkaido.

SUKA AT BAWANG (AKA T.J. MAXX VINEGAR)
SOO•kah aht BAH•wahng
GARLIC AND CHILE TABLE VINEGAR

MAKES 2 CUPS (480 ML)

2 cups (480 ml) unpasteurized apple cider vinegar

12 fresh Thai chiles, slightly crushed but left whole

3 fresh serrano chiles, slightly crushed but left whole

7 cloves garlic, smashed and peeled

½ red onion, sliced into ½-inch (12 mm) wedges

Take a clean, empty vinegar bottle or jar and slip the chiles, garlic, and red onion inside. Pour in the apple cider vinegar and shake.

Cover and store in a cupboard. After a day or two, the vinegar will take on the punchy flavor of the chiles and garlic. Keep it for up to 2 years.

he cultural practitioner Lane Wilcken told me a story about the origin of the coconut tree: In the time before time, the brother of the demigod Lumauig speared an enemy and brought his head—considered the seat of the soul—back to the village, as both proof of victory and a way of making peace, by honoring the loss of life and making the enemy, in death, a spiritual member of the community. The head was buried, and from it grew the coconut tree, which in the Philippines is known today as "the tree of life," because every part of it is used for nourishment and sustenance, from the roots, trunk, and fruit to the pith, leaves, and inflorescence—the unopened flowers of the tree, whose sap is extracted to make sugar, liquor, and vinegar.

Here I use coconut water (from young green coconuts) as the base for homemade coconut vinegar, which is smooth and light in acidity, good for boosting the coconut flavor in Coconut Milk Chicken Adobo (page 20) and a gentle substitute for stronger vinegars. This experiment was inspired by a mishap—when I was in the Cayman Islands during the pandemic, working on this cookbook, my mini-fridge's gasket broke and the gallon of coconut water I'd bought (at the lovely Clarence Farm in Bodden Town, where the trees are nourished by freshly drawn well-water) began to fizz. I added sugar as extra "food" for the natural wild yeasts to turn into alcohol, and apple cider vinegar to help speed up the conversion of alcohol into acetic acid.

You can downsize this recipe, but since the fermentation process takes at least a month—low effort, but lots of patience required!—I encourage you to make a big batch. And don't worry if your coconut water starts off pink, as pictured here, and continues to change color: That's just a sign of natural oxidization and doesn't affect the flavor.

HOMEMADE COCONUT VINEGAR

MAKES ABOUT 2½ QUARTS (2.4 L)

1½ cups (300 g) granulated sugar

1 cup (240 ml) hot water

2 quarts (2 L) coconut water

3 cups (720 ml) unpasteurized apple cider vinegar (I like the Bragg brand)

In a large jar or bottle that can hold about 3 quarts (2.8 ml) liquid, combine the sugar and water to make a simple syrup.

•

Add the coconut water, then cover the container's opening with a folded kitchen towel and secure with a rubber band. This is to keep any bugs or fruit flies from getting into the vinegar, while allowing airflow and oxygen, so fermentation can take place. Put the container somewhere warm-ish and dark where it can sit undisturbed. My favorite spots are under my sink next to the dishwasher and in a cabinet by the stove or above the refrigerator.

•

Let the container rest for a week or two. You should see some activity in the jar—it's fun to watch, so check on it every couple days. Mine formed a bubbling white yeast layer on top and showed lots of fizzing as the sugar turned into alcohol.

•

After a week or so, when the activity dies down, remove the kitchen towel and add the unpasteurized apple cider vinegar, then cover with the towel again. Let ferment for 1 to 3 months or more.

•

When ready, the coconut vinegar should be tangy and tart. Transfer to a couple bottles that have screw-on caps to keep in your pantry. Stored in a cool, dark place away from heat, it should maintain its flavor for 2 years. If sediment forms at the bottom, that's totally normal—just give it a shake.

*P*atis, or fish sauce, is so essential to Filipino cooking that some of us have been known to pack bottles of it on trips abroad and surreptitiously give a splash to foreign dishes. "No matter how strange or different the food, the patis gives it Filipino flavor," the cultural historian Doreen Gamboa Fernandez wrote.

For vegans, I wanted to offer an alternative that still delivers the same deep funk. Simmering and then steeping kombu, shiitakes, and black garlic in water yields this umami elixir. Black garlic brings a beautiful note of dark caramel, but if you can't find it, try plain garlic and a charred onion. Or make your own black garlic: Wrap whole heads of raw garlic in plastic wrap and foil, then put them in a rice cooker on warm for three weeks, until they're soft, caramelized, and dark as jet, thanks to the Maillard reaction (see "Ferment," page 163).

VEGAN "FISH SAUCE"
MUSHROOM, KOMBU, and
BLACK GARLIC MAKES 2½ CUPS (600 ML)

1 sheet of kombu (5 by 6-inch/11 by 15 cm), broken
    up into pieces
1 cup (35 g) dried shiitake mushrooms
1 bulb black garlic (1¼ ounces/35 g)
2 tablespoons kosher salt

Add 3 cups (720 ml) water and all the ingredients to a 2-quart (2 L) saucepan. Bring to a boil, then reduce the heat slightly, so the surface just ripples. Simmer for an hour, letting the broth steep (no stirring), then turn off the heat but keep the pan on the burner. Once the liquid has cooled, put a lid on the pan and let the mixture continue steeping overnight.

●

The next morning, strain the sauce through a fine-mesh strainer and discard the aromatics (the kombu, shiitakes, and black garlic). Pour the liquid into a bottle or jar to store in the refrigerator for up to a month, and use whenever you want a hit of brine and funk.

My dad always kept a store-bought jar of this sweet-and-sour green papaya pickle on hand, to anoint braised or barbecued meats and revive the palate between such rich bites. Like chow-chow, the tangy relish from the American South, atsara typically comes submerged in vinegar spiked with sugar, but here I coax out the flavors through lacto-fermentation, leaving the green papaya to ferment for a few days in a simple solution of water and salt, alongside crispy radish, bell peppers, carrots, and raisins that fatten nicely in the brine. Ginger brings a little humming heat. Start with firm green papayas, as green as can be, for the most satisfying crunch.

ATSARA *aht • CHA • rah*
GREEN PAPAYA TABLE PICKLE

MAKES 1 QUART (960 ML)

- 1 pound (455 g) green papaya, peeled
- 1 medium carrot, peeled
- 6 red ball radishes
- 1 small red bell pepper
- 1 whole small fresh red Fresno chile (optional, for a bit of heat)
- 1 small red onion
- ⅓ cup (50 g) black raisins
- 1 tablespoon sea salt
- ½ cup (120 ml) warm water
- 2 cloves garlic, smashed and peeled
- 2 (1-inch/2.5 cm) pieces fresh ginger, peeled

Using a mandoline or a chef's knife, julienne the green papaya, carrot, radishes, bell pepper, and chile, cutting the vegetables into even matchstick-sized pieces, and put them in a large mixing bowl. Halve the onion, then cut the halves from top to root, slicing them into thin strips, about ⅛ inch (3 mm) wide. Add the onions and raisins to the mixing bowl.

•

In a small bowl, dissolve the salt in the warm water.

•

Cut one clove of the garlic into very thin slices, then julienne one piece of the ginger and add both to the bowl of vegetables. Using a Microplane, grate the remaining clove of garlic and piece of ginger into the salted water, to bring intensity to the brine.

•

Pour the brine over the julienned vegetables and combine using clean hands. Transfer the vegetables and brine to a large jar, ceramic pickling pot, or food-grade plastic vessel that can hold at least 1 quart (960 ml). With your fingertip, gently press down on the vegetables inside the jar to remove as many air bubbles as you can. You should have just enough brine to cover the vegetables; if not, don't worry—the salt will cause the vegetables to release liquid and the brine will rise.

•

Lay a small square of plastic wrap directly on top of the vegetables inside the vessel (in lieu of a lid), in order to limit exposure to the air. Fill a sandwich-size zip-top bag with water, seal, and put on top of the plastic wrap. This should weigh down the vegetables so that they are completely submerged in the brine for the duration of the pickling process.

•

Using tape, label the jar with the start date, so you can keep track of how long it ferments.

•

Store in a cool, dark place where the pickles will not be disturbed. Fermentation should take 2 to 5 days, depending on the temperature of the storage area and the ripeness of the green papaya. On the second day, take a taste, then taste each day thereafter. The pickles will grow more sour daily.

•

When you decide that the pickles have achieved the perfect balance of funky, sour, and sweet, they're done! Remove the water-filled bag and plastic wrap, cover with an airtight lid, and then put in the refrigerator to store. The pickles should keep for up to a month, while continuing to ferment very, very slowly.

For those who grew up in the West, like me, bitter melon can seem like a test: the kind of vegetable you have to learn, begrudgingly, to love. There is no secret to making it gentler on the tongue; salt will temper it only so much. In the end, all you can do is submit. Embrace the bitterness. That's why it's here, to trigger parts of your palate you don't even know about yet, and show you a whole other dimension of flavor. These days I even drink it—my favorite herbalist, Grace Galanti at Furnace Creek Farm, sells fresh-pressed bitter melon juice at the Union Square Greenmarket in New York City, and I mix it with sparkling water or tulsi (holy basil) vinegar, to make a truly grown-up soda.

This is a quick pickle, meant to be eaten in small amounts as a kind of cleansing between other tastes—of charred meats, long-braised stews, salty silogs (see Breakfast and Silogs, page 118)—like pickled ginger at a sushi restaurant. Each bite is a tiny wake-up call.

SALTED BITTER MELON

SERVES 4

1 (4-ounce/115 g) bitter melon, ends and seeds
    removed, cut in half lengthwise
1 teaspoon kosher salt

Using a mandoline or sharp chef's knife, cut the bitter melon halves into very thin half-moons, about ⅛ inch (3 mm) thick.

●

In a small mixing bowl, combine the bitter melon and salt, using your fingers to thoroughly combine. Set aside; the salt will start to extract liquid from the bitter melon, softening it. After 30 minutes, pick up the bitter melon pieces with your hands, ball them up in your fist, and squeeze a few times to wring dry. Discard any liquid, then return the bitter melon to the bowl.

●

Run cool water from the kitchen tap into the bowl. Soak and rinse the bitter melon, discard the water, and rinse again. Wring the bitter melon dry once more and transfer to a small bowl to serve, or store in an airtight container in the refrigerator and eat within a few days.

This is really two recipes in one. Both rely on my mom's technique of blistering eggplant on the stovetop, laying it right on the burner, then breaking the flesh down into smoky velvet. I like to stop right there and just swirl in some garlic cooked super-slow until soft and creamy, and top it off with nothing more than flaky sea salt. But my mom would add raw onion and tomato, for a touch of brightness, and finish it with a dose of fish sauce. (I soak the onion first in ice cold water, rinsing and changing the water a few times, to help mellow the raw flavor.) You can merge the two approaches, as here, but please also try each version separately. Serve this as a side with Pork BBQ (page 41), Pork Bellychon (page 157), or fried fish—or just eat it straight. (I do.)

SMOKY CHARRED EGGPLANT

SERVES 2

6 cloves garlic, peeled
¼ cup (60 ml) olive oil
1 large Japanese eggplant
Flaky sea salt
½ small tomato, diced (optional)
¼ small red onion, finely minced and soaked and
    rinsed in ice cold water (optional)
Fish sauce or Vegan "Fish Sauce" (page 181; both
    are optional)

In a very small saucepan—I once used my metal ½ cup (120 ml) measuring cup as a tiny pot—combine the whole garlic cloves and olive oil so that the cloves are completely submerged. Bring to a boil on high, then reduce to a low, slowly bubbling simmer. Hold the saucepan at the edge of the burner where the heat is lowest, and let the garlic simmer slowly for about 30 minutes, until softened. Set the pan aside and do not discard the oil: You're going to need it.

•

Heat a stovetop burner to medium high. Char the eggplant directly on the burner (electric and gas both work), rotating every minute until all sides are charred, about 5 minutes total cooking time.

•

Once cool, peel the charred eggplant, then cut into 1-inch (2.5 cm) chunks and discard the stem. Smash the eggplant in a small bowl with a fork, and stir until the eggplant starts to look like baba ghanouj. Add the softened garlic and 2 tablespoons of the garlic cooking oil to the eggplant. Crush the garlic cloves into the eggplant mash and stir to combine.

•

At this stage, you can serve as is, with some flaky sea salt to finish. Or follow my mom's lead and add the diced tomato and onion—think of the proportions you would use in adding tomato and onion to guacamole—then season with fish sauce to taste. Serve in a small bowl with a spoon so that everyone can help themselves.

In the West, sweetness can be tyranny, with fruit prized only at its ripest. But in the Philippines, it's used at every stage—partly out of frugality and the desire to waste nothing, but also because sourness is just as delicious, and often necessary to balance out a rich meal. For this tart pickle, you want the greenest, hardest mangoes possible; too ripe and everything will end up mushy. (This is a nice way of making the mango season longer: You get in at the very beginning and enjoy them all the way through that peak of sweetness.)

Be sure to limit how much air the pickle is exposed to during the fermentation process, to keep out potentially harmful bacteria and molds. If some solid, slightly wrinkly white masses appear at the top, don't worry: This is just yeast that you can skim off and discard. (A patch of any other color, however, might mean spoilage, especially if it has a fuzzy texture.) There's no set deadline; you judge by your own taste when the pickle is done. Then use it as a palate refresher with grilled meats and fish, sticky-sweet barbecue (page 41), and braised stews like Pork Adobo (page 23)—or eat it straight.

LACTO-FERMENTED GREEN MANGO

MAKES 1 QUART (980 ML)

2 large green mangoes

3 sprigs fresh dill

1 cup (240 ml) warm water

4½ teaspoons kosher salt

2 teaspoons chile paste or ½ fresh red chile, minced, or 1 tablespoon Lacto-Fermented Hot Sauce (page 175; for a spicy version double or triple these options based on your desired heat level!)

½ teaspoon whole black peppercorns

Peel the green mangoes with a vegetable peeler. Cut the mango flesh away from the flat large seed lodged at the center of the mango's widest part; you can shear off two big chunks on either side, then shave off any strands still attached to the seed.

•

Cut the mango flesh into a few wedges, about ½ inch (12 mm) at the widest part. Layer the mango wedges with the dill and pack snugly into a glass jar or food-grade plastic or ceramic container.

•

In a small bowl, make a brine by combining the water, salt, chile, and whole black peppercorns. Stir to dissolve, then let the mixture rest for about 10 minutes, until it reaches room temperature.

•

Pour the brine over the mango wedges. Lay a small square of plastic wrap directly on top of the mangoes inside the vessel (in lieu of a lid), in order to limit exposure to the air. Fill a sandwich-size zip-top bag with water, seal, and put on top of the plastic wrap. This should weigh down the mangoes so that they are completely submerged in the brine for the duration of the pickling process. Using tape, label the jar with the start date, so you can keep track of how long it ferments.

→

Store in a cool place where the mangoes won't be disturbed. If the brine is close to the edge of the container, set the jar or container on a plate, as the brine may bubble over (a natural occurrence and nothing to worry about).

●

Let the mangoes ferment for 2 to 5 days. The length of time depends on many factors, including the temperature of the room and the ripeness of the mango. On the second day, take a taste, then taste each day thereafter. The pickles will grow more sour daily. After the first two days, don't be afraid to taste the pickles every day. When you decide that the pickles have achieved the perfect balance of funky, sour, and sweet, they're done!

●

Remove the plastic wrap, cover with an airtight lid, and then put in the refrigerator to store. The pickles should keep for up to a month, while continuing to ferment very, very slowly.

SALTED EGG

MAKES 12 EGGS

One day at my lola's house, I found a tall brown glass jar under the sink, full of eggs submerged in brine. I was a young line cook then, just learning how to pickle and preserve, and I was thrilled at the thought of making salted eggs—which I'd always bought from Asian markets—at home. Lola told me the recipe on the spot, and it's pretty much what you'll read below.

It's the simplest of equations: egg, salt, and time. Submerge an egg in brine and the salt will slowly work its way through the porous shell and start to break down the proteins in the egg white and firm up the yolk. Ours wallow just long enough for the white to settle and the yolk to darken slightly and take on the ripeness of aged cheese.

This is the surprise smack of salt and funk that brings depth to Bibingka (page 215), an otherwise sweet, delicate cake. It's also an essential condiment served on the side with charred Pork BBQ (page 41) and long-braised meat dishes: You boil it, cut it in half crosswise—shell and all—then dice it in the shell and scoop out the creamy insides (like you would with an avocado; it has the same texture), then mix it with a little diced tomato. The salt draws out the tomato juices and, with a few stirs, the egg and juices come together to make a sauce, coating the tomato (see photo on page 192).

The salted eggs you find at Asian markets are often duck eggs, which are fattier and have larger yolks, but it's fine to use chicken eggs instead. The key, my lola said, is to "keep adding salt until you can't anymore." If you'd like a bit of color—the ones at the market are often tinted bright magenta, to distinguish them from the fresh eggs in your refrigerator—use food coloring or experiment with grated beet, turmeric, red cabbage, or other natural dyes in the brine, keeping in mind that oxidization could give you unexpected results: As pictured here, I used beet and ended up with a marbling of greys and whites, like Venetian plaster. Once the eggs are in the jar, you can check on them every once in a while, but mostly just leave them alone in their cool, dark hiding place.

½ cup (60 g) salt
1 quart (960 ml) warm water
12 eggs, any size

Pour the salt into a 64-ounce (2 L) nonreactive container like a glass mason jar, ceramic pickle pot, or food-safe plastic tub. This will be your storage vessel. (All the eggs should fit, but if you have only 32-ounce (960 ml) containers on hand, use two and split the brine between them.)
→

SALTED EGG CONTINUED

Salted egg and tomato condiment

Pour the warm water into the container and stir. Carefully put in the eggs, one by one, nestling them in layers and making sure they don't crack. (If using a jar and your hand can't fit through the mouth, take a spoon and guide the egg down the side.) Check to see if the salt brine covers the eggs; if not, make a little more to pour over.

•

Preserve unrefrigerated in a cabinet for 3 to 4 weeks. It's helpful to label the vessel with a start date, so you can quickly calculate how long it's been sitting there. Check on the eggs every once in a while and give them a gentle swirl, so that the brine comes into contact with every egg.

•

After 3 to 4 weeks, carefully rinse the eggs and arrange them in a pot. Cover with cold water and bring to a boil over high heat. When the water starts boiling, reduce heat to a low simmer so the eggs don't knock into each other too much, risking cracks. (If an egg does crack, it's okay to keep cooking it.) Cook for 8 to 9 minutes.

•

Strain the cooked eggs and cool in an ice bath or under cold running tap water. Once cooled, drain and air dry, then store in your refrigerator until needed. They last pretty much forever.

Young green coconut has a jelly-like, scoopable flesh, but in mature brown coconuts, the meat is heartier and clings to the shell, so it has to be pried and scraped out with a knife or specialized tool. Squeezed, the meat yields creamy coconut milk, and from this milk comes latik, the crunchy curds left after the liquid is almost all boiled away, typically scattered over sweet kakanin (see Kakanin, Pastries, and Sweets, page 210), although I like to use it in savory dishes, too, like Laing (page 67). Latik is so coveted, it once caused a war—or such is the story told by the indigenous Filipino folk dance called Maglalatik, in which fighters adorned in coconut shells swirl into battle, clashing the shells in a thunderous beat. To the winner go the curds.

Making latik is simple but time-consuming: It can take from 45 minutes to 2 hours, depending on the fat content of the coconut milk, and you need to keep an eye on the stove. (You'll save yourself some trouble stirring if you use a nonstick pan.) You just simmer the coconut milk (or coconut cream, for a higher yield) until the curds separate from the coconut oil—itself a fantastic ingredient, slightly caramelized, like brown butter, and good to reserve for Coconut Milk Chicken Adobo (page 20), Laing, and Crispy Pandan Coconut Rice (page 79).

LATIK *lah•TEEK*
CRUNCHY COCONUT-MILK CURDS

MAKES FROM ¼ TO ¾ CUP (25 TO 108 G) LATIK AND
FROM 3 TO 10 TABLESPOONS (40 TO 150 ML) TOASTED COCONUT OIL,
DEPENDING ON THE BRAND OF COCONUT MILK OR COCONUT CREAM

2 cans (13½ ounces/400 ml each) unsweetened, full-fat coconut milk or coconut cream

In a small nonstick saucepan, bring the coconut milk up to a boil. Immediately lower the heat to medium low.

Simmer uncovered for 45 minutes to 2 hours, stirring occasionally with a rubber spatula. As the coconut milk reduces, you'll observe something exciting happening every 15 to 30 minutes, signaling a new phase in the cooking process. First, as the coconut milk evaporates, it starts to separate into curds and coconut oil. The color shifts to a light gold, then large bubbles appear, shading into a caramel-colored foam.

At this point, you won't be able to see the curds at the bottom of the pot. As the bubbles shrink and continue to darken, stir to break up the curds. When the bubbles die down, the curds become visible again.

Once the curds are deep brown, pour the pan's contents into a fine-mesh sieve over a bowl. Save the coconut oil in the bowl for future use, storing it in a covered jar or bottle with a screw-top cap at room temperature; it should last for a few months.

Tip the crunchy curds from the sieve onto a paper towel to drain and dry. This is latik. Store in an airtight container in the freezer for a few days until ready to use. If the latik gets a bit soft due to humidity, just pop it into the oven at 325°F (165°C) until it dries out again.

Tomas de los Reyes, now known simply as Mang Tomas—"mang" is an honorific, like mister—was a lechonero who started selling ready-to-go whole roasted pigs in the 1950s in Quezon City, first from the yard of his house to gamblers heading home from neighborhood cockfights, and then from a shop with lechon displayed on vertical bamboo skewers, their skin so burnished from the coals, they nearly glowed. Part of the lure was his special sauce, made of mashed, mineral-rich pork livers, sugar, and vinegar, tangy sweet and just bracing enough to counter the lushness of the lechon's salt and fat.

Today you can buy it in a bottle or make it yourself. My take on it is peppery and almost adobo-like. I add Suka at Bawang (page 177) for extra depth of flavor from the steeped garlic and chiles, but it's fine to swap in apple cider vinegar. You can pair this with Max's Style Fried Chicken (page 35), Pork Bellychon (page 157), or the ultra-luxurious Porchetta Bellychon (page 159). But keep in mind, too, that some people are happy just to use the sauce like ketchup—or even eat it straight, over rice.

PORK LIVER SAUCE ("MANG TOMAS")

MAKES 2 CUPS (480 ML)

2 tablespoons olive oil

2 cloves garlic, smashed, peeled, and minced

1 medium yellow onion, finely minced

1½ teaspoons coarsely cracked black pepper

1 pork or chicken liver, connective tissue removed, cut into ½-inch (12 mm) dice

½ teaspoon kosher salt

½ cup (120 ml) Suka at Bawang (page 177) or apple cider vinegar

¼ cup (60 ml) soy sauce

3 tablespoons (45 ml) molasses

Heat a 1-quart (960 ml) saucepan over medium. Add the olive oil, and when the oil is warm, reduce the heat to medium low and add the onions, garlic, and pepper. Cook, stirring occasionally, for about 10 minutes. Once the onions and garlic are soft, add the liver and salt, and cook for an additional 2 minutes.

•

Add the suka at bawang, soy sauce, and molasses and let the liver braise in the sauce, uncovered, for another 10 minutes. Turn off the heat and let the sauce rest and cool in the pan for about 15 minutes.

•

Add the liver and cooking liquid to a blender and puree for about 2 minutes; the texture should be a little coarse, not totally smooth. Store in a covered jar in the refrigerator for up to 1 week.

Garlic is as essential to Filipino food as olive oil to Italian and butter to French. It appears at every meal, in abundance. I love it in all forms, from the garlic ice cream served at the annual garlic festival in Gilroy, California (a half-hour drive from my hometown, San Jose), to black garlic, which is garlic aged slowly, over low heat, until the cloves turn inky and soft (see headnote for Vegan "Fish Sauce," page 181, to learn how to make it).

Here we fry garlic to a crisp, to sprinkle over Pancit Palabok (page 81), Munggo (page 57), Arroz Caldo (page 51), Filipino Spaghetti (page 89)–really, almost any dish, whether it already has garlic or not. The key is timing, since you can go from perfect fried garlic to bitter rubble in a manner of seconds. Intuitively, you'll want to wait for the visual cue of the garlic turning the right shade of brown in the pan, but by then it's almost too late. Run a test with a few slivers of garlic: As soon as the color turns golden (but not brown), pull the slivers out; they'll continue to cook as they cool, and the color will deepen.

Be sure to find nice garlic at the market, firm and picturesque. This batch is pretty small; I typically double or triple it and easily use it up in a few days. If you make extra, you also get to collect more garlic-suffused oil from the fryer, for adding a kick to other dishes. And you can crush and finely mince some of the garlic before frying if you want smaller crispy bits, as in Pancit Palabok.

GARLIC CHIPS

MAKES ABOUT ½ CUP (25 G)

8 cloves garlic, peeled
⅔ cup (165 ml) canola or other neutral oil
⅓ cup (75 ml) olive oil

Using a mandoline, take 1 clove, holding it by the woody root end, and slice it into pieces ⅛ inch (3 mm) thin. Apply even pressure and take careful strokes. Don't slice the whole clove: You don't want to get too close to the blade and cut yourself. Instead, when you get toward the end, save the last bit for another recipe. You can also use a sharp paring knife to cut the garlic; just try to make the slices as even as possible, so they all cook in the same amount of time.

•

Put a 1-quart (960 ml) saucepan on a stovetop burner, but don't turn on the heat yet. Add the canola and olive oils, then tip in all the garlic. (Starting with cold oil helps the chips fry more evenly.) Set the heat to medium low. After about 1½ minutes, you'll start to see bubbles around the garlic. Stir the hot oil with a fine-mesh sieve.

•

The oil will continue to bubble as the garlic cooks and becomes fragrant. After another 2 minutes, the garlic will turn golden and the bubbles will start to quiet down; this means that the moisture in the garlic has evaporated, leaving the garlic crisp and chip-like.

→

GARLIC CHIPS
CONTINUED

Scoop out the garlic chips with the fine-mesh sieve, or set the sieve over a heat-proof bowl and carefully pour the hot oil and garlic chips into it. (Reserve the oil for future use, for up to a month.) Immediately transfer the chips to a plate lined with paper towels and let cool.

•

You can use the chips right away, or store them in an airtight container for up to a couple weeks.

•

Minced Fried Garlic

Some recipes, like Pancit Palabok, call for smaller crispy bits. Instead of slicing the garlic cloves, crush them and finely mince as evenly as you can, then fry for about 2 minutes, until they are golden.

•

Garlic Oil

The reserved fryer oil can be used to make Garlic Cornick (page 102), Garlic Butter Fried Rice (page 75), or to start Coconut Milk Chicken Adobo (page 20) or Pork Adobo (page 23), or in any recipe calling for garlic. It's a powerful infusion—don't waste it!

Made with starch extracted from the cassava root, sago, also known as tapioca pearls, are translucent, slippery, chewy orbs that squeak between the teeth, a texture that the Taiwanese call Q (or, if something's really chewy, QQ). You find these little spheres in desserts across Asia, studding snowy heights of shaved ice and swirling in the depths of boba tea, aka bubble tea, a drink invented in Taiwan in the 1980s. If you make your own, you can give them any flavor and color you like, but the process is labor-intensive, so you might want to double the recipe—once dried, they can be stored in the freezer in an airtight container for up to 6 months. These get a little molasses in the dough, sticky and sweet, with a hint of smoke. Drop them into Halo-Halo (page 263), Taho (page 241), slushes, and iced milky coffee and tea.

HOMEMADE MOLASSES TAPIOCA

MAKES 2 CUPS (360 G) OR ABOUT 240 UNCOOKED PEARLS, FOR 4 TO 8 SERVINGS

1⅓ cups (180 g) tapioca starch, plus extra for
    dusting
2 tablespoons (30 ml) molasses
⅓ cup (75 ml) boiling water
1 tablespoon brown sugar, plus more for simple
    syrup (optional)

In a small mixing bowl, using a small spatula, mix together the tapioca starch, molasses, boiling water, and brown sugar, if using. When the dough has coalesced into a rough ball, turn it over onto a clean work surface and cut it into eighths, then roll each eighth out to make a log. Cover the bowl with plastic wrap so the tapioca dough doesn't dry out.

•

Roll each log into a longer, skinnier rope, about ⅜ inch (1 cm) wide and 1 foot (30 cm) long. Using a knife or bench scraper, cut these ropes into ⅜ by ⅜-inch (1 by 1 cm) pieces, then loosely cover the pieces with plastic wrap. Working with one piece at a time, roll it between your palms to make a tidy ball shape, then put it on a sheet tray dusted with extra tapioca starch to rest. Repeat with the remaining pieces, then repeat with each rope. You should end up with about 240 freshly rolled pearls, which may be cooked immediately or left on the counter to dry and stored in a zip-top bag or other airtight container in the freezer for up to 6 months.

•

When ready to cook, fill a 2-quart (2 L) saucepan with water 1 inch (2.5 cm) away from the rim of the pot. Bring the water to a boil on high and add the number of pearls you want to use, but no more than ¼ cup (90 g) at a time. Boil for about 30 minutes, then scoop out the pearls with a small fine-mesh sieve—keep the water boiling—and rinse in a colander under cool water. Return the pearls to the boiling water until the centers are cooked all the way through, about 5 more minutes if the pearls are freshly made and 10 to 15 more if dried, then scoop them out into a bowl. (If making another batch, discard the cooking liquid, since it will be starchy, and fill the saucepan with fresh water to start the process again.)

•

Add tap water to the bowl, enough to cover the sago. If you'd like the pearls to be a little sweeter, make a simple syrup by stirring together equal parts brown sugar and warm water to fill the bowl instead. Keep the sago in the water or simple syrup at room temperature. Use within a few hours, before the pearls harden.

*U*nlike Malaysian kaya—which I also love: rich and custardy, suffused with pandan—our version of coconut jam doesn't require eggs, which makes it the vegan equivalent of dulce de leche, coconut milk and sugar held at a low simmer until dark and thick as butterscotch. I use light brown sugar and molasses, for sweetness tinged by smoke, but you can swap out both for 1 cup (220 g) packed dark brown sugar instead. You'll need this for Biko (page 233), but it can also take the place of regular jam in linzer cookies. Stir it into hot coffee, slather it over a hot pan de sal (our daily bread), or eat it on buttered toast with a pinch of flaky sea salt.

COCO JAM

MAKES 2 CUPS (480 ML)

2 cans (13½ ounces/398 ml each) unsweetened,
 full-fat coconut milk
4 tablespoons (60 ml) molasses
1 cup (220 g) packed light brown sugar
2 pinches kosher salt

In a 2-quart (2 L) saucepan, bring the coconut milk, molasses, light brown sugar, and salt up to a boil, then reduce to a slow simmer and bubble over low heat.

•

Simmer for about 2 hours, to reduce the coconut milk mixture until it thickens. As it reduces, use a spatula to scrape the sides and bottom of the pan intermittently. Between scrapes, rest the spatula on a small plate on the counter by the stovetop while you work on other cooking projects.

•

The coconut milk mixture will soon take on the sepia tinge of a café au lait, then deepen several shades as it gets syrupy and almost waxy at the edges of the pan. Close to the 2-hour mark, the jam will start to look translucent and reach the color of dark caramel.

•

Transfer the hot coconut jam to a clean, heatproof container, and store in the refrigerator for about 1 month. Once cooled, the jam will turn opaque again and settle into a lighter amber.

To dismantle a mango, my mom would always shear off the sides first–navigating unerringly around the invisible seed–then score crisscrossing diagonals into the flesh. She'd hand me a half and I'd get to do the magic part, where you flip the mango inside out and find perfect cubes, fanned out like a hedgehog's quills. I'd eat them straight off the peel. If we got to the mangoes too late and they were overripe, my mom would boil the pulp with some sugar to make us mango jam, perfect on buttered toast or with a thick slice of sharp white Cheddar inside pan de sal (the fluffy bread we ate almost every day).

In my version, I introduce a little smoke and heat, inspired by a Jamaican pepper jelly I tried in the Caribbean. It would make a great dollop on a cheese board. If you'd like a more straightforwardly sweet jam, you can leave out the chipotle and Fresno chiles; if you want some spice but can't find the right ingredients, don't substitute canned chipotle, which would overwhelm the mango–go with dried ancho chile instead.

SMOKY PEPPER JELLY–MANGO JAM

MAKES 2 CUPS (480 ML)

1 small dried chipotle chile
4 ripe mangoes, about 2 pounds (910 g)
2 fresh red Fresno chiles, finely minced
    (½ cup/80 g)
1 small lemon
½ cup (100 g) granulated sugar

Heat a 3-quart (2.8 L), preferably nonstick saucepan over high. Toast the dried chipotle in the pan for about 3 minutes, turning every minute until partially charred and crisp. (This releases the chipotle's oils and draws out its fragrance, and will bring some elegant bitter notes to the jam.) Turn off the heat and remove the saucepan from the burner.

•

Break up the chipotle into small pieces and discard the stem. In a clean spice or coffee grinder, crush the chipotle into a fine powder. Set aside.

•

Put the mango on a cutting board with the stem pointing down. Cut off one side, navigating the knife around the flat central seed, then cut off the other side. You will end up with three parts: two curved sides and a narrow middle with the seed. Take the two curved sides and, using a spoon, scoop the mango flesh out of the skin and chop into 1-inch (2.5 cm) pieces. Then peel the skin off the middle section and, using a small knife, cut as much of the mango flesh as you can from the seed.

•

Add the mango to the saucepan you used to toast the chile, along with the chipotle powder and minced Fresno chiles. Cut the lemon in half and juice directly over the mangoes, being sure to catch and discard the seeds. But don't discard the lemon rinds–drop them in the pan. (The pectin in the rinds will help thicken the jam.) Then add the sugar and stir to combine.

•

Bring the mixture to a boil, then drop the heat to a low, slow simmer. Stirring occasionally, cook for 1 to 1½ hours, until thickened. To test, scoop a teaspoon onto a plate and flatten slightly to cool. When you run your finger through the jam, it should hold its shape rather than weep.

•

Turn off the heat and cool the jam at room temperature in the pan. Transfer to a jar (following canning procedures, if you like) or a plastic food-grade container, and store in the refrigerator for about 1 month.

Chocolate was a gift from the Americas, brought to the Philippines in the late seventeenth century via the Spanish galleons that plied the seas from Manila to Acapulco. The first cacao was planted—under the shade of coconut trees, to protect it from wind and sun—in Batangas, where my dad grew up, and the area is still known for making the best tablea: cacao beans fermented, dried, roasted over fire, hulled, then traditionally ground by hand between two stones into a sandy paste, which is then molded into thick coins.

Sometimes a little sugar is added, as here, but you're not meant to eat this chocolate straight. In treats like Tsokolate (page 277), Night Moss Shake (page 269), and Champorado (page 135), it's deployed like cocoa powder—only it's much darker and richer, because the cocoa butter hasn't been squeezed out. As a kid, I was always a little disappointed by the cheap, super-sweet milk chocolate handed out at Halloween. Only when I learned to make my own tablea did I come to love cacao, as an almost savory ingredient.

This homemade version uses cacao nibs, which are cacao beans that have been fermented and cracked; toast them until they sweat their oils a little, then pulverize them with sugar and shape. They make a worthy gift, wrapped in parchment or decorative paper.

TABLEA *tah • BLAY • ah*
ROASTED CACAO NIBS AND RAW CANE SUGAR MAKES 10 TABLEA

1 cup (125 g) raw cacao nibs
⅓ cup (70 g) demerara or raw cane sugar

Preheat the oven to 325°F (165°C). Roast the cacao nibs for 20 minutes, or until they release their oils and turn fragrant. Set aside to cool.

•

Once cool, transfer to a blender, add the sugar, and blend for about 3 minutes. The mixture will crumble, then form a semi-smooth paste with some sandy bits. Tear off two 14-inch-long (35.5 cm) pieces of plastic wrap and layer them on top of one another, oriented so the shorter side is nearest to you. Using a small rubber spatula, scrape the cacao paste out of the blender onto the wrap. Shape it as neatly as you can into a 10 by 2-inch (25 by 5 cm) log, arranged lengthwise at the center of the wrap. Take the bottom edge of the wrap and fold upward just enough to cover the cacao log. The wrap will help the paste hold its shape as you roll it into an even thinner 10 by 1-inch (25 by 2.5 cm) log.

•

Again, take the bottom edge of the wrap, but this time fold it up all the way to meet the top edge. Gently press the wrap against the log and roll the log away from you toward the top edge.

•

Cut two 3-inch (7.5 cm) pieces of kitchen twine. Twist one end of the plastic wrap like a candy wrapper and secure with the twine. Repeat with the other end. You now have a cylinder of tablea—a chocolate torchon!

•

Rest the log for about 10 minutes at room temperature, or until hardened to a clay-like texture. (Don't let it sit for more than 15 minutes, or it will get too hard to work with.) Unwrap the log and put it on a cutting board. Using a sharp knife, trim the rounded ends if you like (but keep them—they're good to use), and cut the log into about 10 coins, ¾ inch (2 cm) thick.

•

Arrange the coins in the same log shape as before and wrap in parchment (or decorative paper if it's a gift). Store in a cool, dry place for up to 1 year. If a white powder appears on the surface, don't worry, it's not mold—just a natural chemical reaction as the fat and sugar bloom from exposure to moisture.

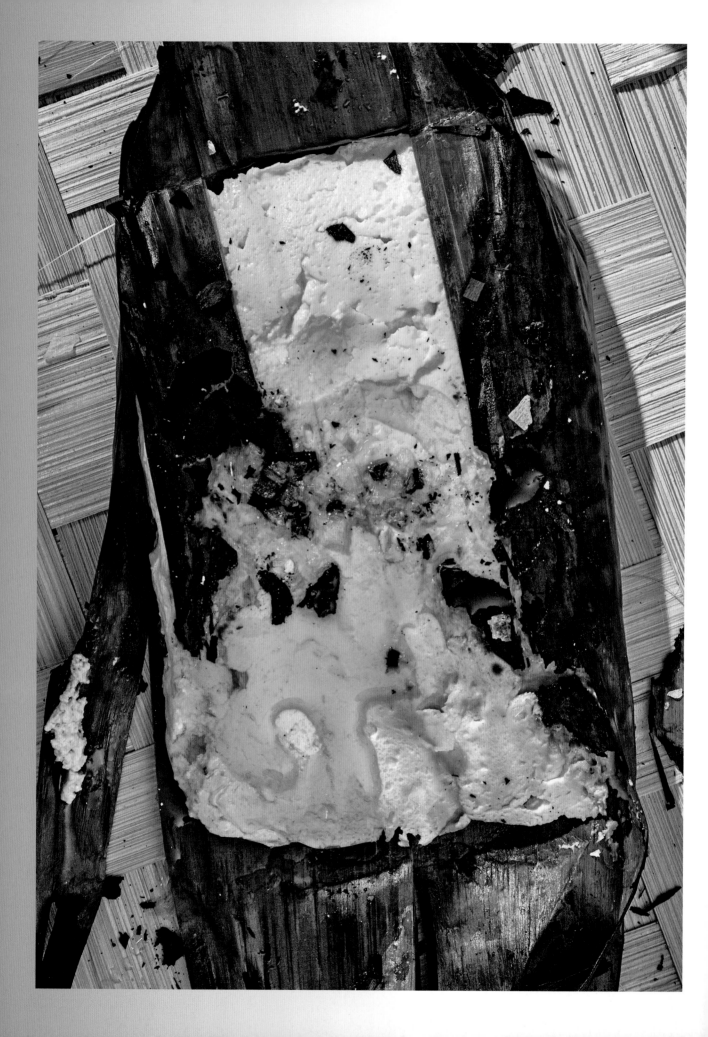

In the Oaxacan town of Ocotlán de Morelos, at the food stall La Cocina de Frida, the chef Beatriz Vázquez Gómez wears flowers in her hair and draws her eyebrows into a single arc, in honor of the artist Frida Kahlo. Beatriz—or Frida, as her customers call her—is famous for her mole and enfrijoladas, and often throws in a gift with the meal: once a blackened, super-ripe plantain that burst open with steam, basking on a bed of orange-pink rose petals; and, on my last visit, a round of requesón, a freshly made cheese so soft and delicate, I almost cried.

It reminded me so much of kesong puti, a Filipino cheese traditionally made with carabao (water buffalo) milk and curdled with calamansi. Frida tucks her requesón into a corn-husk pouch and sears it on the grill; I was inspired to do the same, only with banana leaves, to infuse the cheese with their green scent and a ghosting of smoke. If you can get your hands on raw cow's milk, goat's milk, or buffalo's milk, the taste will be deeper and tangier. Spread kesong puti on toast and top it with flaky sea salt and a drizzle of olive oil or honey, or make it part of a cheese plate, with a daub of Smoky Pepper Jelly–Mango Jam (page 203).

CHARRED KESONG PUTI
KAY •sung pooh• TEH
BANANA LEAF–SCENTED FRESH FARM CHEESE MAKES ABOUT 1 CUP (230 G)

4 cups (960 ml) milk of your choice (see headnote)

½ cup (120 ml) heavy cream

¾ teaspoon kosher salt

3 tablespoons (45 ml) fresh lemon juice

½ banana leaf (see headnote for Suman, page 229), fresh or frozen, cut into two 10 by 10-inch (25 by 25 cm) sheets

Flaky sea salt, for finishing

Olive oil, for finishing

Put the milk, heavy cream, and kosher salt in a large heat-safe mixing bowl. Fill a saucepan or pot with water 1 inch (2.5 cm) deep. Create a double boiler by setting the bowl over the pot. Bring the water to a boil over high heat, then reduce to medium low. With a spatula, stir the mixture occasionally for 15 to 20 minutes to help bring the milk up to temperature (around 212°F/100°C, if you have a thermometer).

•

Remove the bowl from the heat and add the lemon juice. Let rest at room temperature for 1 hour. As the mixture cools, it will separate into curds and whey.

•

Set up a strainer lined with cheesecloth (or a large, clean, thin dishcloth or scrap of T-shirt) over a bowl. Pour the curds and whey over the cheesecloth to drain. Discard the liquid in the bowl. At this point, the fresh, soft, creamy cheese is ready to eat.

•

Lay out the two banana-leaf sheets. Spoon half the cheese into the middle of one sheet and shape it into a rectangle, leaving at least a 2-inch (4 cm) margin on the sides. Take the top edge of the leaf and fold lengthwise to cover the cheese. Repeat with the bottom edge and fold in the sides, pressing to seal. Then repeat with the remaining cheese and the second sheet. You can refrigerate these banana-leaf packets for up to 2 days and move on to the next step when ready to serve.

•

Heat a cast-iron or other heavy-bottomed skillet over medium high. Once hot, add the 2 banana-leaf packets, folded side down, and cover with a lid so the smoke of the charring leaves will infuse the cheese. Sear for about 6 minutes, until the bottoms of the packets are half blackened. Remove the packets with a spatula.

•

Serve warm, unfolding at the table to reveal the cheese. Finish with flaky sea salt and a drizzle of olive oil.

Siya: Decolonizing THE LANGUAGE

(TALKING WITH GEENA ROCERO)

There is no he or she in Tagalog: siya is the word we use when speaking of another person, without specifying gender. Husband and wife alike are asawa, or the poetic kabiyak– your other half. So why, then, do we describe ourselves as Filipino or Filipina? It's a colonial inheritance, much as the name of the Philippines itself, the Philip in question being the sixteenth-century king of Spain, to whom the islands were a mere possession. With the Spanish came their language and the masculine/feminine suffixes -o and -a, embedding a gender binary in the most fundamental of words, what we use to identify ourselves and where we come from.

Still, it's worth remembering that the decision to call ourselves Filipino was initially an act of rebellion against a colonial caste system that discriminated by skin color, imposing taxes on native negritos (descendants of the Aetas, the earliest settlers of the Philippines) and indios (descendants of the Malays who migrated thousands of years ago) but none on blancos (whites). Under Spanish rule, the only people officially recognized as Filipino were those of "pure" Spanish descent who happened to be born in the islands. Not until the late nineteenth century were we able to claim that name.

As a California-born member of the diaspora, I call myself Filipinx, replacing the masculine/feminine suffixes with a neutral x, following the model of Latinx, a term introduced in the United States in the early twenty-first century as a way to break free of gendered language. This is what feels right for me, and I don't impose it on others. It's an act of solidarity, not only with those who, like me, identify as queer and thus stand outside expected binaries, but with my ancestors who took on "Filipino" as a way to unite against an oppressor, and with our culture's long tradition of embracing and celebrating gender fluidity–a tradition that my friend Geena Rocero, the trans supermodel and activist, has studied and graciously agreed to share her thoughts on here.

Geena, me, and Becca McCharen-Tran, founder of Chromat, celebrating the Playboy issue with Geena on the cover as the first trans Asian American and Pacific Islander playmate.

When I moved to New York City in 2005, I'd never seen snow and it was so cold. I called my mom and she taught me how to make sinigang over the phone. It was the first time I'd ever cooked, and it made me feel grounded: This is who I am, this is part of my culture. I needed that, because I was trying to pursue my dream of becoming a fashion model, and I wasn't out as trans—I had to survive by pretending, by being read as a cisgender person. I couldn't just *be*.

Before I came out, I took a trip to the island of Koh Lipe in the far south of Thailand and met an Italian anthropologist on a boat. When I told him that I was from the Philippines, he said, "Oh, you're Austronesian." Back home, I started researching our Austronesian ancestry, which goes back thousands of years. I learned that close to 400 million people speak Austronesian languages, and that more than half of those languages, like Tagalog, are gender-neutral.

The more I studied precolonial history, the more I wanted to drink in that knowledge—of all the ways our ancient, egalitarian culture recognized, accommodated, and honored people without the restrictions of Western constructs of gender. We've never said *he* or *she*; we only use the gender-neutral *siya*. I imagined the Spanish Catholic priests arriving and setting eyes on our katalonans and babaylans, nongender-conforming

The trans advocate and model Geena Rocero with her Playboy bunny-shaped Biko (page 233).

animistic healers who served as conduits to the spirit world and were advisers to kings and queens. They were the first ones shut down: That's too weird, that's too dangerous.

By now I've spent half my life in the Philippines, half in the United States. I think I had to leave the Philippines to fully know it; I had to decolonize my own understanding of who we are. I'm aware of how we've been complicit in a more insidious form of colonialism, with our eagerness to assimilate to Western culture, and how we've supported ideologies that privilege fair skin, from buying whitening lotion to telling kids, "Don't go play in the sun." Even now, when you go to touristy spots, they still say, "When Ferdinand Magellan discovered the Philippines . . ." As if nothing had happened there before!

When I turned thirty, I felt ready to show my true self, hoping it would help others to do the same. First I came out to my friends and colleagues, and then, in a TED Talk, I told my story to the world. I've been telling it ever since.

The paradox is that when I go to Southeast Asia to speak about trans rights, it's seen as a Western concept. Yet I'm Southeast Asian myself, I speak a gender-neutral native language, and gender fluidity has always been part of our culture. I carry that knowledge with me.

We've always been here.

Sweets are the family inheritance: I have so many recipes, I couldn't fit them all in these pages. My lola specialized in Ensaymadas (page 227), spiral pastries golden with eggs and flaking at the touch, a signature of her home province of Pampanga. It was one of her best-kept secrets, revealed to no one outside the family however hard they begged—until now. (Forgive me, Lola!) Then there's my lola's sister, Amalia Hizon Mercado, who was famous for her kakanin, treats made of sticky rice, which she started out selling at drugstores. Her daughter, Teresita Moran, expanded the family repertoire to Western-style cakes, keeping them soft and airy, and in 1979, the two of them opened a small bakery in Quezon City. If you're Filipino, you know it: Red Ribbon Bakeshop, today a brand-name chain owned by the fast-food behemoth Jollibee, with hundreds of outlets in the Philippines and the United States. It's a lot to live up to, but I'm doing my best.

KAKANIN, PASTRIES,

AND SWEETS

**T**aisan means "whetstone" in Kapampangan—a somewhat ironic name for this cloud of a cake, which is a slab in shape but so light it's almost ready to take to the air. It's a great introduction to chiffon, without the trickiness of cutting layers.

Once, far from home and my trusty stand mixer, I had to whip the egg whites by hand. It took forever and was a major workout, but that reminded me of how much labor goes into this cake, and made me extra careful when folding the egg whites into the batter, so as not to waste all that effort.

Think of this cake as a canvas to adorn as you wish. Add crushed dried rose petals, freeze-dried raspberry powder, or finely ground Earl Grey tea leaves to the dusting sugar for different shades of flavor. Or you can top each sugared loaf with finely grated cheddar for a salty-sweet finish.

TAISAN *tie • SAHN* CHIFFON LOAF CAKE

MAKES 2 LOAVES (8½ INCHES BY 4½ INCHES/21.5 CM BY 11 CM EACH)

1 cup plus 2 tablespoons (280 g) all-purpose flour, plus 1 tablespoon for dusting
¾ cup (170 g) granulated sugar, plus extra for dusting
1½ teaspoons baking powder
½ teaspoon kosher salt
3 large eggs, cold, separated into whites and yolks
2 tablespoons pineapple juice
1 teaspoon freshly squeezed lemon juice
3 tablespoons (40 g) unsalted butter, melted and cooled
Crushed dried rose petals or freeze-dried raspberry powder to taste, for dusting (optional)

Preheat the oven to 350°F (175°C).

•

In a large mixing bowl, sift together the flour, ¼ cup (55 g) of the sugar, the baking powder, and salt.

•

Take a separate bowl and whisk together the egg yolks, pineapple juice, ½ teaspoon of the lemon juice, and ½ cup (120 ml) water. (The pineapple is there for a touch of acidity, per Lola; you won't really taste it.) Add the egg yolk mixture to the dry ingredients, whisking until smooth.

•

In a stand mixer with a whisk attachment, beat together the egg whites on low until frothy, then whisk in the remaining ½ teaspoon lemon juice and ½ cup (115 g) sugar and increase the speed to high. Continue to beat until stiff peaks form. The peaks should be shiny and hold their shape when you stop the mixer and pull out the whisk.

•

Using a rubber spatula, gently fold one-third of the whipped egg whites into the egg-yolk mixture. This is the trickiest part: Go slowly so as not to lose any of the volume you've added to the egg whites. Repeat in two more steps with the remaining egg whites, adding half the mixture at a time.

•

Use 1 tablespoon of the melted butter and a pastry brush to paint the inside of two 5 by 9-inch (12 by 23-cm) loaf pans. Add a tablespoon of the flour to one pan and tap the sides to distribute the flour evenly over the buttered walls. When one pan is done, tip the excess flour into the next.

•

Fill each pan with about 1½ inches (4 cm) of the batter. (It will rise to about 2 inches [5 cm].) Bake in the preheated oven on the middle rack for 30 to 35 minutes, until a cake tester inserted in the center comes out clean. Rest in the loaf pans for about two minutes, then run a butter knife along the sides of each loaf and tip over onto a rack to cool.

•

After cooling, brush each loaf on all sides—top, sides, and bottom—generously with the remaining 2 tablespoons melted butter, and dust all over with sugar (if using petals or raspberry powder, mix with sugar before dusting, to taste). Wrap in wax paper to save for later, keeping the cakes moist. Serve within 3 days and cut into ¾-inch-thick (2 cm) slices.

The sixteenth-century Venetian scholar Antonio Pigafetta, who sailed along with Magellan on the first circumnavigation of the globe, recorded that the king of Palawan—the westernmost island of the Philippines—greeted them with food "made only of rice," including "sugar-loaves" that were likely an early form of bibingka, a tender cake of rice flour (and thus naturally gluten free). Sadly, Pigafetta offered no hints of taste or texture, but two centuries later, the Spanish Jesuit historian Juan J. Delgado wrote that bibingka was as fluffy as French bread and outstripped it in whiteness, and was "excellent" when eaten with Tsokolate (hot chocolate; page 277).

That fluffiness: I'd say it's closer to a soufflé, delicate and airy, with just a touch of chew. The cake is traditionally baked atop banana leaves in a clay pot, with hot coals above and below, which isn't particularly convenient for home cooks. Here you tuck the banana leaves into a cast-iron skillet—if you cut off the ribs first, they'll be more malleable—then pour the batter in. As the leaves char, they infuse the cake with smoke, along with a fresh, grassy scent.

About halfway through baking, you pop the cake out of the oven and press in slices of salted egg, available at most Asian markets (or you can make your own; page 190). It's a sly surprise, funk amidst the sweetness, but if you can't find this ingredient, the cake will still be delicious without it. At the end, I like to throw the skillet on a very hot open grill, to singe the leaves further, or else blacken the edges with a kitchen torch, for more smokiness.

BIBINGKA *bee • BING • kah*
BANANA LEAF-ROASTED RICE CAKE WITH SALTED EGG AND CHEESE
MAKES 2 CAKES (8 INCHES/20 CM EACH)

4 large banana leaves (see headnote for Suman, page 229), fresh or frozen

½ cup (1 stick/115 g) unsalted butter, melted

8 ounces (225 g) cream cheese, softened, or Kesong Puti (page 207)

½ cup (30 g) finely grated Parmesan or finely shredded sharp white Cheddar

2¾ cups (440 g) plus 2 tablespoons rice flour

2 cups (400 g) granulated sugar

2 tablespoons baking powder

2 cups (480 ml) unsweetened, full-fat coconut milk

4 large eggs

2 Salted Eggs (page 190) or store-bought salted duck eggs, peeled and thinly sliced crosswise into coins (not ovals)

Preheat the oven to 325°F (165°C) and put a rack in the middle position.

•

Take two 8-inch (20 cm) cast-iron skillets or similar pans and lay 2 banana leaves in each pan, allowing the leaves to overlap at the center and come up the sides. (If a leaf rips, use extra to fill in any gaps.) With scissors, cut off any overhang that extends more than ½ inch (12 mm) beyond the lip of each skillet. Brush 1 tablespoon of the melted butter along the leaf-covered bottom and sides of each pan, reserving the remaining butter for the cakes.

•

In a small bowl, mix together the cream cheese and Parmesan.

•

In a medium bowl, whisk together the rice flour, sugar, and baking powder.

•

In a large bowl, whisk together the coconut milk, eggs, and the remaining 6 tablespoons melted butter. Add about a third of the rice flour mixture and whisk to combine. Repeat twice with the remaining thirds, until the wet and dry ingredients are completely melded.

→

Pour half the cake batter into each buttered skillet and smooth until evenly distributed. Bake the cakes for 30 minutes.

•

While the cakes are baking, shape the cream cheese mixture into 10 logs about ½ inch (12 mm) thick and 2 to 3 inches (5 to 7.5 cm) long.

•

Remove the cakes from the oven. The edges will be set, but the surface at the center will still be puffy and not fully cooked through. Working quickly so the cakes don't cool too much, top each with a few coins of salted egg, arranged at the center, then add 5 cream-cheese logs, radiating outward from the center of each cake, like the arms of a starfish. (The logs will sink a little into the surface of the cake, but should not get swallowed up.)

•

Return the cakes to the oven and continue baking for 10 minutes, then raise the temperature to 425°F (220°C) and bake for another 10 to 15 minutes, until the tops turn deep gold and the banana leaves are slightly charred. The cakes should be fully set. Each cake's surface should curve slightly outward, in a low dome, and spring back when touched.

•

If you have a small propane kitchen torch, put the cakes on a metal tray— there should be no plastic nearby—then carefully turn on the torch with the nozzle pointed away from you. Wait for the flame to turn blue and start to hiss. Sweep the flame over the surface of the bibingka, being sure not to linger in one spot for too long, then aim the torch around the sides to singe the overhanging flaps of the banana leaves.

•

Let cool for 10 minutes before slicing. Serve warm or at room temperature.

My lola made this chiffon cake—akin to Taisan (page 213) but layered with fresh, ultra-ripe mango, and a Red Ribbon Bakeshop classic—for many birthdays, in many shapes: sheets, rounds, dramatic tiers. My mom made it, too, and devoted serious time to decorating, drawing from a suitcase full of vintage piping tips and pillars. My version is humbler: I adorn it with nothing more than sunflower petals, a nod to my mom's other great hobby, floral arranging. (Be sure to use organic flowers that haven't been exposed to pesticides, or look for other edible flowers at the market or online—or be like my mom and freestyle your own decoration.)

You want the ripest fruit, preferably a Manila mango from the Philippines (which the government has officially christened the Manila Super Mango) or a Mexican Ataulfo (also known as champagne mango), descended from Manilas brought over by Spanish galleons. The whipped-cream frosting gets a little cream cheese, to keep it from deflating and give the cake a touch of salt. (Note: There's no sugar in the frosting, because I think the sweetness of the chiffon and the mango is enough, but you're welcome to adjust to your taste.) And I add a swirl of turmeric to half the cake batter, for a tie-dye effect. It brings a subtle earthiness—and is good for you, too.

MANGO–TURMERIC CHIFFON CAKE

SERVES 8

2 tablespoons unsalted butter, melted

2 cups (250 g) all-purpose flour, plus extra for dusting

10 medium eggs, cold, separated into whites and yolks

Juice of ½ lemon

2 cups (400 g) granulated sugar

1 teaspoon vanilla extract

2 tablespoons cornstarch

1 tablespoon powdered turmeric

1 very ripe mango

2 tablespoons cream cheese, cold

1 pint (480 ml) heavy whipping cream, cold

Food-safe sunflower petals or other cake decorations of your choice (optional)

Preheat the oven to 350°F (175°C). Take out two 8-inch (20 cm) round cake layer tins. (Or a 10 by 12-inch/25 by 30.5-cm baking tray, if you'd prefer to make a single sheet cake.) Brush the inside of the tins with the melted butter, then dust with flour, gently shaking and tapping the tins so the flour infiltrates each corner. Remove any excess flour—which might otherwise clump on the surface of the cake—by flipping the tins over and tapping a few times.

In a stand mixer with a whisk attachment, beat together the egg whites on low until frothy, then whisk in the lemon juice and 1 cup (200 g) of the sugar and increase the speed to high. Continue to beat until stiff peaks form. The peaks should be shiny and hold their shape when you stop the mixer and pull out the whisk.

→

MANGO-TURMERIC CHIFFON CAKE CONTINUED

In a separate large mixing bowl, whisk together the yolks, ¼ cup (60 ml) water, and the vanilla extract until creamy and smooth. Add the remaining 1 cup (200 g) sugar. With a clean whisk, in another mixing bowl, whisk together the cornstarch and 2 cups all-purpose flour, breaking down any lumps. Switch to a rubber spatula and add the flour mixture to the yolk mixture.

•

Gently fold the whipped egg whites into the flour-yolk mixture, adding only one-third of the whites at a time and being careful not to overmix. (You don't want to lose the air bubbles you just worked into the whites, which will keep the cake light and fluffy.)

•

Divide the cake batter evenly between two bowls. In one bowl, gently stir in the turmeric until suffused and golden. In the buttered and floured cake tins, alternate pouring in a cup or ladle of plain batter then golden batter, to make a "tie dye" design, until you've used all the batter.

•

Bake for about 25 minutes, until a toothpick or cake tester slipped into the center comes out clean. The cakes will have browned and risen. Run a butter knife along the edges of the tins before carefully inverting over a cooling rack. Let rest for 20 minutes, or until completely cool.

•

While the cake layers are cooling, cut the mango into slices about ⅛ inch (3 mm) thick, then prepare the icing. In a mixer with a whisk attachment, start by whisking the cream cheese until fluffy. Slowly pour in the heavy cream and whisk for 6 to 8 minutes, until whipped and airy.

•

Once the cakes are cooled, arrange the first cake layer on a serving plate with the flat bottom side facing up. Tuck strips of parchment paper under the circumference of the cake, to protect the plate from any wayward icing. Mash one-half of the mango slices in a bowl and mix in one-third of the icing, then spread evenly with a spatula over the top of the cake. (For a simpler cake, just ice the top, then lay the mango slices whole on the iced surface, or else save all the mango for decorating the second layer.)

•

Stack the second cake layer, bottom side up, on the first. With the two layers now merged into a single cake, use a spatula to smear and smooth the remaining icing over the top and sides. Remove and discard the parchment strips. Adorn the cake with the remaining mango slices and fresh sunflower petals—or decorate any way you please.

In my family, making turon—a sweet incarnation of the Filipino version of a spring roll (see Lumpia Shanghai, page 107)—was always a group effort, the recipe easy even for a little kid: Take a banana, peel and slice it lengthwise, then lay it on a lumpia wrapper, give it a whisper of sugar, roll, and fry. My mom guarded the hot oil and handed out the bronzed lumpia as soon as they were cool enough to eat. She let us eat as much as we wanted, because it was fruit, after all.

For big parties, though, we'd order from the caterer and put out foil trays of turon lacquered in caramel, like the cream puffs in a towering croquembouche.

I wanted to recreate that here, with a pinch of salt to tame the sweetness. And I added mochi, the chewy Japanese cake made of pounded glutinous rice, remembering the thrill of eating it hot off the grill one night in snowy Hokkaido, crisped on the outside but still soft at the center.

There are a couple of nerdy cooking techniques here that I love: a shortcut to mochi, via a quick blast in the microwave, and caramelizing directly in the fryer à la minute (to order). It's hypnotic to watch the sugar melt into the oil, bubbling up and changing color—like staring into a lava lamp. But please be careful: the caramel makes the pot extra-extra-hot.

SALTED CARAMELIZED TURON WITH MOCHI *Too•ROHN*

MAKES 12 TURON

⅓ cup (50 g) glutinous rice flour

2 tablespoons granulated sugar

4 ripe saba bananas (see headnote for Beef Giniling, page 29) or 2 ripe plantains

1 large egg, separated into white and yolk (yolk may be discarded or used for another recipe)

12 lumpia or spring-roll wrappers (8 by 8 inches/20 by 20 cm each), thawed if frozen

2 tablespoons brown sugar, plus (optional) ¼ cup (50 g)

2 cups canola or other neutral oil

Flaky sea salt

Ice cream, for serving (optional)

To make the mochi: In a microwave-safe small bowl, whisk together the glutinous rice flour, ¼ cup (60 ml) water, and the granulated sugar. Microwave on high for 1 minute and immediately stir with a small nonstick rubber spatula. (If using the stove, heat the mixture in a nonstick pan over medium high for 1 minute, then cook for 2 to 3 minutes while constantly stirring with the spatula.) The dough will come together in a semi-translucent ball. If it feels too soft, let cool in the refrigerator for 10 to 15 minutes; this will make the mochi easier to handle.

•

Cut each saba banana lengthwise into 3 planks, roughly 1 inch wide by 4 inches long (2.5 by 10 cm) and ¼ inch (6 mm) thick. (If using plantains, cut crosswise into halves, then lengthwise into planks.)

•

Return to the mochi. Wet your hands and a pair of kitchen shears so the mochi doesn't stick. With the shears, snip the mochi into 12 logs that are about ½ inch wide by 3 inches long (7.5 by 12 cm). Set aside on a plate.

→

SALTED CARAMELIZED TURON WITH MOCHI CONTINUED

In a small bowl, whisk about 3 tablespoons (45 ml) water with the egg white.

•

Take a stack of thawed lumpia skins and slowly peel one off the top, using your fingertips and pulling two corners at a time so they don't rip. (If you do get any rips, it's not a big deal; just arrange the lumpia skin so the rips are closest to you, and they will get rolled up into the turon.) Drape a damp paper towel over the remaining skins so they don't dry out.

•

Arrange a lumpia skin on a work surface, angled in a diamond shape. Lay one banana plank down the center and dust with about ½ teaspoon of the brown sugar, using your fingertips. Put a log of mochi on top.

•

Take a little water, moisten your fingertips, and press along the outer edge of the lumpia skin. Lift up the bottom corner of the lumpia skin and fold it up and over the filling, making sure there's no air between the filling and the wrapper.

•

Bring the left and right corners of the wrapper toward the center, pulling and folding them tightly over the filling. At this point, the lumpia skin should look like an open envelope. Brush the remaining upper triangle of the wrapper with the egg-white wash. Then tightly roll the turon away from you toward the top corner. Seal the wrapper closed.

•

Repeat with all 12 lumpia skins.

•

Heat the oil in a 2-quart (2 L) saucepan—you want to leave enough room for the oil to bubble up without brimming over—until around 375°F (190°C). A deep-fry thermometer is a helpful tool here, but if you don't have one, you can test the temperature by tearing off a scrap of a lumpia skin and carefully slipping it into the hot oil, which should start sizzling right away. (You want the oil to be hot enough to crisp the outside of the turon quickly, otherwise too much of it will soak in and make the turon soggy.)

•

If you'd like to caramelize the turon, pour 1 tablespoon of the remaining brown sugar into the hot oil. Once the sugar has melted, put 3 pieces of turon into the fryer. (Adding food to the oil causes the temperature to drop, so you don't want to put in too many at once.) Using a spoon and working quickly, baste each turon with the liquefied sugar, turning to coat both sides.

•

After about 6 minutes, when the turon are golden brown, remove with tongs and rest them on a metal cooling rack. (Do not use paper towels—they will stick to the molten caramel!) While the turon are still hot, sprinkle each with a pinch of sea salt; the flakes will get embedded in the caramel as it cools and hardens. Repeat with the remaining turon in batches of three at a time, waiting for 2 minutes between batches to let the oil come back up to 375°F (190°C).

•

If you'd prefer not to caramelize—which is fine: the turon are also delicious as is!—skip the step of adding sugar to the hot oil and go ahead and put the turon in the fryer in batches of 3 at a time. Fry until golden brown, then set on paper towels to drain and cool for at least 5 minutes, as the filling gets wicked hot!

•

Serve warm on their own or à la mode with coconut, vanilla, ube (purple yam), or your favorite ice cream.

Wrapped in foil and all colors of cellophane, Food for the Gods was Lola's Christmas gift to us grandkids, as if we were little immortals deserving of such grace. (Since her death, my mom has carried on the tradition, and hopes one day to pass it on to us.) These bars, like Lola's, come out golden and dense, loaded with butter, molasses, dates gone almost gooey in the oven and so lovely to chew, and walnuts with their luscious oils and reliable crunch. It's fruitcake reincarnated as fudge, and more tender. For extra nuttiness, I sometimes mix buckwheat flour with all-purpose (¼ cup [30 g] buckwheat to ½ cup [65 g] AP).

FOOD FOR THE GODS
MOLASSES, DATE, AND WALNUT SQUARES

MAKES 16 SQUARES (2 INCHES/5 CM EACH)

½ cup (1 stick/115 g) unsalted butter, softened at room temperature, plus 1 tablespoon to grease the pan

¾ cup (95 g) all-purpose flour, plus 2 teaspoons to dust the pan

¼ teaspoon baking soda

⅛ teaspoon ground cinnamon

¼ teaspoon kosher salt

1 cup (220 g) packed light brown sugar

2 large eggs

3 tablespoons (45 ml) molasses

1 cup (145 g) dates, pitted and cut into ½-inch (12 mm) dice

1 cup (120 g) walnuts, chopped

1 tablespoon breadcrumbs

Preheat the oven to 350°F (175°C) and put a rack in the middle position.

•

Grease the bottom and sides of an 8 by 8-inch (20 by 20 cm) square baking dish with 1 tablespoon butter, using your hands or a pastry brush. Dust with the 2 teaspoons flour, tapping the pan so the flour sticks to the butter.

•

In a medium mixing bowl, combine the remaining ¾ cup (95 g) flour, the baking soda, cinnamon, and salt. Whisk to sift and combine these dry ingredients, getting rid of any lumps.

•

In a large mixing bowl, cream the softened butter and brown sugar together with a whisk. Add the eggs and molasses, whisking to meld. Switch to a rubber spatula and mix in the dates, walnuts, and breadcrumbs.

•

Add the flour mixture to the batter and fold to combine. Pour the batter into the greased and floured baking dish and flatten with the spatula into an even layer.

•

Bake for 30 to 40 minutes on the middle rack. (You're looking for a brownie-like texture; check doneness by gently inserting a toothpick or skewer, which should come out clean.) Remove from the oven and let cool on the countertop.

•

Cut into 2-inch (5 cm) squares and serve. Store leftovers in an airtight container at room temperature for a few days or in the refrigerator for up to 1 week.

The original ensaïmadas are the pride of Mallorca, an island off the coast of Spain: pastries coiled like snail shells, rich with eggs and flaky from a smear of lard (called saïm in Mallorquí, a dialect of Catalan). The Spanish brought them to the Philippines, where local bakers slowly, slyly, upped the level of decadence, folding in more fat and eggs—one recipe I saw called for 60 yolks just to make two dozen ensaymadas!—and layering butter, sugar, and cheese on top. My mom remembers Lola handing them out every Christmas morning when they lived in Pampanga, a province especially famed for its sunny yellow ensaymadas, as tender as brioche. Traditionally the pastry is topped with queso de bola, Edam cheese, which is itself a Christmas perennial, a globe of it sealed in red wax always adorning the festive table. (Edam in turn came to the Philippines from Dutch sailors skirmishing with the Spanish in the seventeenth century—because food history is world history.) I use Cheddar and Parmesan instead, to add that little pang of salt.

ENSAYMADAS
ehn • seh • MAH • dahs
BUTTER PASTRY with CRUNCHY SUGAR and CHEESE **MAKES 12 PASTRIES**

1 packet active dry yeast (about 2¼ teaspoons)

½ cup (100 g) plus 6½ teaspoons (25 g) granulated sugar

½ cup lukewarm milk (around 105°F/40°C)

6 large egg yolks

3 cups (375 g) all-purpose flour

1½ teaspoons kosher salt

½ cup (1 stick/115 g) unsalted butter, at room temperature, plus 4 tablespoons (½ stick/ 55 g), melted and slightly cooled

Nonstick vegetable oil spray

½ cup (50 g) grated Parmesan cheese, plus more for finishing

¼ cup (30 g) sharp Cheddar, Microplaned or grated, for finishing

In the bowl of a stand mixer, use a spoon to combine the yeast, ½ teaspoon of the sugar, and 3 tablespoons (45 ml) lukewarm water. Cover the bowl with a kitchen towel and let the mixture sit for about 10 minutes, until foamy, a sign that the yeast is active and feeding on the sugars, producing carbon dioxide.

•

Whisk the milk, 3 egg yolks, ¾ cup (95 g) of the flour, and ¼ cup (50 g) of the sugar into the yeast mixture until smooth. Cover again with the towel and let sit for 1 to 1½ hours, until very bubbly.

•

To this bubbly mixture, add the salt, remaining 3 egg yolks, ¼ cup (50 g) sugar, and 2¼ cups (280 g) flour. Fit the stand mixer with the dough hook and mix the dough on medium low for 6 to 8 minutes, until smooth and elastic. (It should be sticky.) Add the room temperature butter 1 tablespoon at a time, mixing each tablespoon for about 1 minute, until completely incorporated, before adding the next. At this point the dough should stretch easily. →

ENSAYMADAS CONTINUED

Cover the bowl with a towel and let the dough rise in a warm, draft-free area for about 2 hours, until doubled in size. (If making the dough in advance—you can make it up to 12 hours before baking—do not let it rise; instead, cover with plastic wrap and chill in the refrigerator, and 2 hours before baking let it come to room temperature, still covered, and rise until doubled in size.)

• Preheat the oven to 325°F (165°C). Take two 6-cup muffin pans and coat the cups with nonstick vegetable oil spray, then line with 4-inch (10 cm) squares of parchment paper.

• Punch down the dough and divide into 12 pieces. Take 1 piece and cover the rest with a towel. Roll out the piece of dough into a 14 by 3-inch (37 by 7.5 cm) rectangle. Brush lightly with the melted butter and sprinkle with about 2 teaspoons of the Parmesan. Using a wooden dowel ½ inch (12 mm) in diameter, roll the dough so that it wraps around the dowel, pulling toward you at an angle. Slide the dough off the dowel in tube form; it will scrunch up a bit. Stretch the tube of dough lengthwise until it's 8 to 10 inches (20 to 25 cm) long and coil it around itself to make a snail-shell shape. Put the coil in a muffin cup.

• Repeat with the remaining pieces of dough until all 12 muffin cups are filled. Cover the muffin pans with plastic wrap and let the dough rise for 25 to 35 minutes, until puffy; it should spring back when gently pressed.

• Bake the ensaymadas for 20 to 25 minutes, until slightly domed and golden brown. While the ensaymadas are still hot, brush generously with the remaining melted butter, then sprinkle with the remaining 6 teaspoons sugar, more Parmesan, and the Cheddar.

• Serve immediately, or, when cooled, wrap individually in wax paper or cellophane as gifts. To reheat, pop the wrapped ensaymadas into the microwave for 30 seconds on high—the wrapper will help melt the cheese and leave the buns soft and steamy.

In the Philippines, rice is endless in its gifts, a soothing, earthy backdrop to the salt and sour of a meal, and then the sweet stickiness in dessert. (Sometimes I think we can turn rice into anything.) Before colonial times, kakanin, sticky-rice treats, were made as divine offerings, to please and appease the gods. Suman is one of the simplest, requiring little more than glutinous rice, coconut milk, sugar, and a wrap of banana leaves. It looks like a gift. But the leaves aren't just pretty packaging: They're an active ingredient, steeping in the water as the suman cooks, so that the rice takes on their deep scent and a flavor almost indistinguishable from fragrance. (Banana leaves are fine fresh or frozen; just be sure to rinse them and then warm them over an open flame on the stove–they may appear slightly ashy when first unpacked, but the heat will release their oils and restore their deep green color.) I add black rice to the suman, for a touch of purple– a little surprise when it's unfolded at the table.

SUMAN *SOO•mahn*
STICKY RICE STEAMED IN BANANA LEAVES MAKES 25 SUMAN

2 cups (380 g) glutinous ("sweet") rice

¼ cup (50 g) black rice

1½ cups (360 ml) unsweetened, full-fat coconut milk

½ cup (100 g) granulated sugar, plus more for topping (optional)

1 teaspoon kosher salt

1 package (1 pound/455 g) banana leaves, fresh or frozen

Latik (page 193), fresh-cut mango, grated mature coconut, Toasted Soybean Powder (page 241), crushed pistachios, and/or Coco Jam (page 201), for topping (optional)

Put the glutinous rice in a mixing bowl and rinse under cool running water in the sink. Drain and rinse again, repeating several times. When the water runs clear, drain, add the black rice, and cover with about 4 cups (960 ml) water. Let the rice soak for about 1 hour, then drain and discard the water.

•

Heat a 4-quart (3.8 L) saucepan over high. Add the coconut milk, sugar, and salt. Stir to combine and bring up to a boil. Once the coconut milk is boiling, add the drained soaked rice. Continue to cook, stirring occasionally, until the pot returns to a boil, then drop the heat to medium low. Cook, stirring occasionally for another 15 minutes or until the rice has soaked up most of the coconut syrup and looks like risotto, but is still al dente. (Taste it to be sure.)

•

Transfer the rice mixture to a flat plate or tray and cool. Carefully wash the banana leaves, taking care not to tear them, then wipe each side dry. Using kitchen shears, cut about twenty-five 10 by 12-inch (25 by 30.5 cm) pieces and set aside. (If you wind up with a few smaller pieces, you can combine them to make the necessary size, making sure there's enough overlap that none of the filling is exposed; and if there are any rips, just arrange the leaves so that the rips get rolled up when wrapping the suman.)

•

Then cut about fifty 10 by ½-inch (25 cm by 12 mm) pieces of banana leaf to use like string. You could use kitchen twine instead, but I like the natural appearance of using leaves for both wrapping and tying.

→

SUMAN CONTINUED

Take one of the 10 by 12-inch (25 by 30.5 cm) banana leaves and lay it on a work surface, with the shorter side facing you. Scoop about 2½ tablespoons (55 g) of the rice mixture and spread it out on the leaf in a log shape, about 1 inch (2.5 cm) from the leaf's bottom edge and with an open, even margin on either side. Take the bottom edge and roll it tightly over the rice, turning the log over two or three times. Then fold the left and right sides of the leaf inward, flattening the fold neatly all the way to the end, so both ends rest snug against the rice log, making a taut packet. Keep rolling all the way to the end, and rest the rolled suman on its seam to keep it closed.

•

Take one piece of the banana-leaf "string" and loop it once around one end of the rolled suman, about ¾ inch (2 cm) from the end. Slightly pull the string, loop it once more, and tie it twice to make a secure square knot. Repeat at the other end, then rest the tied suman on a plate. Repeat the rolling and tying process with the remaining filling and leaves.

•

In a 4-quart (3.8 L) stockpot, lay the suman seam side down, stacking them so they all fit. Cover the stack with an extra piece of banana leaf and then add a small plate as a weight, to help keep the suman submerged in the boiling water. Add water to an inch (2.5 cm) above the stack, then put the lid on the pot and turn the heat up to a boil. Once the water is boiling, drop the heat to a low simmer and cook for about 1 hour.

•

Carefully remove the small plate and banana leaf cover—they will be hot; use tongs—and then drain some of the hot water from the pot over the sink. Remove the suman with tongs and let rest for a few minutes, then serve warm. Unfold the banana-leaf wrap to add toppings: sugar for a little crunch, latik, fresh-cut mango, grated mature coconut, toasted soybean powder, crushed pistachio, coco jam—or invent your own!

•

Refrigerate for up to 1 week (or freeze in an airtight container for up to 1 month) and reheat in a steamer basket over boiling water or by microwaving for 1 minute.

here's a hint of molasses in this sticky rice cake, from brown sugar and a gooey topping of melted Coco Jam (page 201), which brings a dark, mellow sweetness. You could make it even more luxurious with brown butter and a finish of chocolate ganache and cacao nibs. Still, the straightforward (and naturally vegan) version is the original, and just how my lola made it.

This is an easy recipe to halve for a smaller group or double or even triple for a party. The banana-leaf base, while optional, imbues the rice with a gentle earthiness. It reminds me of green tea without the bitter edge, or the succulence of steamed dark greens.

BIKO *BEE•koh*
CARAMELIZED COCONUT STICKY RICE SERVES 8 TO 10

3 cups (720 ml) unsweetened, full-fat coconut milk

1 teaspoon kosher salt

¾ cup (165 g) packed brown sugar

1½ cups (285 g) glutinous ("sweet") rice

1 (10 by 10-inch/25 by 25 cm) piece banana leaf (see headnote for Suman, page 229; optional)

½ cup (120 ml) Coco Jam (page 201)

Flaky sea salt

In a 2-quart (2 L) saucepot, combine the coconut milk, 1½ cups (360 ml) water, the kosher salt, and brown sugar and bring up to a boil. Add the glutinous rice, return to a boil, then reduce to a slow simmer. Put a lid on the pot and cook for about 25 minutes, occasionally lifting the lid to stir.

•

Remove the lid and cook for another 5 to 10 minutes, until the rice has absorbed most but not all of the liquid. It should look like risotto. If the center of the grain is still quite hard, add a bit more water, ¼ cup (60 ml) at a time, and continue cooking until the rice is al dente (with just a little resistance left at the center of the grain).

•

Preheat the oven to 375°F (190°C) and arrange the racks so one is at the top level and another at the middle. Line an 8 by 8-inch (20 by 20-cm) pan with the banana leaf, if using. (If not, no need to line the pan with anything else—the rice won't stick.) Transfer the cooked rice to the banana-leaf-lined pan.

•

In a small saucepan over low heat, melt the coco jam into a clear syrup. Using a spoon, spread the melted jam over the cooked rice in an even layer.

•

Bake the biko for 25 to 35 minutes on the middle rack of the oven, then transfer to the top rack and set the oven to broil. Let broil for 2 to 3 minutes, until the surface of the cake is bubbling and takes on the luster of dark caramel.

•

Let the biko cool for about 20 minutes. Cut into 2-inch (5 cm) squares and serve at room temperature with a fillip of flaky sea salt on top.

A pistachio hides at the heart of each of these chewy, mochi-like orbs, which get their elasticity from cassava, a starchy indigenous tuber akin to a potato but more fibrous and ever so slightly sweet. Peeling cassava is labor-intensive but strangely satisfying: You trim off the ends and score the length, pressing hard enough to just penetrate the brown bark, then dig the knife under the bark, as if shucking a tree, and pull it away from the creamy white flesh. (You can also buy it frozen and pre-peeled.)

One tricky ingredient in this recipe is lye water, a corrosive alkaline solution that has to be handled carefully, typically wearing gloves, and is essential to making things likes bagels, pretzels, ramen noodles, and hundred-year-old eggs. Only ½ teaspoon is used here, to give the pichi pichi dough a little bounce. As a substitute, you can toast ¼ teaspoon baking soda in a pan on medium high for about 5 minutes, then add 1 cup (240 ml) hot water and combine; transfer to a bottle for later use.

To shred the cassava and release the juices, I use a standard cheese grater with ⅛-inch (3 mm) holes. Pandan water stains the dough pale green, matching the hidden pistachio. At the end, roll the finished pichi pichi in fresh grated coconut (also available in the frozen section), or take 1 cup (85 g) desiccated coconut and plump it up with ¼ cup (60 ml) hot water before using.

COCONUT AND PISTACHIO PICHI PICHI
PEE • chee PEE • chee
CHEWY CASSAVA BALLS MAKES 24 BALLS

2 pandan leaves, fresh or frozen, cut into ½-inch (12 mm) pieces

1 cup (240 ml) warm water

1 cup (220 g) fresh grated cassava

½ cup (100 g) granulated sugar

½ teaspoon lye water or alkaline baking soda solution (see headnote)

24 shelled pistachios (optional)

1½ cups (165 g) grated coconut (see headnote)

In a blender, combine the pandan leaves and warm water. Blend until the leaves are pulverized and the water turns green. Strain through a fine-mesh strainer.

•

In a small mixing bowl, combine the grated cassava, the pandan water from the blender, sugar, and lye water. Transfer to a heat-safe bowl and put the bowl in a steamer set up in a large pot over 1½ inches (4 cm) water. Bring the water to a boil, then drop the heat to medium low, cover with a lid, and steam for about 45 minutes, until the cassava mixture is clear and slightly yellowed.

•

Carefully remove the bowl from the steamer and let rest for 5 minutes (otherwise the cassava will be too hot to the touch). Heat a metal tablespoon in a cup with some hot water. Take a scoop of the cassava with the heated tablespoon and roll the mixture into a sphere smaller than a Ping-Pong ball. Push a whole pistachio, if using, into the center of the cassava ball, then roll the ball in a bowl of the grated coconut. Repeat with the remaining balls.

•

Eat immediately. If you're preparing the pichi pichi in advance, transfer to an airtight container in a single, spaced-out layer, not stacked and not touching, and freeze for up to a month until ready to use. Steam to soften before serving.

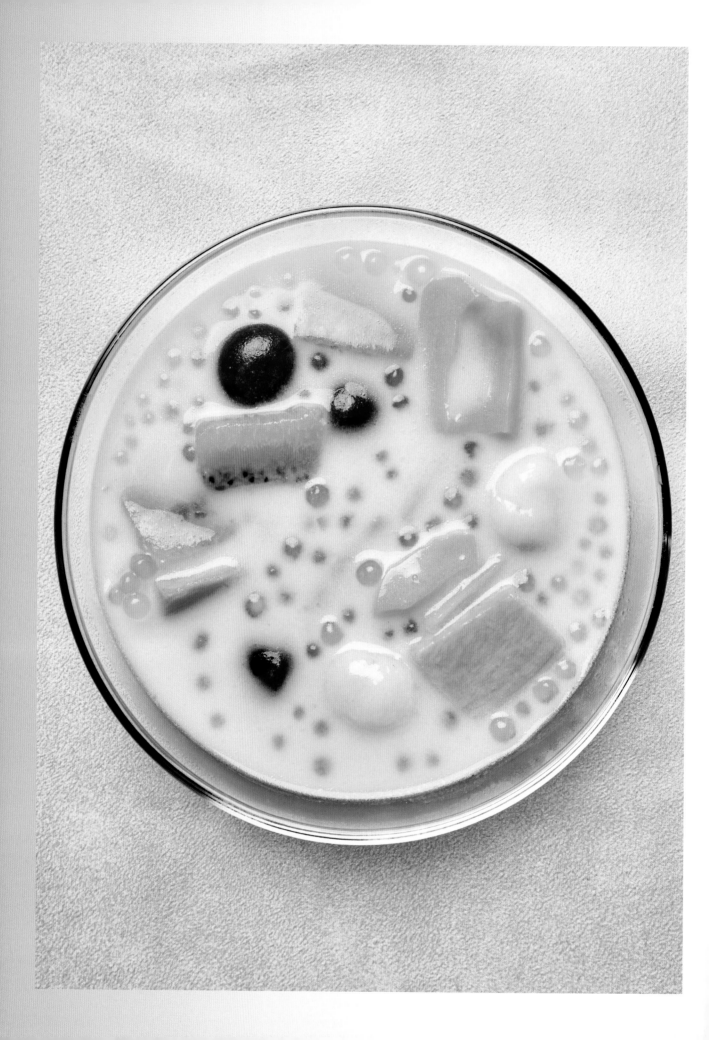

igil is an almost untranslatable word: the sensation of being giddily overwhelmed by adorableness—"when something is so cute you want to bite it," as my friend Geena Rocero (see "Siya: Decolonizing the Language," page 208) explained. That's what I felt as a kid watching Lola roll up bilo-bilo, little balls of mochi no bigger than Milk Duds, and toss them into a bubbling pot of coconut milk on her electric stove. I couldn't resist. I'd stand on tiptoe trying to fish out the mochi with her plastic ladle, until I nabbed all of them, utterly indifferent to the others waiting patiently behind me, hoarding those precious jewels for myself.

Like Halo-Halo (page 263), this dessert is about abundance. The mochi balls are braised in a coconut stew that grows thick with starchy add-ins: sago (tapioca), sweet potatoes, saba bananas, langka (jackfruit). It's traditionally served at New Year's because the round shapes of the mochi and tapioca invoke prosperity, matching the polka dots my sister Mimi wears for the occasion.

In my version, I let chamomile tea steep in the coconut broth, lending subtle floral-woody-tropical notes. Then I double up on mochi, my favorite part of the dish, because there could never be too much. Half the fun is the juxtaposition of colors: One mochi is purple with ube (purple yam), whose earthy sweetness hints at chestnut and vanilla; the other is demurely white with a surprise inside, a goth center of black sesame and raw sugar, bound together by softened salted butter. (I modeled the mochi after Chinese tangyuan, whose thin dough just barely holds back a molten interior that oozes out once bitten; here the dough is thicker and the filling coarsely crushed and crunchy, for more contrast with the warm coconut broth.)

Note: Since it's hard to find ube fresh, you can use dried ube flakes or ube halaya (jam) instead, and amp up the flavor with a couple drops of ube extract.

GINATAANG BILO-BILO
ghee•nah•tah•AHNG BEE•low BEE•low
COCONUT MILK–STEWED MOCHI AND TROPICAL FRUIT

SERVES 6

FOR THE MOCHI:

2 tablespoons black sesame seeds, toasted

2 tablespoons raw cane sugar

2 tablespoons salted butter, softened to room temperature (if using unsalted, add a pinch of kosher salt)

1 cup (130 g) glutinous rice flour, plus extra for dusting

½ cup (120 ml) warm water

2 tablespoons fresh steamed ube, dried ube flakes, or ube halaya

2 drops ube extract (optional; see headnote)

FOR THE COCONUT STEW:

6 tablespoons (55 g) small dried tapioca or 1 cup (241 g) cooked small tapioca or Molasses Tapioca (page 199)

1 can (13½ ounces/398 ml) unsweetened, full-fat coconut milk

¼ cup (50 g) granulated sugar

2 chamomile tea bags

1 small orange sweet potato, peeled and cut into 1-inch (2.5 cm) dice

2 ripe saba bananas (see headnote for Beef Giniling, page 29) or 1 ripe plantain, sliced in half lengthwise and cut into ¾-inch (2 cm) half-moons

¼ cup (60 g) jackfruit preserved in syrup, drained, each piece cut in half

GINATAANG BILO-BILO CONTINUED

Make the mochi: In a blender, pulse together the black sesame seeds and raw cane sugar for 1 to 2 minutes, until the mixture has equal parts fine and coarse granules. (You may also grind them in a spice grinder.) Transfer to a small bowl and fold in the room temperature butter and incorporate thoroughly into a deep black paste. Cover and put in the refrigerator to harden.

•

Divide the glutinous rice flour evenly between two small mixing bowls. In one bowl, add the ube and ube extract, if using.

•

To the bowl of plain glutinous rice flour, add ¼ cup (60 ml) warm water and stir to combine. The mixture should be soft but not stick to your fingers, like a lighter Play-Doh. Cover with a damp kitchen towel and set aside.

•

To the bowl with the ube, add a couple tablespoons of the remaining warm water at a time, stirring to achieve the same lighter Play-Doh texture. If you're using fresh steamed purple yam or ube halaya, you will need less water, and if you're using dried ube flakes, you might need a bit more.

•

Dust a tray (or dinner plate) and a cutting board with glutinous rice flour. Roll the ube mochi dough into a log about ¾ inch (2 cm) wide. Cut the log into 1-inch (2.5 cm) pieces and transfer to the tray. Cover with a damp kitchen towel. Take one piece at a time and roll it between your palms into a sphere ¾ inch (2 cm) in diameter, about the size of a Milk Dud. (There should be enough to make about 12 ube mochi.) Put each sphere back on the floured tray and keep covered with the damp towel.

•

Take the black sesame butter out of the refrigerator. Using a small butter knife, cut the chilled butter into ½-inch (12 mm) cubes, about the size of a frozen pea, and put them in a bowl. If it's hot in the kitchen, rest the bowl inside a larger bowl of ice, to keep the butter from losing shape.

•

Dust the cutting board with rice flour again. Roll and cut the plain mochi dough as you did the ube mochi dough and let rest under a damp towel on the same tray as the ube mochi. Take one piece at a time, roll it into a ball, then flatten it into a round disk about ¼ inch (6 mm) thick and 2 inches (5 cm) in diameter. Working quickly, put one chunk of the chilled black sesame butter in the center of each disk, then pinch the edges of the disk together, completely covering the sesame butter at the center of the dough. Roll each pinched disk into a sphere ¾ inch (2 cm) in diameter and return to the tray under the towel. Repeat with the rest of the black sesame mochi pieces—you should have enough to make about 12—and set the tray aside.

•

Make the coconut stew: If using dried tapioca, bring 3 cups (720 ml) water to a boil in a small saucepan. Add the tapioca and cook for about 7 minutes, then pour the tapioca into a fine-mesh strainer set over a bowl and reserve the cooking liquid. Rinse the tapioca in the strainer under cold running water, then return the tapioca and the cooking liquid to the pan to cook for another 5 minutes, or until the center of each pearl is almost transparent. Strain again, discard the cooking water, and set aside.

•

In a 4-quart (3.8 L) pot, bring 2 cups (480 ml) water and the coconut milk and granulated sugar up to a boil, then reduce to a simmer. Tie the chamomile tea bags to the handle of the pot and steep the tea in the coconut milk broth as it simmers. Add the sweet potato and continue simmering on low heat for 8 to 15 minutes, until the sweet potato is soft to the touch, but not falling apart. Using a ladle, scoop some of the warm coconut broth into the container holding the cooked tapioca, and whisk to loosen and separate the tapioca into individual pearls.

•

Add the banana to the pot and stir to combine. Simmer for about 3 minutes. Stir the broth and add the tapioca, followed by the two types of mochi. Simmer for another 5 to 10 minutes, until the black sesame mochi is semi-translucent, the ube mochi has darkened in color, and the broth has thickened into a light gravy. (The thickening comes from the breakdown of starches.)

•

Before serving, discard the tea bags and stir in the preserved jackfruit. Serve warm in bowls, making sure that each includes a few of every ingredient in the stew. It will keep in the refrigerator for up to 4 days; dilute with a couple tablespoons of water when reheating.

One early morning in Batangas when I was visiting the Philippines, I took a walk on a winding, jungly path, and from far away I could hear someone calling out, "Tah-HOHHHH! Tah-HOHHHH!" It was almost a song. Soon a man came in sight with a long bamboo stick over his shoulders, balanced by two wooden buckets. From one he took fresh warm, creamy tofu, scooping it into a little plastic cup. Then he popped open the lid of the other bucket and ladled out chewy sago (tapioca pearls) and arnibal (brown sugar syrup). It was breakfast, the tofu delicate and sweet, creamy and airy at once, and in that moment, it was all I could want.

The flavors made me think of Japanese warabi mochi: a jelly-like version of mochi made from bracken starch with more texture than flavor, disappearing on the tongue, drizzled with kuromitsu (brown sugar syrup) and dusted with kinako (toasted soybean powder). So in my version of taho, I scatter a little kinako, to enhance the earthiness of the tofu; you can save the extra as a topping for Halo-Halo (page 263) and ice cream. If you have time to make Molasses Tapioca, you'll get some of the same deep malty notes as in Filipino raw cane sugar. Otherwise try to find brown sugar tapioca, although white works fine, too, because what's most important is the tapioca's squeak and bounce, giving way to tofu as soft as custard.

TAHO *tah • HOH*
WARM TOFU, TAPIOCA, AND BROWN SUGAR SYRUP, WITH TOASTED SOYBEAN POWDER SERVES 2

¼ cup (45 g) dried soybeans

¼ cup uncooked Molasses Tapioca (page 199) or store-bought large tapioca pearls

½ package (14 to 16 ounces/396 to 454 g) soft tofu

½ cup (120 ml) soy milk

3 very ripe strawberries, sliced into ½-inch (12 mm) pieces (optional)

Molasses, for finishing

To make the toasted soybean powder, preheat the oven to 325°F (165°C). Arrange the dried soybeans on a small tray and roast for about 20 minutes, until the skins crack and the beans take on a creamy brown color.

•

Transfer to a spice or coffee grinder and process for about 2 minutes, until the soybeans have been pulverized into a very fine powder that's warm, toasty, nutty, and fragrant. (This should yield 6 tablespoons soybean powder.)

•

If using store-bought tapioca pearls, fill a 1-quart (980 ml) saucepan with water and bring to a boil over high heat. Add the tapioca pearls and cook for about 10 minutes. Turn off the heat but keep the pot on the still-warm burner. Cover the pot and let the tapioca rest in the hot water for 15 minutes. Then strain the tapioca through a fine-mesh sieve and rinse under warm water. At this point, the centers of the tapioca should be transparent; if they're still opaque (since large tapioca sizes vary), repeat the boiling once or twice more.

•

If using homemade molasses tapioca, cook following the instructions on page 199.

•

Open the package of soft tofu, carefully drain any liquid over the sink, then score the sides of the tofu away from the packaging and invert onto your cutting board. Cut the tofu block in half. Return one-half to the packaging and store in the refrigerator for future use. Transfer the other half to a small saucepan, add the soy milk, and heat over medium low. Once the tofu is warm, cover the pot and steam the tofu until it's warmed all the way through, about 8 minutes, very gently tilting the pot every couple minutes to help distribute the heat.

•

Using a spatula, transfer the warmed tofu (still in block shape) to a serving bowl. Scatter the strawberries (if using) over the tofu, then spoon the cooked tapioca on top of the strawberries. Dust with a teaspoon or two of the toasted soybean powder and finish with a drizzle of molasses. (Store the rest in a small spice jar or airtight container at room temperature for up to a month.) Serve the taho warm, with two spoons.

*S*ome of the first churches in the Philippines, built of adobe, limestone, or coral, were bound together by egg whites, mixed into the mortar to make it stronger. As the food historian Pia Lim-Castillo has written, millions of eggs were likely sacrificed to the cause—and something had to be done with all those leftover yolks. Rather than let them go to waste, enterprising cooks turned them into desserts, most beloved among them leche flan.

The original recipe, for a wobbly custard with a drape of gooey caramel, came from the Spanish; we made it richer, the better to survive the humidity. This version is particularly luxurious, calling for 4 whole eggs plus 5 separate yolks. You can make it a day ahead and keep it covered in the refrigerator, then invert it from the mold and bring it to room temperature before serving, so the caramel loosens.

It tastes best with a trace of sour-sweet and even a hint of bitterness, which my lola achieved with calamansi in the Philippines and later tried to approximate with lime in the United States. I suggest grapefruit here, but I'm also fond of meatier pomelo and—my favorite—oroblanco, a hybrid of the two fruits, justly named "white gold."

LECHE FLAN WITH GRAPEFRUIT

SERVES 6

1 small grapefruit

1⅔ cups (335 g) granulated sugar

4 large whole eggs

5 large egg yolks

1⅓ cups (315 ml) heavy cream

1⅓ cups (315 ml) whole milk

¼ teaspoon kosher salt

Finely grate all the zest from the skin of the grapefruit and set aside. Using a sharp knife, supreme the grapefruit: Cut a little off the top and bottom—just enough that you can see the flesh inside—so you have two flat sides to work with, then cut away the peel and white pith and discard. Working over a bowl, cut along the membranes and let the grapefruit wedges drop into the bowl; discard the membranes and set the wedges aside.

●

Sprinkle 1 cup (200 g) of the sugar in an even layer in a small saucepan. Cook over medium heat until the sugar begins to melt at the edges, making a dark gold halo at the bottom of the pan. Do not stir. Instead, using a heatproof rubber spatula, drag the hot molten sugar from the edges toward the center of the pan, so it melds with the unmelted sugar. Continue dragging and combining for 10 to 12 minutes, until all the sugar is melted and the caramel is uniform in color and as glossy as amber. (It should smell toasty but not burnt.) If you see undissolved lumps of sugar, take the pan off the heat and gently stir until the lumps dissolve.

●

Pour the caramel into two pans, either 8-inch (20 cm) round pans or 9 by 5-inch (23 by 12 cm) loaf pans, preferably glass or ceramic to maintain the clarity of the caramel and yield the smoothest custard. (Metal typically conducts heat less evenly.) Be sure to divide the caramel equally between the pans, creating a layer ⅛ to ¼ inch (3 to 6 mm) deep. Let cool.

●

Set a rack in the center of the oven and preheat to 275°F (135°C). Bring a kettle or large pot of water, about 2 quarts (2 L), to a boil.

●

In a blender, puree the eggs and egg yolks with the remaining ⅔ cup (135 g) sugar for about 1 minute, until the sugar is dissolved. Transfer to a large bowl and gently mix in the heavy cream, milk, salt, and the reserved grapefruit zest; let rest for 5 minutes. Strain into a large measuring glass, then pour into the prepared baking dishes, dividing into two equal amounts.

●

Line a roasting pan with a thick kitchen towel; this will keep the baking dishes from sliding and protect the flan so it doesn't overcook. Set the baking dishes on top of the towel and put the roasting pan in the preheated oven. Pour very hot water into the towel-lined pan; it should reach the same height as the flan inside the baking dishes. Bake the flan for 40 to 55 minutes, until it looks set—like Jell-O, it should wobble slowly in the center when gently shaken. Transfer the baking dishes to a wire rack and let cool.

●

When ready to serve, run a small knife around the edges of each flan to loosen. Turn upside down over a platter, top with the reserved grapefruit wedges, and bring to the table.

My first pies came from the Wonder Bread discount store, where my mom would buy squashed loaves at 75 cents a pop and little crecent-shaped, individually bagged Home Run Pies. They were ten for a dollar, a better price than at Lucky or Safeway, and she let me choose which ones to bring home to my brothers and sisters. I thought the fruit fillings were too cloying, bound together by a strange, gluey syrup that reminded me of extra-strength hair gel, so I always opted for chocolate or vanilla "pudding" instead.

This recipe is a Home Run Pie in shape, but owes its creamy filling to the buko pies made famous in the 1960s by the Pahud sisters at Orient Bakery in Los Baños, Laguna, just south of Manila. Nanette Pahud, the eldest sister, learned to bake pies while she was a cook for a visiting American professor, and decided to experiment with young coconut meat. At Orient, they use only coconuts harvested the day of baking—a true luxury!—at the mala-kanin stage, when the meat is as soft as boiled rice.

If you can find fresh young coconuts at the market, bring home three of them and scoop out the quivery flesh with a spoon; otherwise, frozen young coconut meat will do. I don't like my desserts too sweet, so the sugar is kept in check here. You can really taste the contrast of the flaky, buttery crust and the lush yet featherweight pudding, as refreshing as a sip of coconut water straight from the shell.

BUKO HAND PIE *BOO•koh*
YOUNG COCONUT PUDDING PIE

MAKES 10 HAND PIES

FOR THE FLAKY PIECRUST:

2¼ cups (280 g) all-purpose flour, plus extra for dusting, chilled in the freezer

1 teaspoon granulated sugar

1 teaspoon kosher salt

1 cup (2 sticks/225 grams) very cold unsalted butter, cut into 1-inch (2.5 cm) chunks, kept in the refrigerator until ready to use

⅓ cup (75 ml) ice water

FOR THE FILLING:

1 can (13½ ounces/398 ml) coconut cream (reserve 2 tablespoons for the icing glaze)

¼ cup (50 g) granulated sugar

⅓ cup (45 g) cornstarch

½ cup (120 ml) plus 2 tablespoons coconut water

1 cup (250 g) young coconut meat, chilled and cut into roughly 1-inch (2.5 cm) pieces

1 medium egg, beaten, for brushing

1 cup (120 g) powdered confectioners' sugar (no need to sift), for the icing glaze

The night before baking, prepare the pie dough: In a large mixing bowl, combine the chilled flour, sugar, and salt. Whisk to sift, then add the cold butter chunks directly from the refrigerator. Toss loosely with a rubber spatula.

Dump the bowl out onto a clean work surface.

•

Take a rolling pin and roll back and forth over the mixture quickly, to flatten the butter chunks. (Try not to handle the mixture too much.) Between every few rolls, use a bench scraper to scrape the mixture into a heap on the cutting board; if the butter sticks to the rolling pin, use the bench scraper to scrape it off, into the heap. Continue rolling until the butter chunks turn into flat, jagged pieces that look like paint chips—they should not be worked in completely, or the crust won't be flaky. After about 2 minutes of rolling and scraping, use the bench scraper to return the mixture back to the mixing bowl.

→

BUKO HAND PIE CONTINUED

Add the ice water to the mixture and loosely combine with a rubber spatula. The mixture should still be rough and shaggy. Immediately dump the mixture onto a flour-dusted surface. Roll and scrape the dough twice more; the water will bring the shapeless mass together. Roll into two 2 by 5-inch (5 by 12.5 cm) logs, then wrap the logs in plastic wrap and chill in the refrigerator overnight. (The dough can also be frozen—give the logs an extra layer of plastic wrap or put them in a zip-top bag—for up to 6 months.)

•

That same night, prepare the pie filling: In a 1-quart (980 ml) saucepan, combine the coconut cream (minus the 2 tablespoons reserved for the icing) and granulated sugar, and bring to a boil over medium heat. While the pan is heating up, take a small bowl and make a cornstarch slurry by whisking together the cornstarch and ½ cup (120 ml) coconut water.

•

After 6 to 8 minutes, when the coconut cream is boiling, whisk the cornstarch slurry once more and dump it into the pan. Immediately turn off the heat but keep the pan on the burner. Quickly stir the mixture, as it will thicken instantaneously. (It's important that the coconut cream is at a full boil, to activate the starches in the slurry.)

•

Using a rubber spatula, transfer the thickened coconut cream to a fine-mesh strainer over a bowl. Press the mixture through the strainer to break down any lumps.

•

Add the chilled young coconut meat and stir to combine. This is the buko filling. Store overnight in the refrigerator to chill and further thicken.

•

The next day, preheat the oven to 450°F (230°C). Cut the logs of pie dough into 10 disks, 1 inch (2.5 cm) thick. Using flour to dust your rolling pin and work surface, roll out each disk to make a larger and flatter disk, 5 inches (12.5 cm) in diameter and ⅛ inch (3 mm) thick, about the size of a corn tortilla. Stack the dough disks, dusting with flour in between, and set aside.

•

Take 1 disk of dough and put 1 heaping tablespoon of the buko filling at the center. Dip a fingertip in water and dampen the lower circumference of the dough, then lift the dampened edge and fold the dough upward over the filling, making a half-moon. Lightly press the edges together, careful not to disturb the round mound of filling inside. Using the tines of a fork, crimp the edges to seal. With a cake tester or toothpick, gently poke about 5 holes in the dough, to let a bit of steam out in the oven. Transfer to a cookie sheet (you'll need two). Repeat with the remaining dough disks and space them out evenly, 5 per sheet.

•

Dip a pastry brush in the beaten egg and delicately gloss the surface of each hand pie, making sure to apply the egg evenly, on all sides. (This egg wash will give the pastries shine and help the icing stick.) Transfer the hand pies to the oven and bake for about 25 minutes.

•

While baking, combine the confectioners' sugar and the reserved 2 tablespoons coconut cream to make the icing glaze.

•

When the pies have turned golden and darker at the edges, take them out of the oven and, while they're still on the cookie sheets, use a fresh pastry brush to generously coat each pie with the icing glaze. The glaze should be thick enough to make a slightly opaque coating. Then use a spatula to transfer the pies to a cooling rack. Try to be patient while they cool and the filling firms. Eat.

Crumble is built into this cookie's name: polvo is "dust" in Spanish. The key here is toasting the flour, as when making a roux, which, like browning butter and caramelizing sugar, brings depth of flavor. Heat also loosens the gluten structure, so the cookies–which require no baking–turn out yieldingly tender, almost like halva. I mix all-purpose flour with oats and black sesame seeds, both ground and whole, for earthiness and contrasts in texture; as the flour darkens in the pan, the kitchen fills up with the scent of roasting nuts.

There's lots of room to play here. You can omit the black sesame seeds and pair the oats with ¼ cup (35 g) toasted soybean powder (page 241) or buckwheat flour (30 g). Or drop both the oats and sesame seeds and use ¼ cup (45 g) fine cornmeal instead, or increase the all-purpose flour to ¾ cup (95 g) and add ¼ cup (30 g) ground pistachios. I've seen recipes that call for Rice Krispies or crushed Oreos, tossed in with the melted butter.

Polvoron molds are available online, but if you can't find one, try packing the dough in an ice cube tray, halfway to the rim. (They just won't be as pretty.) And while it's traditional to wrap polvoron in bright cellophane as gifts, don't feel guilty if you keep them all for yourself. I like to crumble them–fulfilling their destiny!–over ice cream or a simple bowl of fruit and cream.

POLVORON *pohl • vuh • ROHN*
TOASTED OAT AND BLACK SESAME SHORTBREAD COOKIES MAKES 18 COOKIES

½ cup (45 g) instant rolled oats

3 tablespoons black sesame seeds, toasted in a pan until fragrant

½ cup (65 g) all-purpose flour

½ cup (60 g) powdered milk

6 tablespoons (75 g) granulated sugar

¼ cup (½ stick/55 g) butter, melted

In a spice grinder, combine the rolled oats and 2 tablespoons of the toasted black sesame seeds. Grind for about 1 minute, until the oats and sesame have made a coarse flour. (It will be mostly powder, but it's fine to leave a few bigger pieces in there.)

•

Put the all-purpose flour, the oat-sesame mixture from the spice grinder, and the remaining 1 tablespoon black sesame seeds in a sauté pan. (The whole seeds bring a nice contrast in texture.) Toast for about 15 minutes on medium heat, flipping or mixing occasionally so the flour toasts evenly as it shades into gold.

•

Transfer the toasted flour, oats, and sesame seeds to a mixing bowl and let cool on the counter for about 10 minutes. Once cooled, add the powdered milk and sugar and stir to incorporate. Then add the melted butter and combine. While the dough is still warm from the butter, press it firmly into a polvoron mold, packing it tightly. Then release the dough from the mold onto a plate and let cool.

•

Present immediately, or store in an airtight container at room temperature for up to two weeks.

astilla is a Spanish word supple enough to signify a pill, lozenge, or anything of similar shape, or a small pastry. (In Morocco, it's a flaky savory pie.) But the candy of this name is wholly Filipino, from the town of San Miguel in Bulacan province, which neighbors Pampanga, where my mother grew up. Traditionally, pastillas were made with carabao (water buffalo) milk, as a way for farmers to use up any excess, so it wouldn't spoil in the time before refrigeration. Carabao milk is gorgeously rich with a salty tang, but hard to get; a mix of sweetened condensed milk and instant nonfat dry milk is a modern approximation. I add ube, but you can skip that step—milk is the classic flavor.

For decoration, try pressing edible flowers into the dough before rolling them up in parchment paper. If you're feeling ambitious, there's a special (and sadly fading) art to wrapping the pastillas, called pabalat. Using papel de japon (Japanese tissue paper) and fine-point scissors, artisans create intricate cutouts—tumbling flowers, birds mid-soar, dancers and the infinite folds of their dresses—to trail from the candies like streamers.

PASTILLAS DE UBE
pas • TEE • yahs deh OOH • beh
SOFT MILK PURPLE YAM CANDIES

MAKES ABOUT 4 DOZEN CANDIES

2 medium ube (purple yam) or 1 cup (225 g) ube halaya (purple yam jam)

7 ounces (210 ml) sweetened condensed milk

½ cup (35 g) instant nonfat dry milk

½ teaspoon finely grated lime zest

1 teaspoon kosher salt

2 tablespoons granulated sugar or to taste, plus ½ cup (100 g) for rolling

If using ube, preheat the oven to 350°F (175°C).

•

Roast the ube on a rimmed baking sheet for 40 to 50 minutes, until tender. Let cool. Cut in half lengthwise and scoop the flesh from the skins; discard the skins. Press the flesh through a ricer, or push through a fine-mesh sieve with a rubber spatula into a bowl. You should end up with 1 packed cup (about 200 g).

•

In a medium nonstick saucepan or skillet, cook the ube (or ube halaya, if using) and condensed milk over medium heat for 6 to 8 minutes, stirring often, until thickened and jammy. Add the powdered milk, lime zest, salt, and sugar. Continue cooking and stirring for about 3 minutes, until slightly thickened. Transfer to a small bowl and cover with plastic wrap, pressing directly on the surface of the ube mixture. Let cool.

•

Turn out the ube mixture on a work surface and roll into logs ½-inch (12 mm) thick. It will have a texture like Play-Doh, but softer. Sprinkle some sugar over the work surface and roll the logs in the sugar until liberally coated. Cut into 1½-inch (4 cm) pieces.

•

Wrap tightly in little squares of parchment paper, twisted closed at the ends, and put in the refrigerator. Once chilled, they may be eaten immediately or saved for up to 1 month.

Dogeaters

(TALKING WITH JESSICA HAGEDORN)

Dogeaters, Jessica Hagedorn's outlaw novel of life in the Philippines under the compulsive corruption of the Marcos regime—clamorous, kaleidoscopic, a brilliant mash-up of high and low, finding a grubby majesty in the fates of hustlers and aristocrats, shopgirls, and senators alike—was published in 1990.

ANGELA: You're the first Filipino artist I encountered. I read *Dogeaters* at my Catholic girls' school in northern California. All the immigrant moms wanted to send their daughters to the other, whiter private school in the neighborhood, but I fought to go to Notre Dame, which was more diverse, maybe a third Asian, a third Latinx, and really progressive. People would say, "You can't go to Notre Dame, all the girls there end up tattooed, pierced, and queer"—and look, that happened to me! As an adult, I've thought a lot about my intuition and whether it's actually the guidance of ancestral spirits. The teachers at Notre Dame gave us books by writers who represented us, and that led me to your work.

JESSICA: I'm honored that they were teaching my novel. But that kind of breaks my heart.

A: What do you mean?

J: That I was the first Filipino writer you encountered. There were so many who came before me; they just didn't get the attention. Some of them were my mentors. They toiled away and were read by maybe three people. Then publishing opened its doors for a moment. You think, great, this means there will be more of us, more knowledge shared. But then I hear you say . . . what year was that?

A: I was probably fourteen, so it must have been 2000.

J: By then it should've been old hat. You would've said, "Oh, cool, but I've already read so-and-so and

so-and-so." That's why I put together those Asian-American anthologies, to highlight as many different writers as possible. It's hard to sustain yourself as a writer; a lot of writers I know wrote their first novel and then disappeared. It's very hard to keep it up, to fight this fight, to feel that you're part of the conversation.

LIGAYA: Was it difficult to get the novel published?

J: I was turned down by eleven publishers. When publishers talk about the "universal," they usually have a very narrow idea of who their readership is. As if we don't read. We're used to transposing and projecting ourselves onto non-Filipino characters. But why did they think this book was *only* about Filipinos? Now they're publishing more people, but they still don't give you the same support, unless you've already written a bestseller. It's kind of a self-fulfilling prophecy. I think my job is to show that it's no big whoop being Filipino. We're part of the world, not a trope or a catalyst. They act like it's "new" whenever a Filipino book comes out—no, it's not. (It's kind of nice being an old lady: I don't have to make things pretty.)

L: Did the response to the book surprise you?

J: It was a vindication. There was so much stuff in the news about the Philippines then; politically, it was the right time. But a lot of Filipinos hated the title. It was controversial. I had to stand by my artistic decision.

JESSICA HAGEDORN

DOGEATERS

"A surrealistically hip epic of Manila . . . Combines narrative drive with a lyric sensibility."
—*San Francisco Chronicle*

Jessica Hagedorn's groundbreaking 1990 novel, *Dogeaters.*

In Hawai'i, when I went on tour with the paperback edition, I met an old woman who had worked in the fields, this lola, and she said, "I read your book. I loved your book. You have to change the title. Why did you do that to us?" I thought, what are we so ashamed of? I listened; I invited her up onstage; I gave her the respect. "I didn't mean to hurt you," I said. "But I'm not changing it."

A: The other day, someone commented: "Filipinos eat dogs," on one of my recipes for the *New York Times*. I was surprised—not that somebody said it, but that it was my first time actually seeing it. I reposted it so that my friends would know that this is still part of the conversation.

J: Once I taught a writing workshop for these teenage girls who'd never met an Asian person. They asked, "Is it true you eat cats?" I said, "Dogs, not cats." We all laughed. I got to teach them something.

L: I almost did the same thing! I was in Woodside, Queens, on the strip they call Little Manila, and I saw this white guy who was yelling into his phone about his upstairs neighbors. He was stomping up and down, spit flying, screaming that something had to be done about "the smell": "They're cooking a cat up there!" I wanted to tap him on the shoulder and say, very innocent-eyed and polite, "Excuse me, sir? It's dog."

J: I remember my mom, right after we arrived in San Francisco, cooking all this stuff, adobo, relleno, and she said, "Oh, the neighbors are going to complain about the smell." But she laughed it off.

A: Filipinos have to laugh off a lot.

J: Sometimes we laugh too much. I think, "Why are you smiling? You don't have to smile for me."

A: Representation is important, but why does our work *have* to be representational? When the *New York Times* asked me to contribute "10 Essential Filipino Recipes," I was honored, but I also wondered: Why me? Just because I'm Filipino doesn't mean my recipes are definitive; they come from a particular lived experience. I wasn't originally planning to write a Filipino cookbook, but I felt called to it by other forces, as a way to better know my family—and myself.

J: Everybody wants to think we're all the same, that there's only one kind of Filipino. Everybody wants to put you in the box. It's not malicious; it's just that they have no imagination. The same thing happens with food. My mother's pinakbet was really different from my auntie's. They were both great—I was so lucky!—but I couldn't choose between them.

A: What's been so beautiful to me about doing this book is getting to see the different types of people who are part of the Filipino diaspora. It can be lonely and confusing, this gray area between cultures. Thinking about our links to the past through food, I've felt a lightness.

J: For me, the Filipino is like an astronaut. We keep showing up. When I finally became close to my Filipino poet tribe in San Francisco, I realized that they'd been there all the time. In New York there's now this whole family of Filipino diaspora artists. We're all so different; we carry so many different stories. But man, when we get together. You don't have to explain yourself over and over again. You just are.

A: At my school, the most popular club was the Filipino Association. Everyone wanted to join, Filipino or not.

J: Parties! Food!

A: Every year we'd put on a Philippine Culture Night. I did a lot of dancing because my mom was in Bayanihan [the national folk dance troupe].

J: What's your mom's name?

A: Dolly—that's her Filipino name. From Dulce. Sarah Dulce Santiago Dimayuga.

J: Sometimes I sign my emails Dolly.

A: Really?! How did you get that name?

J: My mother's friend Dolly Baker—I called her auntie, but she wasn't—was a torch singer in Japan. (R.I.P. Dolly.) So when a friend of mine went there, I told him, you should meet my auntie, and he went and loved her, and she of course immediately adopted him. He came back and he said, "I'm going to call you Dolly." We both use it when we text.

A: I've had different phases when I wanted to rename myself Dolly, or name my kid Dolly, or take my paternal grandmother's name, Solita, which is my middle name.

J: You can have all those names. You can be all that.

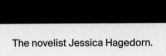

The novelist Jessica Hagedorn.

Ice came to the Philippines in the mid-nineteenth century, giant blocks of it carved out of frozen Wenham Lake in Massachusetts, famous at the time as supposedly the purest ice in the world, as clear as glass. Before that, drinks were cooled in earthen jars, to redress the heat of the climate. By the turn of the twentieth century, as chronicled by the historian Ambeth R. Ocampo, Filipinos were clamoring for ice, which was buried in rice husks to keep it cold and sold from horse-drawn carts. (Refrigerators arrived in the 1920s, too expensive for any but the rich, and only became widely available after World War II.) As with so many imports from abroad, we've embraced ice as our own, turning it into the foundation of one of our favorite desserts, Halo-Halo (page 263). And every drink, even a soda taken straight from the fridge, gets poured into a glass with a stack of ice cubes—although we do make an exception for a few hot drinks, above all Tsokolate (page 277).

COLD THINGS

AND DRINKS

_n summer, my mom used to crack open a can of creamed corn, pour it into bowls over crushed ice, give it a splash of cold milk, then hand around spoons. This is my homage to that memory: sweet kernels straight off the cob, boiled with sugar, frozen, and pulverized into a slush that's creamy without any added dairy—a vegan treat.

Or you could just make my mom's recipe, but instead of creamed corn, crush 3 to 4 strawberries with a fork in each bowl before pouring in the cold milk and topping with icy rubble.

CORN SLUSH

SERVES 2

2 ears corn, kernels cut off the cob

2 tablespoons raw cane sugar, or to taste

½ teaspoons kosher salt

In a 1-quart (960 ml) sauce-pan, bring 2 cups (480 ml) water to a rolling boil over high heat.

●

Add the corn kernels, sugar, and salt. Drop the heat to medium low for a slower boil and cook for about 5 minutes, until the corn tastes sweet and crunchy.

●

Transfer to a shallow heat-proof container and freeze overnight. Let defrost on the counter for about 15 minutes, until you can break up the icy corn easily. Reserve a handful of kernels for garnish and puree the rest in a blender until completely smooth and creamy colored. Pour into two glasses, garnish with the reserved kernels, and serve immediately.

A mango at peak ripeness is luscious, the tropics incarnate, but I love the fruit at every stage. Grab it when it's still green, firm, and tart, and you can eat it simply dipped in salt or Bagoong (page 169), or turn it into a crunchy pickle (Lacto-Fermented Green Mango, page 189). Here I pulverize it into a refreshing slush, with a little pineapple, lime, and ginger for extra contours of flavor. If your mangoes are particularly sour and you'd like a touch more sweetness, add a pinch of raw sugar and drizzle some condensed milk on top.

GREEN MANGO SLUSH

SERVES 1

1 cup (165 g) green mango, peeled, cut into ½-inch (12 mm) chunks and frozen in advance

¼ cup (40 g) fresh pineapple, cut into ½-inch (12 mm) chunks and frozen in advance

Juice of ½ lime

1 cup (125 g) crushed ice

1 (½-inch/12 mm) piece fresh ginger, peeled and grated

Raw cane sugar or sweetener of choice to taste (optional)

1 teaspoon condensed milk (optional)

In a blender, combine the mango, pineapple, lime juice, ice, ginger, ¼ cup (60 ml) water, and sugar, if using. Blend for 1 to 2 minutes, until very smooth.

•

Pour into a glass and add a swirl of condensed milk for extra sweet creaminess, if you choose.

This dessert came to me in a dream: I saw it on a table, in a fogged-up glass, beaded and cold. At the time, I was in the Cayman Islands, where I'd stopped over for a brief cooking residency before flights were suspended due to COVID-19. The tropics are hardly the worst place to be marooned in the middle of an epidemic, but I think my body was craving the flavors of Asia and channeling memories of milk teas I'd slurped down on the streets of Taipei. When I woke up, I jotted down the ingredients. Later I learned that coffee jelly was an early nineteenth-century British recipe that got revived and revamped in 1960s Tokyo, and then made its way to—yes, the Philippines, where wobbly sweets have always been treasured.

I use goat's milk to make this because I love the grassiness, but any milk will do. And you can make the condensed milk jelly on its own, to add to Halo-Halo (page 263) or crushed strawberries and ice milk (a variation on a Corn Slush, page 257).

BLACK TREACLE TOFFEE MILK
AND COFFEE JELLY WITH
BABY TAPIOCA SERVES 2

FOR THE CONDENSED MILK JELLY:

2 teaspoons powdered gelatin

2 tablespoons condensed milk

¾ cup (180 ml) warm water

FOR THE COFFEE JELLY:

1½ teaspoons powdered gelatin

1 cup (240 ml) hot, freshly brewed coffee

1 tablespoon cane sugar

2 tablespoons small tapioca pearls (½ cup/120 g when cooked)

Black treacle

Crushed ice

2 cups (480 ml) milk

Make the condensed milk jelly: Combine the powdered gelatin and 2 tablespoons room temperature water in a small glass or plastic food storage container. Stir thoroughly with a small spatula, then let the mixture rest for a few minutes; the water will activate the gelatin and make it bloom.

•

Add the condensed milk and warm water, and stir to combine. Cover and cool in the refrigerator.

•

Make the coffee jelly: Combine the powdered gelatin and 2 tablespoons room temperature water in a small glass or plastic food storage container. As with the condensed milk jelly, stir thoroughly with a small spatula, then let rest for a few minutes.

•

Pour the coffee into the container with the gelatin. Add the sugar and stir thoroughly to encourage the gelatin and sugar to dissolve. Cover and cool in the refrigerator.

•

To prepare the tapioca, bring 4½ cups (1 L) water to a boil in a small saucepan over high heat. Add the tapioca pearls, reduce the heat to medium high, and boil for 10 minutes, or until the tapioca is two-thirds of the way translucent, with a small white center. Strain the tapioca in a fine-mesh sieve over a bowl and return the collected hot water to the pan.

→

BLACK TREACLE TOFFEE MILK AND COFFEE JELLY WITH BABY TAPIOCA CONTINUED

Over the kitchen sink, cool the tapioca under cold running water for about 1 minute, then return the tapioca to the pan and raise the heat to a medium high boil for another 3 to 5 minutes. Shut off the heat but leave the pan on the burner and let the tapioca soak until fully translucent. Transfer back to the sieve and cool under cold running water again. Store in a plastic container and set aside.

•

When the condensed milk and coffee jellies have cooled for about an hour, they should be set; check to see if the center of each jelly quivers slowly when jiggled.

•

To assemble the dessert, take a paring knife and cut each jelly—still inside its container—into two ¾-inch (2 cm) squares. Prepare two tall glasses for serving. (I like to use a cylindrical tumbler like a Collins glass.) Dip a butter knife into the jar of black treacle and use the knife's tip to drizzle the treacle along the walls of the glass. This is sweet stuff, so adjust the amount according to your taste.

•

Using a spoon, scoop out the coffee jelly squares and put one in each of the glasses as the base of the dessert. After the coffee jelly, add a square of the condensed milk jelly, some cooked tapioca pearls, and crushed ice, then repeat the layers. (You should be able to fit at least two layers of ingredients.)

•

Shake the milk in its carton to encourage foaming, then pour into each glass to the rim. When the milk and the treacle meet, it tastes like toffee. Drizzle a little more treacle on top of the milk as a garnish. Serve immediately with spoons and straws.

alo-halo—properly haluhalo, according to the government Commission on the Filipino Language, but so commonly referred to as halo-halo that I'll use that name here—is one of the great Asian ice desserts, part of a lineage going back to the tenth century, when the Japanese poet and courtier Sei Shōnagon listed "shaved ice mixed with liana syrup and put in a new silver bowl" as one of the world's "elegant things." According to the historian Ambeth R. Ocampo, halo-halo started out as mongo-ya, a treat of ice and sweetened beans sold by Japanese immigrants in the Philippines before World War II. This seems almost ascetic in comparison to our modern version, brimming over with toppings and joyfully verging on anarchy.

The word halo means "mix," but that part is your job. In summer, my mom used to set up a halo-halo buffet on our kitchen counter, putting out jars and bowls of chewy jellies and sago (tapioca pearls); crunchy corn, kaong (palm seeds), and pinipig (young glutinous rice pounded flat and toasted); sweetened beans; creamy macapuno (the consummately tender, jelly-like flesh of a coconut varietal), ube halaya (purple yam cooked down with coconut milk until nearly pudding), and roasted or boiled yam and taro; and fruits both fresh and preserved in simple syrup. There was always condensed and evaporated milk to drench the ice and a scoop of ice cream, with a tiny square of Leche Flan (page 243) as the cherry on top, the impossibly decadent final touch.

This is not a recipe, then, just an invitation—to mix and match flavors, textures, and colors. Pictured on the next two pages is a traditional halo-halo, as described above, alongside its sepia-toned alter ego, a study in coffee, chocolate, and toffee. You could make versions dedicated to shadings of green tea, strawberry, pistachio, coconut: whatever you like! Start by thinking about the ice cream you want and embellish from there.

HALO-HALO
𝓗𝓐𝓗 • loh 𝓗𝓐𝓗 • loh

SERVES 1

Swipe jam (if using) on the side of the glass.

•

Layer ice, jellies, fruits, starches, and chewy bits.

•

Top with ice cream, syrup, and leche flan (if using).

•

Flood the glass with milk.

•

Finish with crunch.

TRADITIONAL

TOASTED
WHITE RICE
FROM RICE COFFEE
(PAGE 275)

CONDENSED MILK

UBE
ICE CREAM

LECHE FLAN
(PAGE 243)

CRUSHED ICE

LANGKA
(JACKFRUIT)
PRESERVED
IN SYRUP

SAGO
(TAPIOCA PEARLS),
SMALL AND LARGE

AGAR-AGAR

MILK

KAONG
(PALM SEEDS)

PRESERVED
ADZUKI BEANS

UBE HALAYA
(PURPLE YAM JAM)

PRESERVED
WHITE BEANS

SEPIA-TONED

BLACK SESAME
POLVORON
(PAGE 249)

COFFEE ICE
CREAM

COCO JAM
(PAGE 201)

CONDENSED
MILK JELLY
FROM BLACK TREACLE
TOFFEE MILK
(PAGE 261)

HOMEMADE
MOLASSES TAPIOCA
(PAGE 199)

TOASTED BUCKWHEAT
RICE FROM RICE
COFFEE
(PAGE 275)

MOLASSES

BLACK SESAME
MOCHI FROM
GINATAANG BILO-
BILO
(PAGE 237)

CHOCOLATE MILK

COFFEE JELLY
FROM
BLACK TREACLE
TOFFEE MILK
(PAGE 261)

COCONUT WATER
GRANITA

*I*n summer, I remember my mom going to the flea market every weekend and coming home with whole flats of mangoes, strawberries, and melons. When I was little, I used to trail behind her; she'd get me a pomegranate at the start of the day and I'd eat it slowly and seriously, making it last for hours, red juice dripping down my face and shirt. Back home, she'd start shredding cantaloupe into a pitcher with a special tool that I wasn't allowed to touch until I was older. It turned the melon into long, skinny, spaghetti-like strands. I'd scrape out any remaining juice in the melon halves, and then we'd add lots of ice, sugar, and water. (You can omit sugar, as here, if you use the ripest possible fruit.) The result was like an agua fresca, but more fun, with those shivery noodles, bright and crisp on the tongue. I consider that melon shredder a family heirloom, and my brothers and sisters better watch out, because I've got my eye on it.

DOLLY'S CANTALOUPE REFRESHER
CANTALOUPE SLUSH WITH CANTALOUPE SPAGHETTI, CRUSHED MINT, AND CONDENSED MILK SERVES 2

2 cups (320 g) diced cantaloupe, frozen

½ cup (50 g) crushed ice

10 fresh mint leaves, plus extra for garnish
(optional)

½ cup (80 g) shredded or julienned cantaloupe, in
long, skinny spaghetti-like strands

Condensed milk, for garnish (optional)

In a blender, combine the frozen diced cantaloupe, ice, ¼ cup (60 ml) cold water, and 5 of the mint leaves. Blend on high for about 2 minutes, until smooth.

•

Pour the slush into two glasses. Add the shredded or julienned cantaloupe (i.e., the "cantaloupe spaghetti"), dividing the amount evenly between the glasses, along with the remaining mint leaves, hand-torn and slightly crushed, so you get chewy bites of cantaloupe and mint while you enjoy the slush. Stir to combine. If you have more mint, use as a garnish. Sometimes I like to drizzle a little condensed milk on top to make this extra luxurious on a hot day.

I got my first "signature dish" from a spiral-bound church recipe book on my mom's shelf. It sounded so fancy to me as a kid: spinach salad with strawberries, slivered almonds, and a raspberry vinaigrette. Since then I've found recipes in many unexpected places, and I firmly believe that the best ones don't always wind up on glossy magazine pages or between hardbound covers. So I was comforted in the middle of the pandemic when my friend Sienna Fekete, a curator and multimedia producer, put together a community cookbook, an homage to those mimeographed pamphlets of old, passed around by hand as a kind of culinary samizdat. She wanted to give people a sense of connection even though we were apart.

The recipe that caught my eye was "Night Moss," a vegan chocolate mousse haunted by the scent of raw mint—the creation of another friend, the performance and installation artist Hayden Dunham. At the time I was experimenting with one of my mom's favorite treats, a voluptuous avocado shake. (Westerners tend to think of avocado as savory and vegetal, but in the Philippines, we eat it as dessert, with brown sugar or mashed with condensed milk.) Inspired, I decided to add mint and a couple coins of my homemade Tablea (page 205), cacao nibs roasted and pulverized, then tossed in toasted sesame seeds, for extra richness. I especially like Hayden's instructions for how to handle the mint: Hold it between the fingers "to wake it up."

NIGHT MOSS SHAKE
AVOCADO, CACAO, AND MINT SERVES 1

½ very ripe avocado

2 tablets tablea (store-bought or homemade, page 205) or 2 tablespoons cacao nibs, plus more for garnish

2 tablespoons toasted sesame seeds, plus more for garnish

1½ cups (175 g) crushed ice

1 sprig fresh mint, plus more for garnish

1 tablespoon demerara sugar, plus more to taste

Flaky sea salt, for garnish (optional)

In a blender, combine the avocado, tablea, sesame seeds, ice, ½ cup (120 ml) water, the sprig of mint, and sugar. Puree until smooth, about 1 minute.

•

Pour into a chilled glass and garnish with extra mint—you can tear a few leaves into small pieces or put in a whole sprig and tear the leaves as you drink. Top with extra cacao nibs, sesame seeds, and a small pinch of flaky salt, if you wish.

Calamansi is our native citrus, the offspring of the ancient elopement of a mandarin and a kumquat, out in the wild, without human intervention. It starts off green and blushes into orange when ripe, the fragrant peel matching its orange flesh. It looks like an orange in miniature—like a Brussels sprout next to a cabbage—but stings like a lime, with only the faintest, tempering sweetness. We squeeze it into almost everything, for a bright flash, sunny and sour.

Ideally for this recipe, you would use ½ cup (120 ml) of calamansi juice, bought frozen or, if you're lucky, squeezed fresh from a friend's backyard harvest—you'll need around a dozen fruits. Otherwise, the juice and pulp of 1 lemon, 1 lime, and 1 orange are a good approximation of the flavor. Salt, both mixed in and dusted at the end as a garnish, brings it into focus and reminds me of Vietnamese chanh muối, a soda made with preserved limes. I like to keep the pulp to chew on as I sip. If you want, add 1½ ounces (45 ml) of your favorite spirit.

PULPY SALTY CITRUS SODA

MAKES 2 DRINKS

2 tablespoons honey

⅛ teaspoon kosher salt

2 tablespoons hot water

½ cup (120 ml) frozen calamansi juice, or 12 calamansi or 1 lemon, 1 lime, and 1 orange, for juice and pulp

Flaky sea salt, for garnish

Ice cubes and crushed ice

1 can (12 ounces/355 ml) seltzer or club soda

2 thin slices of lemon, lime, or orange, for garnish

In an open cocktail shaker, combine the honey, kosher salt, and hot water. Stir to combine. If using frozen calamansi juice, add it to the shaker and skip the next two steps.

●

If using fresh calamansi or lemon, lime, and orange, roll each citrus between your open palm and a cutting board to prepare them for juicing. Cut each citrus in half. Take half of a calamansi or lemon and lightly rub the cut side against the rims of two rocks glasses, touching about a third of the circumference, then dip that part of the rim in flaky sea salt.

●

Place a fine-mesh sieve over the open shaker, then juice the calamansi or lemon, lime, and orange into the sieve. When all the juice is out, squeeze each citrus closed and scrape your thumb or a spoon along the edge of the pulp to dislodge it into the sieve. (No need to get all the pulp, just enough to chew on.) Scoop the pulp out of the strainer, discarding the seeds, and add the pulp to the citrus juice and salted honey in the shaker.

●

Fill the shaker with ice cubes and the rocks glasses with crushed ice (although ice cubes are fine here, too). Close the cocktail shaker and shake vigorously for about 1 minute, until the sound of the cubes change; that's how you'll know the ice has broken and the drink is slightly aerated. Pour the drink through a cocktail strainer into the waiting glasses.

●

Top off each drink with the seltzer or club soda and garnish with a piece of citrus.

In 2018, one of my favorite artists, Meriem Bennani, was working on a video installation, "Party on the Caps," about a dystopian future in which people caught illegally teleporting across borders are imprisoned on an island full of crocodiles. For a collaboration with Meriem at the Biennale de l'Image en Mouvement in Geneva, Switzerland, I came up with a cocktail using ingredients that could be found on an island: sea salt, coconut milk, and spirulina, a blue-green microalgae harvested from saltwater.

Spirulina also happens to have antioxidant properties, in keeping with another avant-garde technology in Meriem's film: age reversal. But the spritz is perfectly refreshing without it. The coconut milk doesn't make it creamy; there's just enough to lend voluptuousness, like adding a splash of milk to hot tea. I go heavy on the lime zest, for a tinge of bitterness, and let the salt underscore the other flavors.

This drink is good with or without vodka, and can be diluted generously with club soda as you wish. It's the ideal thirst quencher to accompany Pork BBQ (page 41).

COCONUT MILK SPRITZ (AKA "REVERSE AGING" COCKTAIL) MAKES 1 DRINK

1 lime, for zest and juice

Flaky sea salt

2 pinches spirulina (optional)

1½ ounces (45 ml) vodka (optional)

1 ounce (30 ml) unsweetened, full-fat coconut milk

1 ounce (30 ml) simple syrup (equal parts sugar and warm water, stirred)

Ice cubes

Splash club soda

Using a Microplane, zest half the lime and set aside. Use the palm of your hand to roll the lime over a clean kitchen surface; the pressure helps prepare it for juicing. Cut the lime in half.

•

On a small plate, mix together a couple pinches of salt, a pinch of the zest, and a pinch of the spirulina (if using).

•

Take a Collins or rocks glass (or your favorite cocktail glass) and run a half-lime along the rim to moisten it. Dip half the rim into the green salt and set aside.

•

Transfer the remaining zest to a cocktail shaker. Juice the citrus (you'll need about 2 tablespoons/30 ml) and add to the shaker. Add the vodka (if using), coconut milk, simple syrup, the remaining pinch of spirulina (if using), and another pinch of salt. Fill the shaker with ice cubes, then secure the lid.

•

Shake vigorously for about 1 minute. Fill the cocktail glass with ice cubes and set a cocktail strainer on top. Pour the cocktail through the strainer into the glass. Add a splash of club soda—it will make the drink foam up beautifully, just like an ice cream float—and serve.

I love the scent and deep, almost buttery nuttiness of Japanese genmaicha, green tea steeped with rice that's been roasted until it pops. There are versions of this drink elsewhere in the world—sungnyung in Korea, ranovola in Madagascar—but I didn't realize until after I worked out this recipe that it's made in the Philippines too. There it's called kapeng bigas, or rice coffee, even though there's no coffee in it.

The roasted grains are a gentle alternative to coffee beans, without the jitters of caffeine.

You can use whatever rice you have on hand (and if you're cooking from this book, you'll have plenty!): brown, white, jasmine, sushi rice. Try a mix, or add other grains; I especially like the toasty, husky flavor of quinoa. Note that if you use barley, the grains will float at first, but after a long steep they'll sink to the bottom.

RICE COFFEE
BURNT GRAIN TEA

MAKES 8 CUPS (2 L)

1 cup (170 to 200 g) uncooked rice (may be mixed
     with your choice of grain, like quinoa or
     barley)
Ice cubes (optional)

Heat a large sauté pan over medium high, then pour in the uncooked rice. (Make sure that the pan is large enough to allow for an even layer of rice, covering the bottom.) Stir and toss the rice for about 3 minutes. Drop the heat to medium low and slowly roast the rice in the pan while shaking and flipping it intermittently for 25 to 35 minutes. The rice will pop as it toasts. You want the grains to brown evenly; you can keep taking the color further by letting the rice rest for a moment, then flipping it again.

•

Once uniformly brown, the grains will start to show speckles of char and smell slightly smoky. At this point, transfer the rice to a large plate or tray and cool completely. Store in a jar or airtight container. (This will keep pretty much forever.)

•

To make the tea, transfer 2 tablespoons of the burnt grains to a mug or heat-proof glass. Pour in freshly boiled water. The grains (except for barley) will stay at the bottom of the glass. Allow the tea to steep for about 2 minutes, until cool enough to sip.

•

If you prefer an iced version, let the tea steep until completely cool. Fill a large glass (like a pint glass) with ice cubes, then pour in the cooled tea. Serve immediately, as a refresher on a hot day.

To my dad, hot chocolate wasn't a postprandial treat, to be sipped in winter by the fire. He drank it with dinner, between bites of salt and sour, whatever the season. Making tsokolate, as we call it, is an art: He takes a batidor—a wooden tool like a honey dipper, only larger and more ornate, and a cousin to the Mexican molinillo—clasps the handle between his palms, and rubs his hands so it whirls back and forth, whipping the tsokolate and bringing it to a froth. (His most prized batidor has a ring attached, carved so it hangs loose save for a small piece anchoring it to the handle, to create extra movement and more bubbles.)

He always used Nestlé brand "Abuelita" Mexican hot-chocolate disks, laced with cinnamon. Only later in life was I able to get my hands on the Filipino version, tablea. Both are potent, delivering cacao in its full savory, bitter glory, and have a subtle sandy texture that lets you almost nibble as you sip. While my dad likes his tsokolate milky, I just use hot water as a base, to highlight the dark notes. The oils from the cacao give a little body to the drink, but if you want it creamier, feel free to make this with your favorite milk or add a splash at the end.

To get good froth, I suggest pouring the tsokolate into an insulated water or coffee bottle with a nice seal (like a screw-on top) and shaking it—unless you own a batidor, of course, in which case please use it for its divine purpose.

TSOKOLATE
choh • koh • LAH • tay
HOT CHOCOLATE SERVES 1

2 tablets (36 g) tablea, store-bought or home-made (page 205)

Add 1 cup (240 ml) water to a 1-quart (960 ml) saucepan, cover, and bring to a boil. Once boiling, stir in the tablets of tablea to dissolve.

•

Transfer to an insulated bottle and screw the lid on so it is securely closed. Shake vigorously for about 2 minutes to help build some froth. (It's wise to do this near the sink and to be careful when opening the bottle, as the contents might spatter with the release of pressure.) Pour into a mug and serve hot.

THE *Filipino* DISCOUNT

Sometimes being Filipino is a golden ticket. At the hospital after I broke my elbow skateboarding, I said salamat (thank-you) to the Filipino woman working the front desk and she whisked through the paperwork so I was seen right away; at a shoe store in Soho where I swooned over a pair of yellow cowboy boots, the impeccably stylish Filipino manager let me talk him down to a quarter of the price. As a minority in the United States, we're often invisible, so it's a relief to be recognized. Sometimes the code word is just saying your name. ("When I saw your name, I said, 'Aha,'" the novelist Jessica Hagedorn told me, with a sly smile.)

And with so many of us in the service and hospitality industries, here and around the world, we find ways to look out for each other. Last March, I flew down to the Cayman Islands for a cooking residency—my chef friend Gerardo Gonzalez, who was based at the Palm Heights hotel, had invited me to work on the cookbook there—and got stranded because of COVID-19. Flights were suspended. I'd planned to visit my family in California, to cook alongside my mom again, and to make a trip to the Philippines as research for the book; instead, I was alone, in a place that was beautiful but far away from all I knew.

Then I found them. At the market, they sold pancit palabok alongside saltfish and ackee, and they hacked open coconuts for me and scooped out the trembling jelly. Filipinos make up one of the largest groups of migrant workers in the Caymans, second only to those from the neighboring country of Jamaica. Thousands are employed at the resorts. There are so many of them, one native-born farmer had started growing Asian ingredients to meet demand: kangkong (water spinach), malunggay (moringa), seventeen varieties of mangoes. He knew all their Tagalog names and what dishes they were meant for.

A Filipino-run stall at a local farmers market.

The freshwater well that nourishes the produce at Clarence Farm in Bodden Town, Grand Cayman.

One of my final Cayman sunsets.

I was confused but excited to see my people. Still, there were barriers between us. I was neither a tourist nor a hospitality worker, and at times I felt uncomfortably like a voyeur. In resort destinations like the Caymans, where the financial gap between visitors and inhabitants is so great, the labor system relies on people who are often marginalized. One young woman who worked at the hotel had to say goodbye to friends who'd been forcibly repatriated to the Philippines. To her, I was rich, because I was American.

I didn't feel rich. I was staying in a spartan room that was under renovation and lacked a proper kitchen. To test recipes, I had to scavenge plates and cooking utensils from the hotel. But even when I was able to cook, making Filipino food for nobody felt wrong. Cooking was supposed to be about sharing.

In August, I finally got a seat on an evacuation flight. On my last day in the Caymans, I went to Smith Cove, a municipal beach, instead of the private stretch of sand in front of the hotel. It was full of families, mostly Filipino and Jamaican, enjoying a day off together, albeit at the pandemic-mandated social distance. I could see my parents in them, young Filipinos come to seek a new life in a foreign country, and it made me understand for the first time what a risk they took, because of the big dreams they had for the next generation.

Maybe loneliness was necessary for me to get here. Away from my family, I had to cook from memory; I had to relearn who I was and where I came from. Some of the dishes I made for this book I hadn't eaten since childhood, and others I'd never tried at all. But even the ones that were new to me turned out to be familiar, each spoonful breaking down into flavors I know like the back of my hand. Like a secret code, and I was home.

KEEP READING

FICTION AND POETRY

Alvar, Mia. *In the Country: Stories*. Knopf, 2015.

Apostol, Gina. *Gun Dealers' Daughter*. Norton, 2012.

Bulosan, Carlos. *America Is in the Heart: A Personal History*. Harcourt, Brace, 1946; Penguin Classics, 2019.

Castillo, Elaine. *America Is Not the Heart*. Viking, 2018.

Gambito, Sarah. *Loves You: Poems*. Persea, 2019.

Hagedorn, Jessica. *Dogeaters*. Pantheon, 1990.

Linmark, R. Zamora. *Rolling the R's*. Kaya, 1995, reissued 2016.

Tenorio, Lysley. *Monstress: Stories*. Ecco, 2012.

ROOTS

Barretto, Glenda, Conrad Calalang, Margarita Forés, Myrna Segismundo, Jessie Sincioco, and Claude Tayag, ed. Michaela Fenix. *Kulinarya: A Guidebook to Philippine Cuisine*. Anvil, 2008.

Cordero-Fernando, Gilda. *Philippine Food and Life*. Anvil, 1992.

Fernandez, Doreen G. *Tikim: Essays on Philippine Food and Culture*. Anvil, 1994.

Fernandez, Doreen G. *Palayok: Philippine Food Through Time, On Site, In the Pot*. Bookmark, 2000.

Rosales-Barretto, Glenda. *Flavors of the Philippines: A Culinary Guide to the Best of the Islands*. Via Mare, 1997.

Sta. Maria, Felice Prudente. *The Governor-General's Kitchen: Philippine Culinary Vignettes and Period Recipes, 1521–1935*. Anvil, 2006.

Wilcken, Lane. *Filipino Tattoos: Ancient to Modern*. Schiffer, 2010.

LIFE IN AMERICA

Hong, Cathy Park. *Minor Feelings: An Asian American Reckoning*. One World, 2020.

Ku, Robert Ji-Song. *Dubious Gastronomy: The Cultural Politics of Eating Asian in the U.S.A.* University of Hawai'i, 2013.

Ku, Robert Ji-Song, Martin F. Manalansan IV, and Anita Mannur, eds. *Eating Asian America*. New York University, 2013.

Mabalon, Dawn Bohulano. *Little Manila Is in the Heart: The Making of the Filipina/o American Community in Stockton, California*. Duke University, 2013.

Ocampo, Anthony Christian. *The Latinos of Asia: How Filipino Americans Break the Rules of Race*. Stanford University, 2016.

Ray, Krishnendu. *The Ethnic Restaurateur*. Bloomsbury, 2016.

Rodriguez, Dylan. *Suspended Apocalypse: White Supremacy, Genocide, and the Filipino Condition*. University of Minnesota, 2009.

Vargas, Jose Antonio. *Dear America: Notes of an Undocumented Citizen*. Dey Street, 2018.

MARAMING SALAMAT

From Angela

To my family and chosen family, book team, guides, North Stars, and inspiration: my lola Josefina, Lolo, Mommy Solita, Mom, Dad, Dundee, Mimi, Aviane, Astrid, Anthony, Lu, Ligaya Mishan, Rica Allannic, Laura Dozier, Alex Lau, Meriem Bennani, Humberto Leon, Sean C. Roland, Orian Barki, Silver Cousler, Precious Okoyomon, Tosh Bosco, Kimberly Drew, Shui, Candice Saint Williams, Dachi Cole, Dicko Chan, Fariha Roisin, Jazzy & Jezenia Romero, Lafawndah, Maia Ruth Lee, Wu Tsang, Alex Patrick Dyck, Arielle Johnson, Geena Rocero, Jessica Hagedorn, Carl Jan Cruz, Lane Wilcken, Shakirah Simley, West Dakota, Sophia Al-Maria, Fran Tirado, Mohammad Fayaz, Oscar Nñ, Jenna Wortham, GUSH, Papi Juice, Anicka Yi, Gerardo Gonzales, Diane Shaw, Jenn de la Vega, Glenn Ramirez, Studio ELLA, Sue Li, Paul Wang, Jami Ginsberg, Nicole Louie, Micaela Go, Chris Hacker, Paige Marton, Alyssa Piro, Wretched Flowers, Chen Chen + Kai Williams, Clue Quilala, Ute Mete Brauer, Jessica Wang, Rene-Rose Island Cuisine, Jean Adamson, Samin Nosrat, Anthony Bourdain, adrienne maree brown, Chani Nicholas, Cosmic Jacqui

From Ligaya

To my husband, Ahrin; my daughter, Calla; my mom and dad, Consuelo and Kenneth Rogers; my brothers, Erik and Kenny; all Velascos far and wide; all Wangers great and small; Angela Dimayuga; Nicole Aragi; Nicole Ponseca; the O.G.s, Jessica Hagedorn and Gina Apostol, and the barkada—Marissa Aroy, Hossannah Asuncion, J. Mae Barizo, Sarah Gambito, Joseph O. Legaspi, Leslie Norton, David Rohlfing, Ricco Siasoco, and Lara Stapleton; Jenn de la Vega; Alex Lau; Laura Dozier; Glenn Ramirez; Priya Krishna; Seth Byrum; Michele Humes; Max Falkowitz; Hanya Yanagihara; Kurt Soller; Thessaly LaForce; Pete Wells; Nick Fox; Sam Sifton; Patrick Farrell; Emily Weinstein; Julia Moskin; Melissa Clark; Francis Lam; Leo Carey; Gerald Howard; Lara Mui Cowell; Valerie Tate Jopeck; Grace Lee

INDEX

Photo credits:

Back cover: Justin Wee
Pages 8, 13: Alex Lau, copyright Condé Nast
Pages 10, 94, 116: Sarah Dimayuga
Page 42: Angela Dimayuga; Sarah Dimayuga
Page 43: Sarah Dimayuga; Brayden Olsen
Pages 95, 278-279: Angela Dimayuga
Pages 136–137: Alex Patrick Dyck
Page 162: Ioanna Morelli, Angela Dimayuga

Page 163: Julie Goldstone
Pages 208–209: Geena Rocero
Page 252: *Dogeaters* cover painting by Papo de Asis; cover design by Gail Belenson; reprinted with permission of Penguin Books, an imprint of Penguin Random House LLC
Page 253: Renee Montagne

Editor: Laura Dozier
Managing Editor: Glenn Ramirez
Design Manager: Jenice Kim
Production Manager: Kathleen Gaffney

Design by: Studio ELLA

Library of Congress Control Number: 2021932491

ISBN: 978-1-4197-5038-0
eISBN: 978-1-64700-468-2

Abrams books are available at special discounts when purchased in quantity
for premiums and promotions as well as fundraising or educational use.
Special editions can also be created to specification. For details, contact
specialsales@abramsbooks.com or the address below.

Abrams® is a registered trademark of Harry N. Abrams, Inc.

ABRAMS The Art of Books
195 Broadway, New York, NY 10007
abramsbooks.com